WHAT IN THE WORLD
IS GOD DOING?

WHAT IN THE WORLD IS GOD DOING?

RE-IMAGINING SPIRIT AND POWER

LEE E. SNOOK

Fortress Press
Minneapolis

*To Lois, my companion and chief conversation partner
during our life in the spirit.*

WHAT IN THE WORLD IS GOD DOING?
Re-Imagining Spirit and Power

Library of Congress Cataloging-in-Publication Data
Snook, Lee E., 1930–
    What in the world is God doing? : re-imagining Spirit and power /
Lee Snook.
    p. cm.
    Includes biobliographical references.
    ISBN: 0-8006-3154-4 (alk. paper)
    1. Holy Spirit. 2. Power (Christian theology), 3. Theology.
Doctrinal—Africa, Sub-Saharan. I. Title.
BT124.S985 1999
231'.3—dc21   98-48894
                                                                         CIP

Manufactured in the U.S.A.   AF 1-3154

03   02   01   00   99   1   2   3   4   5   6   7   8   9   10

CONTENTS

Preface   vii

Introduction   1

1. Re-Imagining the Spirit as God in the World   13

2. Re-Imagining the Triune God as Spirit and Word   23

3. The Power of the Spirit in Ultimate Reconciliation   39

4. The Power of the Spirit in Tragic Conflict   59

5. The Power of the Spirit in Victory over Evil   75

6. The Power of the Spirit in Destabilizing Laughter   95

7. Discerning the Spirit in the World and the Church   119

Notes   135

Selected Bibliography   161

Index   169

PREFACE

Such a small book, on such a cosmic question, written over such a long time—more than six years and on two widely distant and disparate continents—North America and Africa—leaves its author in debt to more people than might be evident from the size of the final product. Without their knowing it, my students have been shapers of this manuscript. Colleagues at the University of Zimbabwe and Luther Seminary at St. Paul have taught me more than they know through all the formal and informal events that make up an academic institution. Paul Sponheim and Lois Malcolm were directly involved as readers of much of the manuscript and asked some pointed questions which I have tried to honor. I am grateful to Henry French, book editor at Fortress Press, for his support in seeing this project through to completion.

Some theologians, it is said, planned their life of scholarly writing and were able to produce their books on schedule as planned. For others, like myself, the writing of books has been contingent on the unforeseen circumstances into which one has been thrown. This book would never have been written if the University of Zimbabwe had not invited me to teach in the Religious Studies department for more than two and a half years. If the faculty and board of Luther Seminary had not given me permission to take that leave of absence more than twelve years ago, my work might never have taken the direction it did. Lloyd Svendsbye, then president, both encouraged the venture and somehow found some funds that made it possible for us to supplement our meager African salary sufficiently to maintain our apartment in the States. And later—when I requested permission to be in Africa for three or four months each year for what turned out to be six years—David Tiede, now president, as well as the board and faculty, made it possible. Grants from Lutheran Brotherhood, Finnchurchaid, the Ulland Foundation, and the Schiotz endowment through Luther Seminary's Global Mission Institute were indispensable for establishing an ongoing program of Luther Seminary in Zimbabwe. Numerous faculty and scores of seminary students have been and continue to be part of that program.

The mind, the spirit, the sense for language, and the wisdom of Lois Snook are imprinted on every page. It was she who said, "Let's go," when in 1985 the possibility of living and working in Africa for several years was first broached. This teacher, writer, editor, broker, wife, mother, grandmother readied our home for tenants, left her employment in Minneapolis, and then—in Zimbabwe—became a student of African literature, teacher of English, coordinator of Luther Seminary's program in Zimbabwe, knowledgeable collector of Zimbabwe stone sculpture, and provider of hospitality for the stream of folks who came to visit in our African and American homes that she had made into places of beauty and comfort.

INTRODUCTION

If I were to identify a precise moment when these reflections on the Spirit and power began in earnest, it was probably at the graveside of Albert Schweitzer nearly twenty years ago. My wife and I were visiting one of our children who—as a Peace Corps volunteer—was building schools in the interior of Gabon. Together we visited Schweitzer's hospital compound, still preserved as a memorial on the banks of the steamy Ogooué River at Lambaréné, where Schweitzer is buried. Not far from Schweitzer's simple grave marker are his room, books, operating theater, and piano, on which he would play Bach to maintain his technique for fund-raising organ concerts in Europe. That experience began to open our spirits to, and to begin my reflections about, the Spirit of God in Africa, although at the time I had no vocabulary in my theological thesaurus that allowed me to express the experience. A few years later, on an extended leave of absence granted by my seminary, I began to teach Christian theology at the University of Zimbabwe. Following that three-year period we have returned occasionally to our little home in Africa, for periods of four months or so, allowing me to read, teach, and write. American theological students come to Africa for study that includes an intensive seminar, "Christianity and Culture in Zimbabwe," in which African scholars, writers, artists, church leaders, and development workers are principal resources. The people welcome the students and us into their families and churches, and our African friends now regularly welcome us "back home." Each time we return to our American home, I often have a sense for what lifelong missionaries must feel on their home visits—the sense of being both at home and being home as a stranger.

American theological students who come to Africa will usually remark that the Holy Spirit is much more evident in the daily lives of most Africans, and certainly more evident in the churches, than in the ordinary lives of Americans or in American mainline churches. No one prompts them to notice such a phenomenon. Faculty colleagues make similar comments, with little embarrassment or hesitation, after a time. What is striking is this simple and spontaneous recognition among newcomers to Africa and that they have a name for what they recognize: the Spirit. They seem already to know what they are noticing. There is cognition, which occurs as re-cognition. It is like revisiting a faintly familiar but long-neglected acquaintance. For Europeans and Americans in Africa this experience of getting reacquainted with the Spirit is often repeated.[1]

Upon leaving the University of Zimbabwe, I was determined not to return to theological business-as-usual. For a lifetime I had been engaged in theology in one sense or another, in what Douglas John Hall calls "thinking the faith."[2] Christian theology is thinking the faith in God as Father-Son-Spirit, but I had never got around to thinking much about Spirit. My vision

1

or perspective on Spirit was determined by two traditions that had shaped my generation of theologians very deeply. First was the theological tradition of the West, which has always and not so subtly subordinated the Spirit to the Son so that—finally—it was often assumed, quite wrongly, that the Spirit was not necessary for understanding the nature of Christ. Strangely, theologians like myself undertook to speak of the nature of Christ with little or no regard for the Spirit of Christ who is, of course, the Holy Spirit of God. Christology—the claim that Jesus is the Christ—has been determined in Western thinking primarily and almost exclusively by the themes of *Son* of God and *word* of God, with scant attention to *Spirit* of God. Before I ever heard the term *filioque* or gave it a moment's thought, my mind had already been shaped by the impact of that late addition to the Nicene Creed, namely that the Spirit proceeds from the Father *and the Son.* In brief, in spite of having memorized Luther's Small Catechism,[3] I never thought the Holy Spirit was that important for coming to believe in Jesus Christ, nor was the Spirit constitutive of the identity of Christ.

The second tradition, the Western mind-set called *modernity,* confined my vision of the Spirit to an even narrower focus. This mind-set made me extremely suspicious intellectually of any reference to the Spirit, spirituality, and the like.[4] It was commonplace more than forty years ago for seminary students like me to make jokes about the Holy Spirit as virtually unreal and, therefore, as unknowable. Later as a seminary teacher, I now regret to remember, I was particularly hostile to students who would appeal to the authority of the Spirit in their lives. In short, Western theology and Western culture have prejudiced whole generations of Christians against the plain teaching of the Bible concerning the Spirit of God in the world. And so it was Africa that obliged me to recognize the Holy Spirit. I realized that my vision of the Spirit had to be revised, that is, re-visioned. Literally, I had to look again (i.e., to re-vision) at what I thought the Holy Spirit is. I came to be more and more suspicious of my own exaggerated and long-standing suspicions of spirit, and that meant re-visioning my lifelong and inadequate vision of the Spirit. It soon became clear that the task of re-visioning what one has taken for granted for a lifetime is no easy task. It seemed that I would have to undergo some kind of intellectual reversal, to go against many of my mental habits and begin to think of God, and especially the tri-unity of God, differently. This process would also mean learning to be more critical, that is, suspicious, that the culture of my upbringing—especially the cultural habit of banishing spirit from all public and secular life into the inward and private realm of religious feeling—was part of the problem, namely the nearly complete separation of mind from body, spirit from matter, private from public, the sacred from the secular, the church from the world, and God from the ordinary.

But the most daunting aspect of my task of re-visioning the Holy Spirit was trying to write when back in the United States, teaching at Luther Seminary in

St. Paul, Minnesota. Teaching has not made it hard to write in the American context. The difficulty has been created by the prevailing ethos, what one might call the "sociology of theological knowledge" at a seminary of one of the mainline churches. I teach at a large school with a splendid array of gifted teachers educated in the best Western graduate schools. The ethos of the school has always been utterly, even jarringly, different from the cultural ethos of Africa. Theology is—of course—thinking the faith, but *how* one thinks can be mightily influenced by the social *location* in which one is doing the thinking. The way one begins to think the faith at a confessional theological school is to begin with the word of God in the historical, written form called the Bible. In the culture of the seminary, thinking the faith begins with engaging the self-conscious functions of the mind in its interaction with the word. In the order of God's being, the word of God is prior to any experience of, or thought about, the Spirit of God. In the ethos of a Western school one rarely if ever begins one's theological thinking by attending to the indwelling spirit of the living God.[5]

The customary European and American way of thinking theologically, then, begins with the word and not with experience. At a theological school, that sequence makes perfect sense because it is the order of being that determines the proper order of thinking. In the order of being, of course, God the Father is the source of all that is created by God, but the creation is not itself any sort of god. But in the order of experience, it is the indwelling Spirit of God in all of creation by virtue of whom the thinking human person has any life at all, let alone the power of thought. We *experience* the Spirit before we formulate any *thoughts* about God. In simplest possible terms, we all breathe the breath (*ruach*) of life, which God breathes into us each moment, long before any of us has any conscious thoughts of God or can speak any word of faith. In the order of the word and of being, of course, God the source is prior, but in the order of our primal knowing—our sensing, breathing, feeling of life—it is the Spirit of God that initiates life and breath. The Spirit eventually stirs our minds to self-consciousness from which comes not only our praise of God but also our resistance to God.[6]

For more than a decade, my way of thinking theologically has bounced back and forth between the culture and ethos of a seminary in America and the culture and ethos of Africa. At the seminary it is the explicit theology of the word that is prevalent. In Africa an implicit theology of the Spirit always insists that, of course, the Spirit of God was active and present in Africa from the beginning, and for centuries before any African ever heard or read the written form of the word of God, the Bible. African theologians are nearly unanimous in their gratitude for the courageous missionary movements that took the Bible story to Africa. I for one have great and deep respect for that missionary history.[7] But now many theologians in Africa suspect that somehow, in telling the Jesus story in Africa, a totally false impression was given concerning the Spirit. These African theologians have no quarrel with the distinctive work of the Spirit in the New Testament, that is, the Spirit by whose power God became incarnate in Jesus Christ as in Matthew's birth narrative, and the same Spirit who raised Christ from the dead as in Paul's Letter to the Romans. Their question is whether that Spirit was absent from the non-Christian world until someone told non-Christians the story of Jesus. There is no question that in the history of Western Christianity, the Spirit has often been thought to be subordinate to Christ; it is an easy step to regard the church of Christ as the sole possessor of the Spirit. The Spirit is put under the control of the institution and structures of the church. By the time of the missionary movement into Africa, the people of Africa were given the impression that—in the Christian view—not only had the Spirit been absent from Africa prior to the Christian mission, but that the Spirit had been replaced by the missionary church.

In researching his book on Pentecostalism throughout the world, Harvey Cox visited Zimbabwe and based one of the chapters on what he learned. I believe he is utterly correct in his assessment of the so-called independent churches of Africa, sometimes called spirit churches or AICs, African-Initiated Churches. Spirit churches are growing rapidly while in much of Africa the missionary churches are not.

The theme of liberation by the power and guidance of the Holy Spirit from European domination is central to many of the African independent churches. In fact, in some the conviction emerged that the Europeans had purposely not told Africans about the Holy Spirit, but had brought them instead a trimmed-down edition of the faith; and it was now the responsibility of the Africans to restore the full Gospel.[8]

One still hears people remark that Africa is backward, that Africa can only show us what human existence *used* to be—in the prehistoric past. Along with Cox I don't think the truth is that simple. Along with him I ask this question: Is it America alone that shows us the promise and the peril of the future, or can we also discern something of the world's future from Africa? We shudder to hear of the ravages of AIDS in Africa, but will our health-care system be able to cope while we maintain a form of health care that treats the body like a spiritless machine—all while consuming huge portions of our material resources and natural wealth? We Westerners are still scrambling to understand the mysterious but real link among the body and the mind and spirit, but in Africa the churches have always maintained the strong connection between the spirit and healing. Cox writes, "I am convinced that healing is the area in which the African indigenous churches have most to offer to other Christians and to the world at large."[9]

Re-visioning the Holy Spirit and the power of God means that we must "have another look," which is the literal meaning of *revise*. The proposal in this book is that we reverse our normal way of speaking of God as Father, Son, and Spirit. Instead of following this logic, which is the preferred sequence in the order of being, what would happen if—now and again—we followed the logic of experience and cognition? Our faith in God as Father, Son, and Spirit will always begin with the experience of the breath of life, the Spirit. It is the Spirit alone who moves us to recognize in Jesus the Word of God, providing that someone communicates the word to us. Knowing the story of Jesus is a historical contingency. No one is born with the knowledge of Jesus already implanted. Such knowledge can only come from outside ourselves. The knowledge of God then arises from the Spirit who brings us to recognize Jesus as God's Word for us, *pro nobis,* and who shows us that God is as good as God's word. The Spirit already dwells in every living creature as the primordial breath of life, but the news of the Christian story can only be communicated from the outside. Self-conscious faith in God as Father, Son, and Spirit begins with the experience of the Spirit and moves to the Son, who shows us that God is the loving Father of the Son. Such a loving God is this that the One to whom Jesus prays as Father is equally the suffering vulnerable parent many know as Mother.

By re-imagining spirit and power, I don't pretend that the African cosmology or any cosmology can be adopted wholesale, but I do strongly question whether the modern paradigm that has captured the Western imagination ever since the Enlightenment is adequate for Christian thought into the next millennium. A new sense of the world is emerging. The end of the modern age, most seem to agree, means that we will in the future perceive the world "less cerebrally and more intuitively, less analytically and more immediately, less literally and more analogically."[10] African forms of Christianity, which can strike a Westerner as pre-modern, may in fact be closer to the emerging "postmodern" ways of thinking and living the faith, and at the same time may retain a livelier sensibility for the power and presence of God's Spirit in the world, and hence a greater openness to the question, "What in the world is God doing?"

The failure of pastors and theologians like myself to consider the Spirit in our theological work has been largely a failure of imagination. But our imagination is often held captive to the old habit of speaking of the Spirit in terms of the *filioque,* a habit reviewed in chapter 2. By insisting in the Western form of the Nicene Creed that the Spirit proceeds from the Father *and* the Son, it is virtually certain that we will always think of the Spirit as subordinate to the Son, as if the Spirit does not come equally from the Father as the Son comes from the Father. Having been educated to think that modern Western culture was normative for all ideas about reality, there was little room for Spirit in our worldview. We found no other way to imagine reality.

Long before the African experience pushed me to recognize the Spirit as God's pervasive presence in the world, I had been working out what I called a "typology of power." I would occasionally present the idea in lectures, but I did not know where to position it in my overall theology. Out of my dissatisfaction with conventional views of God's power as totally overpowering and as dominant over other powers, I had been provoked to find different ways of thinking. The work of earlier process theologians like my teacher Daniel Day Williams and John Cobb encouraged me to break with simplistic notions of divine omnipotence, and to imagine the omnipotence of God in terms that would be closer to the dynamic mode of scripture. The Bible provides little warrant for viewing God's power as totally overpowering and as a force that can determine the exact details of every event. Without being fully conscious of it, I was trying to articulate the many *other* forms of power that one can imagine impinging upon every human and natural event. Power is everywhere; it is omnipresent but it takes many forms. When in Africa I allowed myself to think of spirit as omnipresent and in many forms. I began to notice how spirit and power are linked not only in the Bible, but also in experience. It was then that the shape for this study clicked in my mind. The Spirit is God's power in the world, as the Bible makes clear. But the words *power* and *Spirit* in that straightforward sentence had been completely split from one another in the vocabulary of modern imagination, and certainly in my own imagination as well. *Spirit—in modern imagination—had come to have no connection with real powers in the secular realm.* Power in the modern imagination means but one thing, namely "power over" another or "domination from above." So this book began as one effort to repair the split between power and spirit by suggesting ways of re-imagining both power and spirit and their inseparability in both the world and the church.

Christians can be so completely captured by the so-called modern imagination that they cannot deal with the simple idea that the Spirit is the secular form of God's power in the world. It is widely supposed among Christians that God is not in the world at all, widespread talk about "discerning God in my life" notwithstanding. For modern Christians, speaking of the Spirit as God's power in the world can only mean the Spirit as found in the church. For some churches, of course, the Spirit is found only where there is a proper bishop; for others the Spirit is present only where the word is rightly preached; for others the Spirit is found only in churches where the gifts of the Spirit, like speaking in tongues, are manifest. To re-imagine the link between spirit and the secular forms of power is not to launch an attack on the doctrine of the Spirit, but to release the power of the Spirit from bondage to cultural ideas and from captivity to theological habits that confine spirit exclusively to forms of religion or to exercises in personal and church-sponsored spirituality. Nor is re-imagining the Spirit a betrayal of the Bible's witness. There is ample warrant for making the claim that the Bible also witnesses to the Spirit as the power of God pervading all forms of secular power.[11] Re-imagining the Spirit is not a departure from scripture but a return to scripture.[12]

* * * * *

The general rule in journalism is that reporters should not make themselves part of the events they are investigating. In practice that is impossible, because the fact that an occurrence is observed alters the behavior and speech of the central players. In theory, the rule restrains any impulse reporters may have to misrepresent the events according to political or ideological biases, but the very presence of observers will influence the course of events to some degree. The questions reporters ask the president at a White House press conference help shape that news event and will influence the president's standing in opinion polls, and for a time at least will either diminish or increase his political leverage.

In the case of a theologian reflecting on the question, "What in the world is God doing?" the investigation concerns events not in the near or distant past, but the totality of ongoing events in the whole world—indeed the cosmos.[13] The investigation concerns the totality of the rule of God in every event without exception. A theologian cannot stand outside the world or beyond the presence of God and view the ongoing and all-encompassing events from a spectators' gallery, or—as in some psychology experiments—from behind a one-way mirror that makes the observer invisible to the participants and presumably unmoved and disinterested in how things unfold.

Theology is a strange business. Anyone who undertakes such reflection will already have made a faith commitment, having acknowledged that the question—what in the world is God doing?—is urgent and important and worth the effort. Such inquiry entails further the belief that God is creator, redeemer, and sustainer of the world. Furthermore, any believing theologian, including myself, cannot presume that the world is *totally* other than the human being addressing the question. We are, after all, immersed in the world, and the world is in us and around us. Nor can a believer consistently presume that God is *only* "out there, over there, up there," and therefore not a factor *within* each human being's existence, including that of the theological investigator. By attending in this book to the largely neglected doctrine of the Spirit of God, I have tried to catch the reader's interest. At a number of places I will note how the word *God*—unlike *spirit*—can be thought of almost exclusively as representing the Most High One, who dwells in a realm other than ordinary time and space, or in a transcendent realm. I contend that this view is still dominant. To speak of God in this view is to speak of the One whose presence in the world is only a now-and-then occurrence, and that God's presence only occurs in a special building or ritual or text or person.

It is much more difficult to think in such ways when referring to *spirit*. Perhaps that is why some theologians seem to avoid the language of spirit altogether, because unlike word, spirit is beyond utterance. Theology that is so focused on the word, or *logos*, soon gives way to talking, preaching, and proclaiming, and to "doing" theology, which is the theologians' strong suit—as in *theos-logos*, the study of, or words about, God. To be sure, faith in Christ comes from hearing the Word that was promised in the Hebrew Scriptures and that is manifest in Jesus as the incarnation of the Word. But before anyone can hear the Word, or any word, one must first be made alive in the Spirit who permeates all living. The Spirit is "the Lord, the giver of life." It is that same Spirit of God within us by whom the Word can be heard at all. Martin Luther, in a sermon on John 16:13, spoke of the Spirit as the listener, who is distinct from the speaker (God the Father) and the Word (God the Son). "For it stands to reason that there must be a listener where a speaker and a word are found. But all this speaking, being spoken and listening takes place within the divine nature. . . ."[14] Luther was aghast at those whom today would be called Pentecostals, "gaping toward heaven in search of [the Spirit], . . . divorcing [the Spirit] from the oral Word. . . ." He uses this sermon to warn Christians that "Christ sets bounds for the message of the Holy Spirit." If we take Luther to mean that Christ the Word is the criterion for discerning the work of the Spirit, one could readily agree, but I cannot agree that the Spirit is not present in human experience until the word is preached.[15] Such a "theology of the word" usually never gets around to spiritology—the proper academic term, of course, is *pneumatology.* In the language of Christian faith, then, Christology guides the Christian's belief concerning God's ultimate purpose for the world, but pneumatology prompts the Christian's question, What in the world is God presently doing?

As I shall note repeatedly, the Spirit of God is the breath of God, alive and life-giving in all things. The Spirit lives in all things as surely as all things live in the Spirit, but that does not mean that everything is God's Spirit. To recover the biblical vocabulary concerning the Spirit of God is to recover the language of divine immanence. It is this investigator's view that the otherness or transcendence of God is God's unsurpassable nearness, within-ness, or immanence, usually designated as the indwelling Spirit of God. Only God, as Spirit, is so necessarily and intimately related to every event in the universe. Such pervasive presence transcends the capacity of any creature. No creature can be as radically immanent as God, nor can a creature transcend creation like God alone. It is because God the Spirit is radically immanent that God transcends all creation. It is, in fact, because God the Spirit is present in all things that human creatures, of all creatures, often mistake the creation (alive as it is with presence and power of the Spirit) for the creator. (See Rom. 1:19-25.) No creature, not even the totality of creation, is God or equal to God, but there would be no creatures if they did not have life by the Spirit (breath) of God (Psalm 104). God's radically immanent presence is God's transcendence. God is totally unlike every creature in that, by being radically immanent or present in all creatures, God radically transcends every creaturely being.

As a theologian responding to the question What in the world is God doing? I have not tried to keep myself out of the investigation. That would be theologically inconceivable and would betray an impermissible assumption of objectivity, as if I were not involved with what God is doing in the world.

I have not tried to keep myself out of this investigation, because the world and God are inseparably related to my experience. The world and God can live without me, of course. When I consider the expanse of time and space I have no illusion that I am necessary for the existence of God and the world (Psalm 8). But this book would not be possible if I did not live in the world, draw my sustenance from its resources, and also live in and by the power of the Spirit of God within me (1 Corinthians 6). This theological report concerns the world and God. The world and God, not myself, are the primary subjects of theology, but I cannot extricate myself from an immersion in the two.

The nature of the world in which I am immersed and the reality of God—from whom and through whom and to whom are all things (Rom. 11:36)—are such that there is no way to be utterly objective. Even when theologians have the reputation of living in another world—an ivory tower—no theologian can in fact be so uninvolved with the world and so remote from the Spirit of God that his or her experience is of no value in answering the question, What in the world is God doing? And there is little danger that a theologian would be totally subjective either. The world and God are not the subjective creation of the theologian, spun like a spiderweb out of one's own mind. Theologians do not create God, nor are we self-made. We do not create ourselves nor give life and breath to ourselves moment by moment. We are all so inextricably related to, and sustained by, both the world and God that we can neither be objectively removed *from* them nor subjectively certain of our identity over *against* them. The only way to avoid the false extremes of objectivism and subjectivism is to tell the story of the world and the story of God as one interrelated narrative in which the theologian-narrator is involved.

I am involved in what I have written, and I have not tried to conceal that fact with a facade of academic objectivity. On the other hand, throughout these reflections God the Spirit is the subject to such a degree that I am confident that no fair-minded reader would conclude that it is I and not God who is the subject of these chapters, or that I am merely giving subjective impressions of my life in Africa and in America instead of a proposal concerning the Spirit's power and presence on two continents and in the world.

Chapter 1 is a brief account of why I have come to believe that there is great relevance and urgency in reclaiming what Alfred North Whitehead called "the secular functions of God." *Spirit* is usually not regarded as a "secular" term at all. But *power* is regarded as a secular term, even by those who might be hard-pressed to give a definition of power beyond the physical ability to move an object by superior force. Yet in scripture and in Christian vocabulary *spirit* is a word for the power of God in the world. Chapter 1 sets out the thesis that the power of God in the world is the Spirit of God at work in all the forms that power takes. The difficulty that "modern" people in the West may have with such a notion is in their limited imagination; that is, their images of Spirit and power have split. Thus, *imagination* is the third principal term introduced. Other theologians have begun to take seriously what I will be calling the structures of imagination. Some people prefer to speak and think in abstract concepts, logical symbols, mathematical relations, and the like. It is my belief that the vocabulary of faith, for most people, is full of pictures and images, of narratives and human relations—hence the proposal is that we restructure our imagination. I am not trying to defend a system of abstract thought, even though my own thinking owes much to the descriptive metaphysics of the aforementioned Whitehead.

Some readers may wish to skip chapter 2 when they realize it is primarily historical, asking how the doctrine of the Trinity arose and about its significance for a book on the Spirit, and methodological, inquiring after the nature of religious language and its relationship to other languages, particularly scientific language. Others, however, may find the discussion an important step for understanding my treatment of power and spirit. The chapter provides an argument for how religious and scientific thought are parallel ways of structuring and relating experience, imagination, beliefs, and concepts.

The next four chapters I prefer to call essays or "emplotments." They represent the ways of structuring a narrative, or developing a plot, in the classic sense, namely, comedy, tragedy, romance, and satire. All four plots imply a view of power. Features of all four can be found in Christian discourse. For much so-called systematic theology, however, doctrines of the church are usually explicated by summarizing the scriptures, the creeds, and dogmatic teaching and then by using one philosophical system or another to relate the teaching of the church to human existence. In these four chapters I depart from that strategy and use literary, not philosophical, tools. I am interested in how, once our imagination is set free from certain constrictions, experience, stories, historical events, and key notions like *power* and *spirit* can be more richly perceived and recognized in real life.

A word about the goal and context for these four reflections. The goal is a biblical one: to discern the Spirit at work in the world of power, understanding that there are other forms of power than oppressive domination by force. The "world" or social location for discerning the power of the Spirit is the continents of Africa and North America. In the essay on reconciliation (chapter 3) I focus on the power of order and the power of unity. In the next essay, on tragic conflict (chapter 4), I offer a discussion on the power of freedom and justice. Then follows chapter 5 on victory over evil, in which I consider the reality of power in beauty and love. The last of these four essays, chapter 6, takes up the decentering, destabilizing power of dissent. Throughout I concern myself with the "so what" question. What practical difference does it make to rethink or to re-imagine the secular forms of the power of the Spirit?

In the final chapter I offer the reader proposals for how to discern the Spirit in the world beyond the church. I ask the reader to consider the difference such discernment makes in how existence is lived out within a community of believers who confess the church to be apostolic, catholic, one, and holy. To reimagine the Spirit and power will require that we also re-imagine, or think differently about, the church.[16]

Readers should not expect detailed descriptions of what scholars now call African traditional religion, or African indigenous religion. Nor do I try to summarize the wealth of scholarship concerning the so-called independent-church movements that account for most of the amazing growth of Christianity in Africa. The bibliography supplies resources for such descriptions. On the other hand, I am indebted to the specialists in these fields, scholars fluent in some of the hundreds of African languages, for their empirical work. They have helped me understand why even the most Westernized African intellectuals recognize that traditional religion and the many Spirit-filled churches have imbued the continent with a sense for the powers beyond humanity.

That all things are alive by the power and presence of the Spirit of God has become a stronger realization since I first started writing this book seven years ago, looking out on the sun-drenched streets of Harare.

RE-IMAGINING THE SPIRIT AS GOD IN THE WORLD

It may be that Marx and Freud cannot satisfy our desire for understanding this enigmatic thing which we call power, which is at once visible and invisible, present and hidden, ubiquitous.

—Michel Foucault, *Language, Counter-memory, Practice*

Perhaps there is no other word in the Christian vocabulary which is in our day more confused or subject to dismayingly inadequate understanding than this word, Spirit.

—Joseph Sittler, *Faith, Learning, and the Church College*

For we know, brothers and sisters beloved by God, that he has chosen you, because our message of the gospel came to you not in word only, but also in power and in the Holy Spirit. . . .

—1 Thessalonians 1:4-5

Calamities of the twentieth century have made it almost impossible for many people to imagine God as a presence and power in the world. It has been hard to imagine—or even to want to believe—that God has had anything to do with what is reported on CNN and in the daily press. A student once burst out in class, "God would not be caught dead in a world like this." As we shall notice in the chapters that follow, academic theology has often hastened to stress the transcendence of God to the point that the only instance of God having been in the world is in the One who was in fact caught dead—on the cross. Theology could assert that God was doing something in Christ, but nowhere else, lest we overidentify God with the world and its political or nationalistic agendas. In much of theology, God has been so far removed from the world that it seems to make no practical or publicly observable—that is to say, worldly—difference whether God even exists or not.

There are signs that what in the 1960s was called the "God question" is being asked quite differently in the 1990s. Now that the end of the century and of the millennium is upon us, it is far more common to hear people ask, "What is God doing in the world and in my life?" than to trouble over the question of God's existence. A generation ago, when human beings first set foot on the moon, it was commonplace to marvel at what humans could do. Now it seems we are more alarmed than awestruck. What human beings are doing to each other, to themselves, and to the earth is at best ambiguous, and more often it seems frightening to contemplate. We know what we humans are doing, but what in the world is God doing?

The thesis throughout this book is that all creatures experience the reality of God as the power and presence of the Spirit within, between, and among all things great and small. No creature initiates its own life or is able by its own power to sustain its existence. As we humans grow into consciousness, we can easily adopt the idea that we are largely self-made, and that any idea of God is itself a projection of our self-made ideals and desires onto a cosmic screen. The reality of God is viewed as a human doctrine that we can either accept or decline. And so when most of us are taught to say "God," what comes to mind is an idea, an idea that refers to a distant and totally other reality whose existence cannot be proved. The word *spirit* is usually tacked onto the idea of God as a secondary notion to stand or fall with the idea of God.

To repeat, the thesis of this book is that the Spirit is the breath of God, without which we could not live, let alone come later to think or to speak the word "God." What I have written corresponds closely to the view of Elizabeth Johnson. In her utterly masterful treatment of the mystery of God, Johnson writes that God is first experienced by all creatures as the indwelling Spirit and only later thought of as the ungraspable and transcendent God whose mystery eludes all rational categories. But we who are brought up in the West have been captured by a particular notion of transcendence that trivializes the presence and power of God's Spirit in all things. In Roman Catholic piety, the presence of the Spirit is transferred to the pope, the sacraments, or the Virgin Mary. In Protestant piety, the Spirit is reduced to the work of justification and sanctification, or in Pentecostalism to the largely emotional effects of life in the Spirit.[1] These pieties, or ways of imagining the power and presence of the Spirit, are deficient for responding to the question, "What in the world is God doing?"

This book was conceived in Africa. It was in Africa that much of the reading and research as well as the pondering, writing, and revisions took place. It has been my family's privilege to live and work in both Africa and America for more than a decade. I write as an American, not as a specialist in African studies, yet Africa has provided the impulse, and African people have taken up residence in my consciousness. I am not an African American, but I sometimes wonder if I have not become, at least in part, an Africanized American, which is perhaps my version of being a postmodern American.

Most Americans who have lived in Africa, or who have traveled briefly in the continent, return to speak of their experience as life-changing. When asked, they find it difficult to explain exactly what they mean, because in fact the external circumstances of their lives have not changed that much. What is life-changing occurs in the alteration of consciousness, the transfiguration of imaginations. Africa, like other places that have not yet become total imitators of Europe or America, can easily insinuate itself into one's consciousness and subvert customary ways of imagining the world.[2] What sociologists term "the social construction of reality"[3] is more than a theory of knowledge in Africa. It is a lived experience.

In Europe and America the commonplace and erroneous impression of Africa is that the people are still largely superstitious and uncivilized, that they are "animists," roughly defined as those who believe that everything is inhabited by powerful spirits. Africans, it is thought, have not yet learned to put religion in its proper place, but continue to believe that mysterious powers pervade their lives, the natural world, and human events. They are "premodern" in their modes of thought about reality, whereas most Europeans and Americans are still "modern" in the sense that the religious or mysterious is located in a separate sphere. The presumptions of "modernity"—this separation of religion from life being just one such presumption—are now often being called by another name: Eurocentric cultural arrogance.

The historical development of modern Western civilization includes the history of colonial conquest, the domination of others which the colonizers justified on the basis of an assumed cultural superiority.[4] The disdainful claim that European cultures are the universal hallmark or norm of what it means to be rational, moral, and truly civilized has become the synonym for modernity, now being challenged by the so-called postmodern outlook.[5] This latter viewpoint is not yet widely held or even understood among contemporary Americans. Yet when so-called postmoderns seek an alternative to Eurocentric modernism, which they regard as morally, culturally, and spiritually bankrupt, they look to Africa, to the native peoples of America, or to the Orient for values, worldviews, and modes of thought that are not destructive to the environment, to human communities, or to personal integrity and wholeness.[6]

Meanwhile, the growing concern to compensate for this bankruptcy through programs in "spirituality" within American churches, and the apparent interest in "new age" forms of religion outside churches, are certainly symptoms—but perhaps not a cure—of a malady that is deeper than usually supposed. That deeper ailment is the immense gap between the spiritual and the secular, the religious and the profane. "Spirituality" cannot cure "secularism" because most talk of spirituality is still captive to the popular notion that the Spirit and the secular are two different realms.[7] An emphasis on spirituality can too easily intensify the problem of separation. Spirituality as it is sometimes practiced both takes for granted, and is based upon, the very premise that must be challenged. It assumes that there is a sphere outside, or alongside, or apart from, or totally independent of, spirit. Spirituality is often set over against the scientific or rational as an opposite, assuming that the realm of science and of rational discourse is incompatible with and separable from spirit. This way of imagining spirit is alien to many of the traditional cultures in Africa.[8]

One soon discovers in Africa that wherever its traditional cultures have not yet been captured by the modernist paradigm, the opposition between the Spirit and the secular does not control the imagination.[9] What foreigners in Africa improperly call "animism" is more accurately a worldview or cosmology which recognizes that there is no power or entity—whether human, animal, "organic," or "inorganic"—which can be fully accounted for without the Spirit.[10] In African cosmologies, nothing exists without spirit.[11] But this traditional African way of imagining the world is simply preposterous to the modern imagination. In the imagination of the modern person the world of daily experience is spiritless. African imaginations, from the modern perspective, are dismissed as superstition.

Simultaneous with these developments, biblical scholars, theologians, and historians of culture have reached a consensus about so-called pre-modern or traditional worldviews, such as those of Africa. The consensus is that these views may be close to the sense one finds in scripture, that the whole creation is alive with the breath or Spirit of God.[12] In the present crisis of imagination passages like the following have taken on potency: "By the word of the Lord the heavens were made, and all their host by the breath of his mouth" (Ps. 33:6). The following refers to all creatures, to springs of water, grass, trees, birds, young lions, and creeping things: "When you [God] hide your face, they are dismayed; when you take away their breath, they die and return to the dust. When you send forth your spirit [or breath], they are created; and you renew the face of the ground" (Ps. 104:29-30).

What the Bible assumes about the intimacy of God's Spirit the modern imagination has typically ruled out as unreal, as an otherworldly superstition. The "modern imagination" as I have designated it may not describe the reader's imagination, but it is an exact description of my long-standing consciousness as a white American male born in 1930. By the early 1960s I was serving as a university pastor at Cornell University. My ministry was in two worlds. One of my responsibilities was a town-gown congregation of students, faculty, and residents of Ithaca, New York, whose splendid English Gothic chapel is located at one of the gates of Cornell's exquisite campus. Each day I would also walk to my other office on campus, crossing the deep gorge which forms the border between "Collegetown" and the university, across the stone-arch bridge at the chapel door. I shared a building with other campus clergy, Roman Catholic, Jewish, and Protestant. We also participated in various social service projects on campus and in town, and there, in Anabel Taylor Hall, the civil rights and antiwar movements were centered. We shared in teaching noncredit religion courses, because the university would not offer such courses for academic credit. The tradition dated to Cornell's founding, when Andrew Dixon White, the author of the influential *History of the Warfare between Science and Religion*, was Cornell's first president and insisted that no religion ever be taught there.

It was the decade of the civil rights movement, the "death of God" theology, the Vietnam War, and widespread student protests. It was a spirited decade, but no academic discipline at Cornell considered the Spirit a fit topic for study. The Spirit had been banished from the life of the mind. Carl Sagan of Cornell would later initiate a popular television series on the cosmos, rhapsodizing about its beauty and the astonishing intricacy of its evolution, but the Spirit was neither visible on the screen nor was the word part of Sagan's vocabulary.

And so I lived week after week apparently in two spheres. When I prayed, worshiped, and sang with Christians at the campus gate, when I preached and celebrated Holy Communion with them, I was conscious that our actions assumed the presence and power of God. Yet across the gorge, in the sphere where world-famous philosophers dismissed Hegel's magisterial work on *Geist*—the Spirit—and Nobel physicists tracked what they hoped would prove to be the fundamental particles of reality, there was apparently no need of the reality of spirit. What happened at the altar, or what was said from the pulpit, had no connection to what was happening at the lab table or lecture stand across the gorge.

My extreme intellectual and spiritual discomfort with this split in consciousness—between my "modern imagination" shaped by the university and my Christian sacramental consciousness shaped by the language of the Bible and of worship—eventually led me to a leave of absence in New York City and to a doctorate in theology, with a view to building a mental bridge that would cross the physical and intellectual gap. My doctoral dissertation explored the possibilities for speaking intelligibly of the real presence of God in Christ in *both* worlds. I came to believe then and now that the metaphysics worked out by Whitehead, Hartshorne, and Wieman, and employed by theologians like my teacher Daniel Day Williams and John Cobb, and by theologian/physicists like Ian Barbour, allow Christians to live in one world. This world can be fruitfully described from more than one perspective without assuming that either the Bible or scientific theory is adequate. The Bible and scientific theory do not contradict, but complement and correct each other.

What was missing from my dissertation was consideration of the biblical sense of the intimacy of the Spirit of God in all things. At the end of the 1960s I left the university ministry to teach at a large mainline seminary in the Midwest. For sixteen years I urged my students to take seriously this gap between modern consciousness and Christian piety, and to "minister to the minds" of their parishioners. With that goal in mind, I tried my hand at a book on a theology of preaching, and was quickly discouraged about finding a publisher. Nowhere in that ill-fated manuscript did I take up the question of the power and presence of the Spirit in those who preach the word! After several years of teaching a seminar on Jesus, with particular attention to how modern-day theologians have understood Jesus as Savior, I published *The Anonymous Christ*, in which I proposed that the saving presence of Christ is both ubiquitous and appears in many forms (Luther would have agreed with the term *ubiquity*), but that salvific experiences are not everywhere named as Jesus Christ. Now, more than a decade later, I am chagrined that my Christology did not attend to the richness of trinitarian thought. The Spirit was missing in my thoughts about Christ and in the work of all the other theologians I had read.

By that time, our four children had graduated from college, gotten married, and taken up their lives all around the world. We became global parents, and by now have visited our children in Africa, Japan, Canada, and Australia. Just as *The Anonymous Christ* was being completed, we began to consider taking a leave of absence so that I could take up a new post in Christian theology at the University of Zimbabwe, formerly the University College of Rhodesia and Nyasaland. Little did I know at the beginning of that venture how my consciousness—my residual "modern imagination"—would be challenged and, indeed, how there would be wholesale attacks on modernity to the degree that the "pre-modernity" of traditional African cultures would be seen as having much in common with the emerging postmodernity of the late 1980s and 1990s.

Africa indeed had become the occasion for me to take up the topic that most academic theologians in the West have neglected for hundreds of years. Perhaps traditional cultures like those of Africa will not much longer retain their sense for the omnipresence of spirit. African societies are engaged in the struggle to become self-reliant partners in the political and economic world community and to overcome the condition of dependency and indebtedness. They are undergoing massive cultural transformations. Even so, aspects of these traditional cultures are still available and might be teachers and guides for Christians in the West, who, often quite dimly, recognize that they need to re-imagine God's Spirit as the power that energizes every form of power in the world, and without which there would be no power.

*   *   *   *   *

The thesis of this book is that the religious imagination of people today—in particular Christian people—can be, and should be, transformed for the sake of God's revealed purpose for the world, for the sake of what God is doing in the world with and among the creatures. These chapters on the Spirit and power are intended as essays on practical Christianity. Like any author I am dependent on the patient reader's judgment as to the success of this venture. To the degree that Christianity is imagined to be impractical— that is, powerless to make a real difference toward realizing God's purpose in the world—that deficiency of present-day Christianity can be traced to the way spirit and power are disconnected in Christian imagination. So-called modern Christians, like their so-called secular contemporaries, find it unimaginable that spirit is located in the world of power, and would never speak of spirit in such a way lest they be thought religious fanatics. Instead, spirit is commonly imagined to be private, inward, otherworldly, and necessary only for those with a religious bent.[13] Power, on the other hand, is imagined as a public phenomenon, everywhere present in some form, and capable of empirical description without resorting to such "otherworldly" terms as *spirit*. The thinking is that no purpose can be served without power, that no action can have any practical effect or value without power of some sort.

In short, power is typically described as so utterly secular, public, describable, and empirically measurable that it is outlandish to suppose power to be in the slightest degree a matter of imagination. It would surprise proponents of such views that their images of power are culturally shaped structures of imagination. They might argue that only other people (like "animists"?) suppose that power is a manifestation of spirit. We can hear their objection that power is not a matter of imagination, that it is really the only force that makes things happen. But spirit, they would say, *is* imaginary, and at best only a private opinion. Therefore, the reality of spirit is judged to be impractical and doubtful.[14]

This widely held spiritless view of power challenges any proposal for rethinking what God is doing in the world. The challenge is that no purpose can be served without power, not even God's purpose, to which Christianity witnesses in word and deed. Given this challenge, re-imagining power and spirit is a theologically urgent enterprise if the church's mission in the world is to go forward. But can the world manage just as well with what seems to be the dominant spiritless view of power? The answer to that question probably depends on which part of the world—which image of the world—we are talking about. A subordinate thesis in this book is that a spiritless view of power is only partially true, and that it has proven dangerous when taken as the only view. "The war horse is a vain hope for victory, and by its great might it cannot save" (Ps. 33:17). In order to make good on the effort to relocate the Spirit in all forms of power, and thus to overcome the split in the modern imagination concerning power and spirit, several premises must be stated, at least tentatively, at the outset.

First, to paraphrase a saying from politics, we can begin by asserting that "everything is spirit, but spirit is not everything." With this admittedly playful contention, we can attempt to speak of the pervasiveness of spirit, and to provoke our imaginations toward a more unitary vision of what constitutes the world, in which every human being is embedded. It seems easy for so-called moderns to suppose that "nothing is spirit, and spirit is not anything at all." We are trying of course to imagine spirit as that which pervades everything, but spirit is not a discrete entity among other entities. No thing in the world is detectable as spirit along with other things that are not spirit. Any "thing" imagined as detectable could not be pervasive, omnipresent, necessary. To the modern imagination *Spirit* (usually the lowercase *spirit*) has come to signify ghostly figures that might be detected in haunted houses, when in our right senses, we know such figures are not real. They are not anything at all, which is to say they don't refer to anything in the real world or in any other world.

But must we banish spirit just like that? We can because it has been done by anyone who imagines the world as spiritless and then confirms that view by failing to detect such things as spirits. But to equate spirit with spooks and goblins and "things that go bump in the night" bears not the slightest resemblance, for example, to the biblical sense of the power of God, the breath or spirit or presence (*shekinah*) that pervades all creatures and without which nothing would exist.[15]

But can we alter the way we imagine the Spirit even if we sense there might be good reason to do so? Are modern imaginations open and changeable? Can spirit be imagined differently and viewed as pervasive in the world of ordinary, modern experience, rather than as a discrete entity among other detectable entities? Consider the new public consciousness of the environment.[16] Ecological awareness is a prime example of how human imaginations have been transformed so that a nontangible, pervasive, and necessary factor—relatedness—is imagined as real, inescapable, and necessary for the existence of everything real, even though it is not capable of being isolated, nor of being seen or touched. Everything is related, but relatedness is not everything. The heightened awareness of relatedness and interdependence is relatively recent among citizens of the developed world.

Consciousness and imagination *can* be altered. It would not be altogether inconceivable or exceptional for modern people to re-imagine spirit as pervasive and necessary for the existence of everything, rather than as an isolatable, detectable thing among other kinds of things, or as an exclusively inward and private experience. How and why such an exercise of re-imagination might occur is one of the questions underlying and prompting the creation of this book.

Second, "everything is power but power is not everything."[17] This assertion, which, except for the substitution of the word *power* for *spirit*, is identical with the statement above, would not surprise anyone steeped in the writings of the Old Testament. The Spirit of God is the power of God in the world. It is that equation that is most difficult for modern imaginations. The equation is further complicated for anyone whose religious consciousness has been influenced by the theme of divine omnipotence and divine omnipresence. God's Spirit is none other than God present in the world as power.

Theologians for centuries have debated and continue to debate the nature of divine power as it relates to other powers.[18] There is growing consensus that omnipotence cannot mean that God wills everything to happen exactly as it happens. It is inconceivable that God should be solely and directly responsible for every occasion in the universe. This view, called divine determinism, has been rejected by theologians, who are more of a mind that God's power, God's Spirit, is involved somehow in everything that happens. It would be disastrous for the Christian faith if God were "let off the hook" as uninvolved—which is to say unloving and indifferent—in the world. It would likewise be a contradiction to the Christian claim if God were absent from any domain. If the Spirit and power of God can be imagined as absent, let us say, from the horrors of Hiroshima, the Holocaust, starvation in Africa, religious conflicts in India, or the decaying cities and rural poverty of America, then faith too would be powerless in those circumstances. If God's Spirit and power are unimaginable in some sectors of the world, such failures of imagination would be indistinguishable from practical atheism.

To relocate the Spirit in the powers of the world cannot mean that God's power and Spirit are present only where human beings would feel comfortable as God. Practical Christianity cannot be limited arbitrarily to preferred zones of privilege and safety, beyond risk or challenge, without collapsing, in effect, into practical atheism. This book assumes a particular view of God's power while rejecting three alternative views, none of which is biblical or helpful to the mind of faith today. The first rejected view is that God determines from a safe distance everything that happens, often referred to as classical *theism*. The second view is that God is uninvolved in catastrophes and holocausts (*practical atheism*). The third view sees God as absent from the world of causal connections (*atheism*). The alternative shaping the thought throughout this book is usually called *panentheism*, a word that must never be confused with *pantheism*. Pantheism (literally, "all-is-God-ism") asserts that God and the world are identical. When the following chapters relocate the Spirit in the world of power, we are re-imagining the Spirit of God in ways much closer to the increasingly accepted term *panentheism* (literally, all things are in God and God is in all things) than to traditional theism, or to practical and theoretical atheism, or to Spinozistic pantheism.[19] This book seeks to describe God's power and Spirit as pervasive of all creatures, and to think of all creatures as present and alive within the power and Spirit of God. This does not mean that everything is God. The position is not pantheism but panentheism.

Third, if as Christians we are to imagine the Spirit within, and not separate from, the powers that constitute the world of lived experience, we must try to imagine God as the source—the "whence" of all power—and as the end—the "whither" of all power—without imagining that God alone is the only user of the power which God gives through the Spirit. Because God is the giver of power in all its forms, the generosity of God—that God would give away power so extravagantly—presses our imaginations to the limit.

Should we imagine God keeping all power to Godself and reserving as a divine privilege the exclusive use of power in the world? That exclusivistic sense of omnipotence is precluded in this discussion. Yet can we not imagine omnipotence in another way, in the sense that there is no power whose ultimate source is other than God?[20] This would be a precaution against what is often called metaphysical dualism, an understandable but finally wrongheaded effort to safeguard the goodness of God from all contaminating contact with human beings who grievously misuse God's generosity. Dualism asserts that the power of evil is not from God but from another, evil god. This dualistic view may seem to protect God's good name from contamination, but (1) it compromises the omnipotence of God as the sole source of power; (2) jeopardizes the belief that there is but one God; (3) presumes that the goodness of God is a divine "hands-off" policy toward corruption in the world; and thus (4) is in complete contradiction to the scriptural narrative of God's way—in Word and Spirit—of being involved in the world. Irenaeus, one of the earliest Christian theologians, held the view that God's way of dealing with the creatures to whom God had given power and life is not a hands-off policy. Irenaeus proposed that we imagine God with two hands.[21] God relates to and is responsive to the world by the Spirit, and God creates and redeems the world by the Word—supremely incarnate in Christ who is God's pledge, or testament, of love to the world.

These three opening propositions for re-imagining the Spirit within and inseparable from the forms of power in the world set the program for the following chapters, which will attempt to provide (1) a more ample description of how to imagine the Spirit as pervasive in all powers; (2) a warning against imagining the presence of the Spirit as a guarantee that power will not be misused; and (3) a proposal for imagining God as the sole source and the ultimate end of all power—neither as a hands-off actor aloof from power, nor as the only agent using power in the world.[22]

* * * * *

What in the world *is* God doing? My answer is that God is not doing everything, simply because the world has its own integrity as the creation to whose inhabitants God has entrusted genuine power. God is doing everything *God* can do without violating the integrity that God has given to the creatures. At the same time, let us not imagine the world as an autonomous, complex machine that only needs occasional tune-ups from God. Rather, imagine the world as a vast organism, infinitely complex and interrelated, and alive with the Spirit of God as the breath, the energy, the power behind all that exists. If we are to imagine what God is doing, we have to free our imaginations from mechanistic portrayals of the world. No portrayal can ever capture the mystery of God's presence and power in the world, but the idea of the world as a machine—whether from scripture or science—cannot be commended to thoughtful people who believe that God is alive. By recovering the neglected reality of the Spirit as God's power and pervasive presence, we can go far toward a richer and more intelligible way of speaking of what in the world God is doing.

CHAPTER TWO

RE-IMAGINING
THE TRIUNE GOD
AS SPIRIT AND WORD

T
he homiletical announcement that "God is at loose in the world" has gained considerable currency in the waning years of what seems to have been the most secular of centuries. There is rhetorical virtue in this pronouncement. It can disturb any residual mental habit of supposing that the world is a safe place in which to protect oneself from divine influence or intervention. It cuts against the presumption that one can flee from God within the secure confines of worldliness. The obverse is to suppose that one must flee the world in order to be with God. What the declaration that God is at loose in the world can easily obscure is the underlying assumption that there could be a world at all without the pervasive, already, and always present power of the Spirit. In short, for all its homiletical shock value, the question of what the terms God and world refer to goes begging.

This book is written from a different point of view, namely that *God* and *world* are inseparable from the beginning—as in the Genesis account of creation—and that to speak of God's presence as spirit is our best way of avoiding the unfortunate habit of thinking that the world is far removed, and therefore safely sealed, from the presence of God. By recovering the neglected language of the Spirit of God, we open ourselves to a far more fruitful conversation. The question is not so much, "Is God at loose in the world?" but "What in the world is God doing?"

To use the term *spirit* for God, however, raises its own questions. For one thing, it plays right into what Elizabeth Johnson calls "the intractable dualism of Western thought, which dichotomizes body and spirit, matter and spirit, flesh and spirit," a stubborn mode of thinking that undercuts any theology of wholeness and relationality.[1] Spirit language also seems far too impersonal and shapeless. Conversely, it invites overemphasis on the human world, to the neglect of the presence of the Spirit in the whole cosmos. One must mention the troublesome history of conflict in the church over the Spirit. Theological debates concerning the Spirit have led to a great chasm between Christians in mainline churches who elevate the word over the Spirit and those in pentecostal and so-called independent churches who elevate the Spirit over the word. The casualty for Christian theology has been a deficient understanding of the Trinity, as we shall see in this brief review of history.

There has always been tension about the Spirit among Christians, a tension already present in the New Testament. Perhaps the most familiar instance is the controversy over speaking in tongues as a gift of the Spirit, which occupies much of Paul's correspondence to the Christians at Corinth (esp. 1 Corinthians 12-14).[2] As with any group, the church at Corinth was made up of people with a variety of skills and abilities. Each of the people's many gifts resulted in different activities, but Paul writes, "It is the same God who activates all of them in everyone. To each of them is given the manifestation of the Spirit for the common good" (1 Cor. 12:6-7). Corinth was not an inactive community of Christians; it seemed to lack none of the gifts of the Spirit, and Paul was at pains to affirm all of them. Paul leads us to think that every member of the community was "activated by one and the same Spirit" (1 Cor. 12:11), and that even the weakest member was indispensable. So what was the problem? Surely it was not that they lacked the energizing Spirit. Rather, they did not know how to coordinate all that diversified energy. Such a lively group can become chaotic and ineffective if it loses sight of its mission, of the goal or purpose for which it was formed.

The history of the Christian movement could be written as a continuation of that tension between the power of the Spirit and the necessity for order, purpose, and an authoritative word. God comes into the world as Spirit and as Word. They are the two hands of God, and yet the history of the church makes them appear as competing, even contradictory, versions of God's way of relating to the world.[3] Christianity today presents itself as the conflict between energizing spirit and ecclesiastical authority.[4] The various branches of the church suggest that either the Spirit and its gifts alone guarantee the purity of the church, making issues of doctrine and structure secondary, or that the true doctrines as safeguarded by church structure and order alone guarantee the presence and power of the Spirit. Stated so baldly, the choice obviously presents a false alternative in theory, but at the level of practical Christianity it describes rather accurately the condition of the late-twentieth-century church.

This same apparent conflict also has played itself out as Christian thinkers attempt to clarify the Christian message based on the New Testament witness, and to strengthen the life of the church in its worship and in its mission in the world. At the center of these efforts is the narrative concerning the life, ministry, death, and resurrection of Christ. This narrative has been variously summarized: (1) as the fulfillment of God's testament to the world; (2) as the story of God making good on his promise to redeem what God had created; (3) as God's enfleshed Word in the story of a rabbi named Jesus; and (4) as the story of the only-begotten Son given to the world so that all might believe that God is as good as God's word.

At the center of Christian thought and action, then, is the narrative of Jesus as God's way of living and ruling in the world.[5] God and Jesus are the two who dominate the narrative that—as noted above—can be variously summarized. At the center of every summary or version of the Christian story there are always the two: God the Father and the Son Jesus whom God begets and sends into the world. For the first two centuries, Christian thinking about God's relation to the world focused almost exclusively on God and the Christ, the anointed one of God. The relationship of the two—how they are in truth and action one and yet two—was the topic of fierce debates, finally settled in the year 325 at an assembly of bishops, called and paid for by the emperor—the ecumenical council at Nicea. The council, with significant input from the emperor, agreed upon the Nicene formula, which affirmed that God and Christ are one in essence or substance and at the same time are two distinct *hypostases*, a Greek term that Latin speakers later translated as "persons." Christ, the one person, is nevertheless of two natures, divine and human. With that formula as a creed summarizing its faith and mission, the church was able to safeguard the message of salvation implied by the central narrative: only God can save the world, but in order for God to redeem the world God had to assume human nature. As one of the early Christian thinkers, Gregory of Nazianus, wrote, "What God has not assumed God cannot redeem."[6]

Having found a way to summarize Christian faith concerning the two, God and Christ, the creed ended simply and with startling brevity, "And we believe in the Holy Spirit." Nothing more was said about the Spirit, but in 381 the brief statement was amended to read, as many Christians now confess, that the Holy Spirit is "the Lord, the Giver of Life, Who proceeds from the Father, Who with the Father and the Son together is worshiped and glorified, Who spoke by the prophets. . . ." Many other Christians—Roman Catholics and most Protestants—use still a different version, adding the famous and controversial *filioque*: "Who proceeds from the Father *and the Son* . . ." In the background of these additions is the protracted and complicated debate that contributed eventually to the split between the Western church, centered in Rome, and the Orthodox churches.[7] The later version of the Nicene Creed, with its expanded section on the Holy Spirit, obviously completes the Christian commitment to God as triune. Together with all other monotheists, Christians affirm that God is one, but Christians believe that they have not spoken of the reality of the one God fully and truthfully if they neglect God's coming into the world as Christ *and* as Spirit. God is one but God is not silent, for God gives his word to the world. God is one but God is not inactive and distant, for God is intimately involved in the world, activating and energizing every being with the Spirit. God is one, but the Word is God in the world; God is one, but the Spirit is God in the world. The trinitarian way of speaking of God is Christianity's utterly distinctive way of being truthful to God's revelatory activities in the world as Word and Spirit.[8]

So the two main branches of Christendom—the several churches of Eastern Orthodoxy and the so-called Western churches, Roman Catholics and mainline Protestants—are agreed on the necessity of confessing God as triune, and thus agreed that the Spirit is truly God. Nevertheless, they have for centuries disagreed on how to describe the *relation* of the Spirit of God to the Word or Son of God, and the *relation* of the Spirit to the Father of the Son. At the level of practical Christianity, we have noted how the Spirit (as power and energy) and the Word (as expressed in order, structure, creed) are often in competition as the guarantor of truth in the church. There has been a corresponding debate about the Spirit and the word in the context of the doctrine of the Trinity. The sticking point for many is the *filioque*. The argument is not *whether* God's Spirit comes forth from the Father to empower creatures. Both sides of the debate agree on that point. (See John 14:16; 15:26.) But the Roman Catholic and Protestant churches have insisted that the Spirit proceeds from the Father *and* the Son (John 16:7), not just from the Father alone, which is the preferred statement among the Orthodox. Those who defend using the term *filioque* intend to ensure that the central, normative, and definitive place of the Word not be softened or qualified by the Spirit. In a sense, the *filioque* is a tribute to the universality of the Spirit. It implies that, even among non-Christians, the Spirit is a necessary and universal power, but the Spirit alone is not sufficient for receiving the fullness of God's saving grace. The counterargument from the Orthodox, who do not accept the *filioque*, is that the formula encourages the subordination of the Spirit to the Word, thus, in effect, denying that the Spirit is equal to the Son in being one with God. Any hint that the Spirit of God is subordinate to the Son of God implies that the Spirit is not equally from God, and so the tri-unity of God is compromised.[9]

Many might regard the discussion as tiresome until they recognize that it is a debate, at the level of doctrine and theory, that has a practical counterpart in the life of the churches. For example, among Protestants it is still a plain fact that, in practice, the Word and the Spirit are not the equal and coordinated "two hands of God," but are typically perceived as competitive claims to authority. So-called Pentecostals and many neoevangelicals are more likely to grant greater authority to spirit-filled preaching, spiritual interpretation of scripture, and charismatic leadership, whereas so-called mainline Lutheran, Presbyterian, or Episcopalian churches expect their leaders to adhere to the greater authority of the Word as expressed in the doctrines, polity, and liturgical forms of their tradition.[10]

To most observers, the two branches differ in priorities. One gives priority to Spirit over Word, the other to Word over Spirit. In practice they act out the age-old conflict concerning the doctrine of the Trinity: how to avoid subordinating the Son to the Spirit, or the Spirit to the Son, and how to avoid neglecting—or even the appearance of neglecting—one or the other altogether. The "quibble" about the *filioque*, as reflected in practical Christianity, could help both branches see how each idea, isolated from the other, is a distortion of God's mission to come into the world as both incarnate Word, the Son, *and* empowering breath, the Spirit. Christians from both branches would benefit if they were to revisit the continuing discussions concerning the Trinity. The churches that seem so divided over the question of the Spirit, among other questions, can discover and strengthen their unity when together they explore the mystery of that unity which is the oneness of the triune God.

The Word of God and the Spirit of God are not two Gods set alongside the first of three Gods. That would not represent the tri-unity of the one God but tri-theism, a committee of three Gods. But the "mystery" of God's unity as *tri-unity* should not be taken as a term beyond sensible thought or speech. No speaker, for example, can utter a word without breath. We would hardly suggest that by distinguishing the speaker from her words, and her words from her breath, we destroy her integrity in expressing her true self, as though there were three of her—the speaker, her word, and her breathing. Or consider how most Christians would regard their praying.[11] We pray to God with the confidence that the hearer is as trustworthy and ready to hear as the loving Father we believe God to be. We pray in the name of Jesus, whose life and death are God's final testament or Word that God is as good as God's incarnate Word, that the deepest nature of God is invested in that Word. Yet it is not we who, solely by our own wit or wisdom, pray, for when we truly pray we sense that it is God's own breath or Spirit by whose power we can pray at all. If it were up to our human intelligence, we would have no good reason, for it would be intellectually embarrassing, to close our eyes and speak into an empty room as if someone were listening. We cannot pray on our own; the Spirit intercedes for us with sighs and breathing too deep for words (Rom. 8:26). We cannot pray without that power. Spirit is the power of God by which prayer is possible, and the word or testament of God is the warrant by which we can claim the right to address God at all. It is the warrant by which, most especially, we can address God as confidently and intimately as a son or daughter would address their father, whose love is known to be trustworthy.

THE SPIRIT AND MISSION OF THE TRIUNE GOD

The aim throughout the following chapters is to re-imagine the Spirit and to reconsider how we typically imagine power in the world, but to do so under the guidance of the Christian belief that the unity of God can only be honored—and imagined—as tri-unity.

We have already observed how the Spirit, in Western or so-called secular imagination, has been banished from the images of power that constitute what most people in Europe and North America think of as "the real world."

Among many contemporary Christians, imagination regarding the Spirit is scarcely different from secular imagination. Cultural and intellectual influences have affected Christians and non-Christians. But within the Christian community—the churches—another factor has contributed to the failure of Christian imagination to grasp the power of the Spirit within the powers of the world. That factor is the neglect of the tri-unity of God.

The usual first step whenever the tri-unity is neglected is the subordination of the Spirit to the twoness of the Father and Son, as though the Spirit is not a person in the tri-unity of God in the same sense as the Father and Son are persons, but that the Spirit is nothing more than the relationship that binds God the Father with the Son of God. In short, there are really only two in this version of Trinity: God the loving Father, Christ the beloved Son, and the love or spirit by which and in which they are truly one. That way of imagining Trinity denies that the Spirit is equal with the Word, and is virtually a binitarian doctrine.[12] Christian imagination then can suppose that the Spirit is present only when Christians explicitly confess that Jesus Christ is indeed the Son of God. Soon Christians imagine the Spirit in the captivity of the church, with the practical effect of altering the Trinity to Father, Son, and Holy Church. Whenever in the history of Christianity this movement has occurred, it has often provoked a reaction, known in the present day as Pentecostalism or as the charismatic movement. These expressions protest what is perceived as the cold, spiritless, and formalistic condition of the churches. The pentecostal protests, in turn, are also inclined to confine the Spirit to special, designated manifestations, and thus to imply that certain experiences of, or expressions of, the gifts of the Spirit, especially speaking in tongues, are the only reliable sign of the true Christian church. In practice, these churches frequently subordinate the Son, the incarnate Word of God, to the Spirit, again implying that unless a person has received the Spirit, as these churches understand the Spirit, even faith in Christ is suspected as formalistic, insincere, and of questionable sufficiency for salvation.[13] In actual practice, both word and spirit churches have neglected our question, What in the world is God doing?

The back-and-forth argument about which is greater, the Spirit or the Son, can never be settled merely by referring to the Trinity as a formal reminder to theologians in debate to be fair and to keep the two hands of God in balance. To do so restricts the question to an in-house argument among Christians, usually theologians, battling for their version of the true church. Theologians might all agree formally that God is triune and then disagree about what constitutes the one true church: is it guaranteed by priestly authority (Roman Catholic), by true interpretation of scripture (Protestant), or by prescribed gifts of the Spirit (Pentecostal)? The point of the doctrine of the Trinity is not to regulate in-house debates among Christians.[14] Such use typically turns the church in on itself, worrying about its true identity as distinct from the world.

Such irony! The doctrine of the Trinity serves as the occasion for churches to turn their backs on the world and to have in-house disputes about the Son and the Spirit. Yet the point of the doctrine is that God continuously and universally comes into the world as the Father by whose Spirit faith in the Word is engendered. God is not an autistic, anxiously self-absorbed deity, caught up within an isolated realm of divinity, incapable of genuine relation with others, or uninterested in going out into the world. God goes forth into the world as breath, and that breath communicates and gives life to the Word, which calls forth a living faith. It is the Word that discloses the purpose of God's power and breath, everywhere in the world. No longer must spirit be regarded primarily as a vague, ominous threat that must be cajoled, appeased, and contained. In many forms of African traditional religion, spirits are omnipresent powers that must be placated. The Word offers salvation from such fearful experiences of the Spirit of God.[15] The tri-unity of God emphasizes that God goes forth ceaselessly as Spirit and as Word, but the church that God has commissioned to make God known in the world too often uses the tri-unity of God as an excuse to turn away from the world.

The tri-unity of God is not a debating point that can be clarified by in-house arguments about how to define God's true identity, whose identity is then promulgated in the world. The point about God's tri-unity is that God goes forth as the Word and the Spirit of the Father into the world, a point that can only be discovered by turning to the world, where the tri-unity of God directs the church to be in mission.[16]

The failure of Christian imagination to grasp the full power of the Spirit in the world can be traced, though only in part, to the domination since the Enlightenment of reductionistic, spiritless, and machinelike images by which to imagine and thus to represent the forces and powers that constitute "the real world." The failure can also be attributed to the neglect of the distinctly Christian understanding of God as triune, by which the Christian tradition faithfully imagines God's going forth into the world as Word and Spirit.

God as triune is the theological warrant, or starting point, in the Christian tradition for re-imagining the Spirit and the images of power. Such re-imagining, in turn, determines the church's mission in the world.

RECLAIMING IMAGINATION IN THEOLOGY

One might think it odd to rely on imagination while writing in support of practical Christianity. Should not "practical Christianity" be based on observation and on the clear teachings of the scripture and doctrine? What could be more impractical, and more likely to go astray from tradition, than imagination? These questions state an important caution against unrestrained flights of fancy. Yet, as some theologians and biblical scholars have made clear in recent decades, theology is not an exhaustive attempt to define and preserve the identity of Christianity. Rather it is a quest for possible new meanings and appropriate actions in the contemporary world. Theology has become a probe for the meaning of life, with the Word of God as the measure or standard and the Spirit as the empowerment. So theology has come to reclaim the necessity of imagination for its proper work. Questing, searching, exploring, or probing is impossible without imagination.[17]

Thus far this chapter has argued that much thinking about the Spirit has been a failure, not of will or intelligence, but of imagination. Much thought has shrunk the scope of the Spirit to restricted domains that can then be held hostage to ecclesiastical structure.[18] Theology without imagination probably does not kill faith, but it can surely put the faithful to sleep, render faith impractical, and confine the Word and Spirit of God to places where the authority of unimaginative theologians and clergy is still obeyed. At best such theology renders Christianity ineffective in the world of power, regardless of how "orthodox" its doctrine may appear. At worst, some Christian communities have turned into sects and cults whose leaders on occasion have driven members to suicide. The failure of theological imagination has often been prompted by fear, by craving safety in disputes about Christian identity, and by turning away from mission in the world. One symptom of this failure is the often-heard cry, "We must not let the world write the agenda for the church."[19] Yet, if God is triune, what agenda could God have if not the care and redemption of the world, which is God's creation? It is precisely when Christians fear contact with the world that whole provinces of the world are lost. The aim of theology cannot merely be preserving Christianity's identity without regard for the world; its aim should be to reclaim lost provinces. "But," writes one theologian, "this aim cannot be realized except in terms of *theological imagination* which sees that [humanity's] encounter with the divine does not take place in a special section of . . . life, in . . . religious moments, but in the entire process, personal and social, by which [the human] comes to be."[20]

A number of studies have shown the pervasiveness of imagination in all disciplines, in the arts and also in history, theology, and biblical interpretation, in communication and even science. Advances in any intellectual pursuit are impossible without active imagination. Science, however, is often thought, or popularly imagined, to be the exception, because it is the down-to-earth discipline that can be counted on to expose the fakery of charlatans and quacks, the illusions of madmen, and the wishful thinking in religion. Yet when viewed by scientists themselves, contemporary science has been portrayed as a far more subtle, complex, human, and often imaginative enterprise than commonly supposed. Physicist and theologian Ian Barbour has analyzed how imagination functions in scientific and religious thought.[21] In practice, imagination is indispensable in both, but is the sole factor in neither. Even though imagination is indispensable, we cannot suppose that its work is utterly random, whimsical, or fanciful. Imagination cannot be used to justify the attitude that "anything goes." The way human beings think religiously or scientifically has a definite structure involving, among other human capacities, imagination. Barbour offers helpful diagrams to demonstrate that point.

Modern science has two prominent features: (1) experimental data based on observations carried out directly, or with instruments; and (2) scientific concepts and theories. It has often been assumed that a direct line moves from data to theory, as though theories are found in the data and simply lifted out, like so:

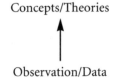

Concepts/Theories

Observation/Data

Barbour agrees that a direct line exists but that the development of theories, and their verification, does not result *only* from a direct connection between data and theory. Theories are not simply "found" embedded in observable data. Theories influence observation, and, as most agree, are not based solely on what is observed. What we call "data" can be observed only when our observations are guided by the appropriate theory. That "all data are theory-laden" is now taken as a matter of course. So the line between theories and data must be augmented by another consideration, providing an additional and indirect connection between theory and data:

Concepts/Theories

Influences of Theories on Observation

Observation/Data

Historians of science such as Thomas Kuhn, who is perhaps the best known, having made *paradigm* almost a code word for comparing different modes of thought, have shown how science is the history of a series of dominant paradigms. "A paradigm implicitly defines for a given scientific community the kinds of questions which can fruitfully be asked and the types of explanations to be sought."[22] The debate about paradigms has underscored what often goes unnoticed in the work of science, namely that concepts and theories, while necessarily related to the observation of data, do not arise directly from observation. In other words, the arrow linking theories and data in Barbour's diagram does not move directly or inductively upward. Rather, theories are "acts of creative imagination." One does not simply stare at the data to find a self-evident theory, and formulate that theory according to accepted rules. The diagram must be modified further:

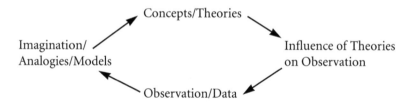

Concepts/Theories

Imagination/
Analogies/Models

Influence of Theories
on Observation

Observation/Data

This more ample diagram Barbour calls the "structure of science." By calling attention to the necessary role of imagination, Barbour is not suggesting that science is merely a fiction of the imagination. He terms his position "critical realism." It is realism because there is a real, but not solely direct, connection between scientific concepts and observation; and it is critical because of the interactive and unavoidable role played by the observer, whose observations are never totally objective, and whose theories are never merely lifted directly out of the data.

Turning, then, to religious thought, Barbour writes, "The basic structure of religion is similar to that of science in some respects, though it differs at several crucial points."[23] For instance, just as data is always "theory-laden," religious experience and religious narratives and rituals can never be represented without being interpreted by a concept or belief concerning religion. Every religion is constituted by two main features that can be substituted in the diagrams above to represent the structure of religion:

Concepts/Beliefs

Religious Experience/Story and Ritual

An *uncritical* realist would suppose that the connection between these two components is direct. Some theologians, for example, would draw the line solely in a downward direction, from a theory or theology of divine revelation to revealed story. Others would draw an arrow going up, asserting that beliefs and religious concepts are based on experience. Neither option is plausible, because the two features are interactive; they influence one another in ways that this diagram does not take into account. Although "religion, more than science, is influenced 'from the top down,'" the influence from the bottom up is not absent. For the purposes of our discussion, it must be noted that religion cannot be reduced to an "upper" and a "lower" component. As in science, indirect but real influences do not appear when religion is reduced to such simple terms. The dynamic, interactive nature of religion is better seen in the following:

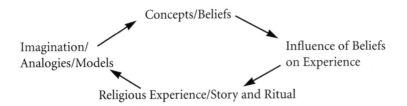

The structure of religion as shown above is both similar and dissimilar to the complex diagram showing the structure of science.[24]

The history of Christianity reflects how beliefs and the biblical story embedded in rites of faith have been passed from generation to generation, but it also tells how these beliefs have had to be reinterpreted and the rituals revised.[25] The history includes both continuity and change. One need only remember how the concept of creation has had to be altered in interpretation and formulation in order to accommodate scientific theories about the origin of the cosmos. This change in turn has meant dramatic shifts in the way one imagines God as creator, calling for new images and models by which to re-imagine God's relation to the world.[26]

Re-imagining is not a departure from what Christians have always had to do, but is an inevitable part of thinking and living as Christian believers. It is all the more urgent in our own time that Christians be more intentional about re-imagining the Spirit and the images of power. The reason for that urgency comes readily to mind.

One of the greatest challenges to Christians in the twentieth century has been the problem of evil.[27] For most of human history natural disasters such as floods, earthquakes, and plagues have devastated populations, raising the theodicy question: how can one reconcile the goodness and almightiness of God with the evil and destruction such disasters bring? Historically, the capacity of mere mortals to inflict harm seemed minuscule in comparison to those of nature, the so-called acts of God. In recent times, humans acting against humans and against nature itself have provoked the question, "What is God doing in a world full of destruction?" Is God, imagined as all-powerful and all-good, involved in these events? How can we imagine God as Lord of the history human beings are making? Such questions may be the most poignant way of focusing our discussion of the Spirit of God in the world of power. Can we re-imagine the Spirit as the power of God, so, as some would wish, the problem of evil is not imagined out of existence? Rather, can we re-imagine the Spirit in a way that will remain realistic about evil and that can engage the question critically and hopefully, trusting that our hope and our efforts are not in vain?

PATTERNS OF IMAGINATION

The next four chapters will probe the various ways in which religious, and specifically Christian, imagination has portrayed and can fruitfully continue to portray the Spirit and images of power. Power is such a widely used word that it is easy to suppose that everyone using the word is clear about its meaning. The phrase "images of power" can be interpreted to mean "power as it is variously imagined," or as "images that have power"—as in, "That is a powerful image." A subtle, intricate relationship exists between image and power, as even a casual acquaintance with commercial advertising or propaganda would demonstrate. The phrase "images of power" elides quite easily into "power of images."[28] Many who use the word power as a matter of course might want to dismiss this discussion as academic game-playing, perhaps contending that power is not tied to imagination, and that real power has nothing to do with spirit or spirituality. Many would likely not join in the explorations that follow. That is a pity. So-called power struggles are clashes in which the imagery and spirit of power are rarely brought into the open, similar to failures in understanding between men and women that result because of a neglected relation between power and symbols.[29]

The above discussion of the place of imagination in science and religion does not imply that the uses of imagination in the disciplines are identical. Religious imagination is much more difficult to describe, especially when dealing with the Spirit and power, which are, by nature, dynamic, pervasive realities. Yet subsequent chapters will submit that, although Spirit and power cannot be confined within boundaries, religious imagination nevertheless organizes their boundlessness. Consider the surface of a globe. It has neither boundaries nor center. (To have a global consciousness is to be aware that Eurocentrism is an arbitrary imposition.) Yet a globe is, or has, a spherical configuration. Similarly, religious imagination seeks to discern the distinctive shapes of the seeming boundlessness of power and the Spirit.

Both religious faith and scientific knowledge make claims about the world, though each uses language differently. But as we have seen, religious beliefs, as well as scientific theories, cannot be applied directly to data and experience. An interactive relationship gives believers and scientists influence, by virtue of their beliefs and theories, on what they observe and experience. Scientific data and religious experience influence but do not control creative leaps of imagination, thus allowing reformulation of both belief and theory. At the "upper" region, in which one locates the claims of faith and knowledge—beliefs and theories—religious dogma and scientific law are not fixed and beyond revision. Similarly, in the "lower" region, there cannot be irreducible, self-evident religious experiences, or completely "objective" data.

Having noted the structural similarities between religion and science, one must then acknowledge a major dissimilarity. Religious language, bearing all the complications peculiar to faith, is far less precise than scientific discourse.

The language of faith—in prayers, creeds, hymnody, liturgy, gestures, and preaching—is ultimately evocative, calling for response. Religious language intends to put the reader, hearer, or pray-er in contact with a reality or power that remains unheard, unseen, and unknowable. When religious language refers to a measurable object among other measurable objects in the visible, audible world, the intent is to go beyond a literal reference. As the speaker addresses others besides herself, she wants the language to refer to more than itself. Such language, in other words, does not primarily transmit information about the objective world or about the speaker, because it is not denotative. Religious language is evocative and performative. It intends to call forth and make real what otherwise would not be called forth if the speech had not been enacted.[30]

The language of the sciences, both natural and social, does not intend to be evocative and performative, although its theories might disturb the religious consciousness of some. Scientific language is denotative. Its intention is to report, to transmit information, to seek explanations, to trace causal connections, and to construct theories that best account for scientifically observable, quantifiable phenomena. Politics and commerce may often use science to evoke support for their programs and products, to make things happen in government or the marketplace, but such uses violate the intention of the scientific community.

Scientific language has usually intended to be descriptive and thus to be a "mirror of nature."[31] This widely accepted self-definition has proven beyond the reach of science, which has directly and indirectly altered the face of nature rather than giving an accurate scientific picture of it. In large measure, the inability to offer an accurate mirror of nature occurs because science is carried out by human beings who are part of nature. No scientist has been able to completely untangle "description" from culturally shaped "prescription." Nevertheless, the ideal of scientific language is to keep the prescriptive to a minimum, an ideal that can be approximated but never achieved.

Today all descriptions of the world—historical, economic, political, ideological, and so on—are heavily indebted to the scientific intention of staying close to the factual, the publicly verifiable. Every such description seeks (1) to organize the factual data, (2) which are gathered according to a theory, (3) which is dependent on a model, (4) which in turn is imaginatively constructed (5) in light of the manifold, buzzing world of experience, which does not enter human consciousness neatly organized. So-called scientific descriptions, while not arrived at casually, as these points make evident, are more factually precise than religious utterances, even though scientific observations cannot be generated apart from imagination.

Religious language also intends to describe the world—the same world depicted by scientific facts and theories—because faith both embraces the world and is embraced by it. Yet description is secondary to religious language. It "is not primarily a description of reality to be formulated in factual beliefs but a redescription of reality . . . opening us to new worlds of possible experience. In that sense there is in religious language a suspension of reference to present reality."[32] Religious language seeks to go beyond describing the world and to redescribe the world, and for that reason the language of faith has a close kinship to the language of the poet. A redescription evoked by prophetic religious language challenges the imagination. It is as though the poet holds before us a vision, and we are led to consider the vision a description of what the world could become. The vision does not describe, nor does it legalistically prescribe, but it redescribes—and thus engages our imaginations in a way that empowers us to hope and to act differently in light of that hope.

In summary, imagination plays a distinctive role in both religion and science. In science, however, imagination is restricted for reasons suggested above, perhaps especially because science, unlike religion, restrains itself from going beyond the descriptive. Religious imagination seeks to redescribe. This fact makes any effort to probe the scope and depth of religious imagination all the more daunting.

* * * * *

Each of the next four chapters will discuss four patterns of imagination concerning power. Each pattern includes two images of power—or two powerful images—which shape human life. There are eight images of power in total. For the scheme I am indebted to Hayden White's *Metahistory* and to Charles Davis's use in Davis's own attempt to assess the current status of Christianity at the close of the millennium.[33]

In simplest terms, the patterns of imagination can be likened to four different ways in which a story can be plotted or shaped. For example, what shape would one give American history if there were only one hour for telling it, let's say to an African not yet familiar with the five hundred years of North American history? The American ambassador's version would probably take the form of *comedy*. In the classic sense of comedy, the narrative reinforces the confidence that everything concludes harmoniously, with misunderstandings, hardships, and conflicts resolved. This way of imagining the "plot" would show how events adhere to the principles of a liberal democratic order and unity. The two dominant images of power would be military, economic, and technological superiority, and truth expressed in the ideals of the Declaration of Independence and the Constitution. Power as domination or superior force, and power as truth, are the images under the structure or emplotment of classic comedy, treated in chapter 3.

Suppose an African American—visiting the continent of his ancestral origin—were to tell the story of America to the African in our example? The telling would set events in the pattern of *tragedy*. The classic view of tragedy emphasizes unavoidable conflicts arising when one version of goodness clashes with another, and the history of America is the history of conflict between several versions of the good life. The freedom of the American marketplace drove the industrial revolution, yielding a life of prosperity and opportunity for many. But the African American would be quick to point out that limited American prosperity was achieved through the horrors of the slave trade, which denied life and freedom to millions of black slaves, whose conscripted labor supported the agricultural economy of the southern states prior to the Civil War. The power of economic freedom—a real but limited good—clashed, tragically, with the power of justice—another actual but imperfectly realized good—with which African Americans would later fight in courts and legislative forums for a share of freedom. Power as freedom and power as justice are the images represented by the emplotment of tragedy, the subject of chapter 4.

If a patriotic moralist, or a radical reformer, were to tell, in one hour, the American story to the inquiring African, the plot would take on the character of a romantic tale—that is, *romantic* in the classic sense of the term. In short, the imagination of moralists and reformers is typically structured to see events in a certain way. History for them is not so much the clash between limited goods as a struggle between good and evil. The classic romantic, often despite the evidence, will usually view history as proving that good wins over evil. For such storytellers, the loftiest forms of power, and the most lasting, are the power of beauty and the power of love. These are the images employed by romanticism, the topic of chapter 5.

These first three versions of American history might seem deficient for capturing the untidiness of American reality. Tenured scholars and established intellectuals may be the least likely to notice the failure of any "plot" to make sense of the dismaying commotion of history. Perhaps the best teller of the story would be one with no professional or existential stake in defending a thesis. We might suppose the story as told by an American equivalent of the court jester, rather than by the king's official mouthpiece. The plot would be a joke, jest, or trick that lays bare the pitiful inadequacy of all plots. The story would be an anti-plot, or satire. In satire two images of power are at work. The first is the power of equality: all listeners are made aware that their perception of events is no more and no less limited than those who pretend sophistication. Anyone who has ventured into a neighborhood crowded with impoverished but street-smart city dwellers has experienced the power of equality that the poor have on their own "turf," and how easily they can satirize any visitor's pretension of superiority. Closely related to the power of equality is the power of dissent, which often arises from those who satire privilege. The power of equality and the power of dissent, falling under the rubric of satire, will be the images considered in chapter 6.

These eight images of power, or powerful images, would not affect human experience if they did not somehow capture the human spirit. Imagination, I argue, is the human spirit's way of envisioning (or re-imagining) the power of the Spirit to effect new possibilities for the future, so that when by the power of the Spirit people make these possibilities actual, persons are no longer held captive to mere matter-of-factness. The many images of power result in many forms of practical Christianity, which says that Christianity as practiced is pluralistic. We should be able to sort out the multiplicity of forms by paying attention to which images dominate in a given version of Christian faith and practice. In the final chapter we will return to a discussion of the Trinity—God the Father coming into the world as breath and as Word—and take up a practical question of extreme urgency, namely how this understanding of the secular powers of the Holy Spirit can guide communities and persons in the discernment of the Spirit, and thus toward a more ample, though still limited, sense for what in the world God is doing.

CHAPTER THREE

THE POWER OF THE SPIRIT IN ULTIMATE RECONCILIATION

D uring the months we are in Africa each year, our home is a small flat in Hanate, the capital city of Zimbabwe. We frequently drive near the home of the national president and have, more than once, been forced to pull close to the curb on a four-lane street to allow the president and his entourage to pass. The entourage uses all four lanes to allow for the outriders on motorcycles and the numerous trucks carrying soldiers with menacing automatic weapons. The Mercedes limousine is equipped with smoked bulletproof windows so that the president is never visible. Except when he is running for election, the people only see their leader on state-controlled television and in pictures in newspapers. This pattern typifies the image of power that African leaders seek to project, that of a lofty figure far removed from people, as one who alone has power to enforce unity through intimidation and coercion unleashed from on high and to disseminate "truth" through the mass media. This image has for centuries captured the imagination of most people, and certainly has captured the imagination of religious believers.

According to one scholar, virtually every theologian in the history of Christian thought has encouraged Christians to imagine God in isolation from the world of ordinary experience.[1] This charge cannot be leveled against all theologians, of course, and not against Paul. He understood well that the human mind and spirit are by nature hostile to God, that when the mind is set "on the flesh" it is impossible to please God. "But," writes Paul to the Christians at Rome, "you are not in the flesh, you are in the Spirit, if in fact the Spirit of God [Spirit of Christ or Christ] dwells in you." For "[i]f the Spirit of him who raised Jesus from the dead dwells in you, he who raised Christ Jesus from the dead will give life to your bodies also through his Spirit which dwells in you" (Rom. 8:9, 11). This earliest of Christian theologians did not imagine God as distant from human life and experience, even when the human spirit rails against God. The hostility of the human spirit does not drive God into the most remote otherworldly realm, at least not for Paul and probably not for most first-century Christians. Yet at the close of the second millennium, this world, the realm of ordinary experience, continues to be imagined as God-less. The Spirit or presence of God in the world is simply unimaginable to many if not most citizens of contemporary Western societies. In these chapters I am trying to re-imagine the Spirit as present and active in the world, and again to locate the power of God as Spirit within— but not to correlate such power with—the powers of the world. We are investigating, then, the phenomena of human imagination, of power and of spirit, in order to redescribe the Spirit of God in the world.

These chapters on power and the Spirit will follow a general pattern, but will depart from the pattern in chapter 6 when examining the power of satire to destabilize all patterns. The baseline assumption is that every description—whether of a historical event, natural occurrence, or human action—is an imaginative construction, not an objective account created as if the mind were a passive receiver of data. Every description implies imaginative thought, according to which the elements comprising that description can be structured and organized. Each chapter, then, will uncover and elaborate how every notion of power is guided by a particular mode of imagination.

Furthermore, every reading of scripture depends on how the reader imagines the power of the Spirit of God. No reading of scripture is neutral or innocent. Every reading will be guided by one or more of the modes of imagination under consideration. In each chapter we ask not only how each redescription of the power and presence of God as Spirit draws on a responsible, imaginative reading of scripture, but also how it bears upon the practical life and witness of those who carry the Christian message into the world of power.[2] There are, as previously noted, four fundamental structures of imagination by which the reality of the Spirit and power can be understood, analyzed, organized, and discussed with some degree of consistency. These ways of imagining spirit and power are not offered as types, or pigeonholes, into which every theory or purported experience can be categorized. At the very least, this exercise may demonstrate that the Spirit of God is open to a variety of imaginative interpretations, and that each interpretation spreads a web of implied practical consequences. Readers should not be surprised to find more than one of these structures helpful for organizing their own musings about the power of spirit and the spirit of power. In the end, intelligible resources exist for answering the question, What in the world is God doing?

THE POWER TO RECONCILE

At the close of chapter 2 we pictured an American ambassador telling the history of his country as a grand comedy in the classic sense of that genre. The plot of a comedy aims toward reconciliation, toward harmony. "When the Christian story is emplotted as a comedy, the drama of the fall and redemption . . . are inserted into the wider theme of creation and restoration which softens the dualistic and tragic elements."[3] The point of comedy is reconciliation of all conflicts and disagreements that arise. By way of illustration, the following is my suggestion of one possible reading of the Christian story as comedy in the classic meaning of the term.

The agony of the crucifixion endured by Jesus is not the end of the Christian story, nor does the resurrection merely cancel or nullify the significance of the cross. Resurrection is God's vindication of the crucified one. It does not "take back" the crucifixion as if it had been an avoidable mistake, but as in comedy, the denouement of the resurrection discloses what was really going on when the various forces conspired to kill Jesus. The point of the resurrection was a reversal of the expectations of the various and conflicting human uses of power. Human power and God's power cannot be compared. God's power is made perfect—it achieves God's purposes—in another way than that of the high and mighty Caesar. And those who "got the point"—in much the way one catches the point when events in a comedic plot go against the inflated expectations of the high and mighty—are those in whom the Spirit dwells, the same Spirit of God who raised Jesus from the dead. The point or purpose of the Spirit of God who raised Jesus from the dead, then, is that all conflicting uses of power in the world be reconciled to God and be harmonized with each other. The power of the Spirit of God who raised Jesus from the dead is the power to reconcile. When imagination is thus guided by the notion that all conflicts will be brought to reconciliation, other characteristics of such an outlook become apparent. First is the concept of a primal order, an Eden corrupted and a relationship with God betrayed—the Fall. The world of ordinary experience and the language by which it is interpreted and understood are at best a flawed version of what "might have been" and what—because of the rebellion—has been irretrievably lost. The human order is so profoundly alienated from the divine order that reconciliation between the two can never be a human possibility. Only God can reconcile the two orders. Even so, in this broken order which we call the human world, and in our groping efforts to express awareness of that brokenness, we are not speechless regarding the divine order.[4] That we retain in our consciousness some sense of brokenness implies that within our awareness lies a faint trace of that order from which we are alienated. How else could one speak of fallenness? The reality of a primal order to which we are meant to belong is implied by the sense of lostness. It is that sense of lostness which engages the imagination.[5] The drama—whose end is reconciliation of the divine and human orders—is the ultimate comedy.

A second characteristic of this structure of imagination is a commitment to analogy and metaphor as speech for expressing what cannot be represented literally. To be sure, no human word or language replicates the divine word, but God's word somehow can be represented in human words. The best candidate is metaphorical language.[6] One might object: "Is it not naive to believe that everyday language can refer to that which is radically other than the ordinary human order of things?" Perhaps, but no more naive than to adopt the structure of imagination that sees in the Christian story a divine comedy. How else to refer to the divine order or the ultimate purpose of the story than with metaphors and analogies ? Metaphor is simply a way of representing divine order in language derived from experience in the human order and that is suitably "transferred." The two orders are utterly different, of course, but when we speak in metaphors, we express confidence that there is enough similarity between the divine and the human that a metaphor can adequately represent the divine in the language of the human. This topic bristles with difficulties and arouses strong passions, as in the debate regarding whether "Father" is God's proper name, authorized by revelation, or a human and therefore less than perfect metaphor.[7]

What of the language of the Bible? While there are analogies and metaphors throughout the Bible, the scriptures as a whole cannot be regarded as one grand metaphor. Instead, the Bible is taken more or less in its literal sense. The Bible is the primary historical source for all theology, that is, for human thought about God. This understanding of the priority of the Bible cannot be equated with a literalist or historicist view of scripture. Because language, in this scheme of imagination, is capable of grasping the nature of things, there is confidence that the truth of the Bible will be self-evident and will not have to base claims of veracity on the philosophical cleverness or worldly sophistication of the interpreter.[8]

Typically accompanying this view of the Bible's priority is a distinctive conception of the church. The church is imagined as that community which makes visible, or is in some important way the locus of, the divine order within the human order. The church is the bearer of eternal values in the world of transience. It is the foretaste of what is to come, and its mission in the world is somehow to show—and this "somehow" is the occasion for frequent disagreement—what the dominant culture should become.[9] It is usually assumed that the mission of the church is a corporate enterprise, and that no individual could presume to embody this task. Therefore, activities essential for the identity of the church in the world are typically corporate activities involving the sacraments and other distinctive rituals, teaching, and preaching. Further still, when there are disagreements about what constitutes the truth of teaching and preaching, or about the appropriate form of ritual and the liturgies of sacrament, arguments take a fairly consistent path. These arguments will usually appeal to principles, ideas, and a certain organic lawfulness that must always hold without much regard for extenuating circumstances. In short, the divine order determines how things are to be done in the human order.

POWER AS COERCIVE FORCE AND AUTHORITATIVE TRUTH

When the imagination of a population is governed largely by a sense of human history as a divine comedy, at the end of which the divine order will reconcile all to all, people will almost always favor two images of power: power as domination and power as truth. If the ideal of any culture, of which the church is somehow the foretaste, is the order ordained by God, then the telos or purpose toward which the story is being driven will be the same. The story will point toward divine order and unity, which will reconcile all the calamitous disorder and chaotic disunity characteristic of human history.

Dictatorships have usually traded on their presumed godlike power to bring order out of chaos and to win assent, because they alone are thought to have a grasp of the truth, which they disseminate through state-controlled media. One of the longest dictatorships of the twentieth century was that of Mobutu Sese Seko, who ruled Zaire, formerly Belgian Congo, for more than three decades, from 1965 until 1997. Mobutu came to power in part because he was able to project a unified goal for the vast territory in central Africa, which is the size of the United States east of the Mississippi River. Zaire had fallen into chaos when the Belgian colonizers pulled out, leaving behind only a handful of educated Zaireans. Mobutu's rule brought an end to three years of postcolonial unrest that claimed half a million lives. Because he seemed to offer unity for the more than two hundred different language groups, he was able to wield power and, in the process, to accrue vast wealth. His ability to dominate the region was based on his military and economic strength, supported by the United States, which needed him as a buffer against the communist bloc that—in turn—supported the Marxist regime in neighboring Angola. He kept churches, universities, and the press submissive, either with money or outright violence. He took unto himself such titles as guide or savior.[10]

The fact is that Mobutu did bring order and a semblance of unity into a setting of near total chaos. He came up from humble circumstances, much like his compatriots, who could identify with him far more readily than with foreigners. There is no denying that his regime represented rule by thieves, and was utterly corrupt and oppressive. On one visit into what was still Zaire we witnessed soldiers, who were often not paid, robbing citizens at gunpoint. Was the power of the Spirit absent from this shabby semblance of civil order and unity? The logic of faith's creed is that the Spirit is the Lord and giver of life—all life. However this kleptocratic order favored a few and degraded the many, its power was not totally self-generated. It was an extreme and grotesque case of using the God-given power of the Spirit against the will of the giver of the Spirit.

In spite of such abuse of the power given to all creatures, there are still many for whom power as dominating force is the best means for restoring and maintaining social order. For others, the power of truth to persuade, through enlightened reason or rational discourse—or in Mobutu's case, money—is the best means to achieve unity among those deeply divided in thought and belief. Closely related to these two images of power—power as domination and power as truth—is the issue of authority. Who has the authority to use dominating, coercive force in order to bring order out of chaos? And from whence comes such authority? Does the authority to use force come from divine order, conveyed through traditional means of religious custom and hierarchy? Or is the authority to use force conferred upon the ruling party by the people, who have been given certain inalienable rights as well as sufficient reason to recognize those truths that they hold to be self-evident?

The tendency toward authorizing force in the name of supreme order is strong when imagination is structured along the lines we have noted. It is little wonder that, to many in the churches, the ideal of unity can best be accomplished by those who have the authority (the magisterium) to teach the truth, in which alone the many can be made one. Within churches the dispute about "teaching authority" has become acute, and is most visible where feminist theologians have challenged the traditional roles of men as the arbiters of theological questions, or where women are denied ordination.[11] In such situations the close connection between power (the power of truth) and authority vested in the teaching and sacramental ministries of the church is apparent.

Whenever there is any social *order* in the civil realm, one can infer that it has been coerced or imposed by power vested in public figures like monarchs, dictators, magistrates, or military commanders. In the church, the Spirit gives such power to bishops or to their equivalent. When one senses that there is social *unity*, it seems fair to assume that the people share common beliefs and values that have the power of truth—truth that transcends all conflicting opinion and that is vested in teachers, philosophers, or guardians of the dominant ideology. In the church, such power is given by the Spirit and exercised by those authorized to teach and safeguard true doctrine.

To round out a description of the structure of imagination guided by comedy, we observe how the two forms of power—power as domination and power as truth—promote or favor certain social images, which then set the terms for distinguishing virtue from vice, correct behavior from incorrect behavior. Images of battle, warfare, and governance are frequently employed when power is imagined primarily as domination. Power as domination is a zero-sum game in which one party's quotient of power is subtracted from other possible holders of power. Power imagined as domination is a possession of some—"the power elite"—and is inflicted on others who have less power, or who are powerless. Virtue accords with behavior best described as obedience and loyalty to those in power, and disobedience and disloyalty are the hallmarks of vice and wickedness. In short, to imagine power as domination is to constrict images of power to politics and warfare.[12]

Power as truth favors images of the academy or university as a community that accumulates power in the form of knowledge. The quest for knowledge is closely allied to the quest for research grants and alliances with those who wield economic and political power. The corollary virtue is right thinking, that is, learning and adhering to the controlling paradigms of one's discipline. The obverse vice is to question the orthodox paradigms that are assumed by the leading authorities in the field.

In summary, the ideological conservatism implied in this way of organizing one's existence is fairly obvious. To identify the style of thought as conservative is neither to praise it uncritically nor to damn it wholeheartedly. "The fundamental principle of conservative ideology is a prior normative order."[13] That prior order can be imagined as a static, finished realm of ideas such as those present in a golden age of faith (the medieval church or Reformation protest), or as dynamic storehouse of possibilities, but the point is that it is a prior and higher order that impinges on the human order from the outside. As the normative order it is given objectively, not subjectively invented or chosen. Ultimately the order cannot be defied or overthrown, but must be obeyed, rightly understood, and taught. The work of the Spirit of God in such a scheme is to enforce in the human realm what has been decreed in the divine order. The secular power of the Spirit would exist as power as domination and power as truth. The image of power can reconcile conflicts that bring disorder and disunity, but as we have seen in the twentieth century, this image of power has been largely discredited by the way it has been abused.

THEOCRACY, DEMOCRACY, AND THE POWER OF GOD

Democracy and theocracy—the rule of the people and the rule of God—are surely not compatible, at least not as usually defined or exhibited in practical politics. In most self-declared democratic societies it is assumed—for all practical purposes—that there is no higher authority than the will of the people. The will of the people is expressed in laws generated through a democratically ordered process, and executed by enforcement agencies democratically chosen to carry out that will. In theocratic systems such as Ayatollah Khomeini's Iran or the apartheid system of South Africa before Mandela, there is no higher authority than the will of God. The will of God is expressed in laws that accord with revealed scripture as interpreted by divinely authorized clergy, who also oversee and direct the courts and law-enforcement procedures.[14]

From the perspective of democracy, a theocracy is the preposterous illusion that fallible human beings can be reliable instruments of the infallible will of God. The history of theocracies includes repeated atrocities against human dignity, carried out by men deluded by visions of themselves as divinely appointed to rule over subjects whose only role is to obey. From time to time religious cults will arise, led by a self-declared divine figure whose charismatic rule over the faithful is totalistic, and then sadly end in mass self-destruction. These theocratic experiments are based on nondemocratic principles, and their failure is seen as testimony to democracy as the better of two imperfect systems.

Conversely, from the perspective of theocracy, democracy is the illusion that human beings have the ability, apart from revelation or divine help, to determine the destiny of humankind. The brief history of democracy encompasses warfare between tribes, nations, and empires as each seeks to establish its supremacy. Every democratic experiment has been guilty of atrocities (witness Hiroshima, Nagasaki, and the firebombing of Dresden), even proclaiming that these actions were the will of God and in the defense of democracy.[15] These rough comparisons notwithstanding, and in spite of the failures of both theocracy and democracy, virtually every society at the close of the second millennium has at least given lip service to the idea of democracy as more desirable than a theocratic system. We cannot read the Bible as though God rules in the world through one of the two systems. It is a false choice. There is no warrant in the Bible for the theocracy exhibited in certain cults, nor is there warrant for supposing that human destiny lies in the hands of human beings, as though that is what democracy requires.[16] The rule of God (Greek, *basileia tou theou*) is assumed throughout the Bible, but God's way of being ruler cannot be reduced to a political system or sociological theory. Nor can the rule of God be reduced to the spiritual, separate from political factors. The kingdom of God, or the rule of God in the world, is nothing if it has no bearing on the way human beings arrange their lives together, called politics. "Thy Kingdom come, Thy will be done on earth as it is in heaven." The history of theocratic experiments has no doubt spoiled the word *theocracy* in ordinary discourse, but its use in the heading for this section at least calls attention to the fact that there is no way to read the Bible as though God were not ruler or theocrat. God as theocrat raises the question whether and how God's Spirit or power rules within and over the world's manifold powers.[17] As theocrat, what in the world is God doing?

That is the question with which the writers of the Bible wrestle on virtually every page, most notably perhaps in the book of Job and in the psalms of lament. Jesus' parables call on hearers to imagine the kingdom of God as depicted in stories about workers in the vineyard, about a Samaritan who stops to assist a victim of crime, and about a father who receives a young son who has squandered his inheritance. God's rule transcends every political order, relativizes every system of governance, and yet is present within the powers of this world. The history of Israel from the time of Abraham, as gleaned from the biblical record, records humans struggling with the meaning of God's covenant with them, that God has chosen them to be the instrument of divine purpose. The biblical theme of covenant is one of the threads running throughout scripture. It is one of the codes by which to decipher God's otherwise hidden presence in the tangled, ambiguous events of Israel's history. Covenant, as a major interpretative principle, is to the history of Israel what comedy is to human history.

Biblical scholars tell us that God's covenant with Israel is not a symmetrical relation. It is not an agreement between equals as in legal covenants between business partners. God is the transcendent authoritative partner who alone initiates and sets the terms of the covenant. God elects the chosen people for the covenant. The people do not elect God.[18] God is not a democratic God, whom the people elect to high office. God is theocrat, and alone does the electing. God is the faithful, never-failing, and always transcendent partner in the covenant, whereas the people predictably fall short. God is the faithful one who always keeps promises, while the people repeatedly forsake God's ways. As in comedy, in which one can count on the final reconciliation of conflicting interests, the covenant reading of the Bible narrative assures the reader that God's purpose in electing Israel will prevail.

The story of Joseph demonstrates that the power of God transcends—even as it is present in—*all* earthly powers, without exception. It is instructive to recall some of the details in order to illustrate a covenantal reading of scripture. The Joseph story (Genesis 37–50) is one of the most poignant and memorable narratives in the Old Testament, a story of one reversal after another.[19] Having the fortune of being favored by Jacob, his father, Joseph nevertheless experiences the misfortune of being sold into slavery by his understandably jealous brothers. He is sold to Potiphar, the captain of the guard, "an officer of Pharaoh. . . . The Lord was with Joseph and he became a successful man." Indeed, the Lord's presence with Joseph is so evident to Potiphar that Joseph is entrusted as an overseer. Joseph is so "handsome and good-looking" that Potiphar's wife tries to lure him to her bed. But Joseph steadfastly refuses until she brings false charges to her husband, who throws him into prison. The Lord stays with Joseph even in that circumstance because, as a slave accused of adultery, he could have been executed. "The Lord was with him; and whatever he did, the Lord made it prosper."

As prisoner, Joseph earns a reputation as a successful interpreter of dreams. This comes to the attention of the Pharaoh, who himself wishes to have his dreams interpreted. Pharaoh's dreams, as interpreted by Joseph, forecast what "God was going to do," namely to send seven years of rich harvests and seven years of famine. Joseph's administrative guidance is for the Pharaoh to select a man to organize and control the storage of the bumper crops as a shelter against the seven years of famine to come. Seeing the wisdom and necessity of this advice, the Pharaoh asks, "Can we find such a man as this, in whom is the Spirit of God?" and then answers his own question by setting Joseph over Egypt, apparently recognizing that "God has shown you all this."

According to the Joseph cycle, the efficacy and presence of God's power, within but at the same time transcending the twists and reversals of human fortune, are not in question. Where is the Spirit? It is in Joseph "in whom is the Spirit of God." Furthermore, the Spirit of God exercises power through Joseph's role in the political system. We are left in no doubt that if Joseph had not been given the authority and power to organize both the collection of grain and its distribution, there would have been starvation, and the concluding reconciliation of Joseph with his brothers would never have come to pass. Joseph's rise to power was a reversal of his brothers' intention when they consigned him to slavery. But God was with Joseph, indeed the Spirit of God was in him, and the outcome was a vindication of God's covenantal relation with the children of Abraham and the descendants of Noah. "God sent me before you to preserve for you a remnant on earth, and to keep alive for you many survivors" (Gen. 45:7). In the final chapter of Genesis, shortly after the death of their father, Joseph's brothers come to ask his forgiveness, fearful that he would pay back the evil they had done to him. "Fear not," he said, "for am I in the place of God? As for you, you meant evil against me; but God meant it for good, to bring it about that many people should be kept alive . . ." (Gen. 50:19-20).

"Am I in the place of God?" is an obvious rhetorical question emphasizing that a human can never usurp the rule of God. Theocracy as a *political system* is disallowed, but God does rule through political figures like Joseph in whom is the Spirit of God. In this story we are invited to imagine the Spirit of God in the form of coercive power exercised by political systems. Power as force or as domination is not in itself contrary to God's way of keeping the covenant. Israel was saved through the political, forceful intervention of Joseph—in whom was the Spirit of God—who was able to impose the kind of order, organization, and structure necessary to avert the forecast disaster. Yet surely brute force is not in and of itself divine, nor is it sufficient evidence of divine favor, let alone the only way by which the power of the Spirit keeps the covenant and reconciles the conflicting forces of history. The temptation to equate brute force with divine power is strong. Indeed, by the time of the Christian era ruling classes of Greco-Roman societies regularly ascribed divine status to the likes of the emperor Augustus, who after the murder of Julius Caesar gave himself the title *divi filius,* "son of the deified one."[20] The peace of God and the peace of Rome were identical: the *Pax Romana.* Such deification of human political power meant that power as political domination was not only divinely established but that it was a religious duty to obey the emperor, whose authority was beyond question. As Martin Hengel remarks, "There was virtually no opposition to this 'imperial metaphysics' with one exception—that tiny nation of Jews and the community of Christians that emerged therefrom."[21] Brute force could not compel Jews and Christians to be one in loyalty of spirit with the Roman Empire.

As noted, power as force can achieve order and is sometimes necessary to forestall disaster, but unity of the many is possible only as the many are one in truth—or truly one in freely consenting to one truth. Under the interpretive rubric of covenant and kingdom of God, one cannot fail, in reading the biblical narrative concerning Jesus of Nazareth, to pay special attention to how Jesus relates to the powers and authorities of his time.[22] Jesus is nowhere presented as a pitiful or powerless figure. There is genuine power in Jesus, but what sort of power does he wield? Was he a political revolutionary? Or was he an otherworldly, apolitical preacher?

In Luke's telling, the power of Jesus is the power of the Spirit. John the Baptist foretold the coming of Christ who would "baptize you with the Holy Spirit and fire" (3:16). When Jesus was baptized, "the heaven was opened, and the Holy Spirit descended upon him in bodily form like a dove" (3:21-22). After his baptism, "Jesus, full of the Holy Spirit, returned from the Jordan, and was led by the Spirit" (4:1) to undergo forty days of temptation. Then "Jesus, filled with the power of the Spirit, returned to Galilee" (4:14), and entering the synagogue at Nazareth, he looked for the passage from Isaiah which begins, "The Spirit of the Lord is upon me . . ." (4:18). When he finished reading he said, "Today this scripture has been fulfilled in your hearing" (4:21). The power of Jesus, in Luke's account, is clearly the power of the Spirit. If we combine that theme with Mark's emphasis on Jesus' message that "the kingdom of God is at hand," then surely the power of the Spirit incarnate in Jesus is the power by which God rules the world. It is the power of God's kingship.[23]

The power of the Spirit in Jesus, then, is neither the "power of powerlessness" as some have written, nor can it be reduced to power as domination, as Jesus makes clear. Again in Luke's account, when at the conclusion of the Last Supper there was a dispute about which of the disciples was "the greatest," Jesus said, "The kings of the Gentiles lord it over them; and those in authority over them are called benefactors. But not so with you; rather let the greatest among you become like the youngest, and the leader like one who serves. . . . I am among you as one who serves" (22:24ff.). Jesus explicitly rejects the notion that the power of the Spirit in him is primarily power as a dominating political force for the sake of "lording it over" others.

In the case of Joseph, we are presented with one who had the power to "lord it over" others. Without such power he could not have organized the relief program that saved both Egypt and Israel from starvation. But in the gospel narrative, the power that Joseph had from God in Egypt is now in the hands of the "kings of the Gentiles." These passages offer us no reason to deny that the Gentile kings received their power of domination from the same source as Joseph. One can readily imagine that Jesus regarded the authority of these kings as legitimate because it came from the same source as his own authority. He distinguished his authority (leadership as service) from their authority (lordship over others) but did not call for an overthrow of the Gentile kings, presumably the Roman occupying forces, arguably because both his and their authority derived from the same source.

We are trying to imagine how the Spirit as coercive power, as in the Joseph story, is related to the power of the Spirit in Jesus. An incident in the Gospel of John—the conversation between Pilate and Jesus at Jesus' trial—depicts an encounter between these two forms of power. In Mark's account, the earliest record of the event, Jesus is silent. John's version shows the influence of the evangelist's theology.

> Pilate entered the praetorium again and called Jesus, and said to him, "Are you the King of the Jews?" Jesus answered, "Do you say this of your own accord, or did others say it to you about me?" Pilate answered, "Am I a Jew? Your own nation and chief priests handed you over to me; what have you done?" Jesus answered, "My kingship [basileia] is not of this world; if my kingship were of this world, my servants would fight that I might not be handed over to the Jews; but my kingship is not from the world." Pilate said to him, "So you are a king?" Jesus answered, "You say that I am a king. For this I was born and for this I have come into the world to bear witness to the truth. Everyone who is of the truth hears my voice." Pilate said to him, "What is truth?" (John 18:33-38; emphasis added)

Jesus clearly does claim kingship or power, but it is not the power that can be used arbitrarily, such as the power Pilate had at his disposal. That is why Jesus makes it clear that the struggle is not a contest between two politically powerful forces; if it were, then the servants of Jesus would fight Pilate on his terms of brute force. There is not the slightest hint in the words of Jesus that Pilate's power has no political or even theological legitimacy. In the Lukan version of the passion, Pilate would be one of the Gentile kings with power to lord it over others. But when Jesus links his own kingly power to witnessing to the truth, he exposes the limits of coercive power *without* calling for its abolition. The question with which Pilate ends the conversation, "What is truth?" certainly does not show Pilate to be a skeptical philosophical sophisticate. Rather, it reveals the limits of trying to live by intimidation and coercive power alone.[24] The question shows how far Pilate is from understanding any power except his own, by which Jesus, rather than Barabbas, is sent arbitrarily to his death.

Also in the Fourth Gospel, but prior to the conversation with Pilate at his trial, Jesus makes a connection between the Spirit and truth. The Spirit who descended upon Jesus in John 1 is also the Spirit whom Jesus promises to send upon his disciples in 14:16-17: "And I will pray the Father, and he will give you another Counselor to be with you forever, even the Spirit of truth whom this world [read, "this system which lives by the power of force alone"] cannot receive, because it neither sees him nor knows him; you know him, for he dwells with you and will be in you." Jesus, who witnessed to the truth before Pilate and thus exposed the limits of power as brute force, also promised to send to the disciples "from the Father, even the Spirit of truth, who proceeds from the Father. He will bear witness to me" (15:26). "When the Spirit of truth comes, he will guide you into all the truth. . . . He will take what is mine and declare it to you" (16:13-14).

By the power of the Spirit that descended upon him at his baptism, Jesus witnesses to the truth which limits and relativizes—but does not destroy or repudiate—power as domination and coercion. Jesus also promises those who believe in his witness that they, in turn, shall have the same power, the Spirit of truth who will be in them ("for he dwells with you and will be in you"). In John 17 we behold Jesus praying for those to whom he has promised to send the Spirit of truth. "Sanctify them in the truth; thy word is truth. As thou didst send me into the world, so I have sent them into the world. And for their sake, I consecrate myself, that they also may be consecrated in truth" (vv. 17-18).

When we try to sift through the implications of these Johannine texts, it is clear that brute force can be described as a possession, external to one's being, or something one has in the form of money, academic or ecclesiastical status, military weapons, or political clout, and with which one can impose order. The Spirit of truth is power of a different sort. The Spirit of truth is "objective" or external because it does come from another and is not self-generated. The Spirit of truth comes "from the Father" and is sent by the Son to persons, but it is also internal ("dwells with you and will be in you"). The Spirit of truth does not originate internally, nor is it captured or acquired by force—if that were true, Pilate would not have asked his question. But the Spirit of truth does "dwell with you and will be in you." Behind Pilate's question was a failure of imagination. He could not imagine what truth might be, especially in this Galilean prisoner who was witnessing to the truth, because the truth is not susceptible to absolute control or to capture by force. One can be grasped by the Spirit of truth. One can receive the power of the Spirit inwardly, but its power utterly transcends, exceeds the boundaries of, and eludes control by Caesar's and Pilate's power to "lord it over others."

The covenant or promise of God implies that God has and can employ whatever power it takes to make good on that promise. The survival of Israel in famine required the use of (that is, God's use of) political and economic power in the person of Joseph, to whom Pharaoh gave the required authority. Yet that is not the only form of power, nor is political power sufficient for ensuring that God's covenant will be sustained in the world. The power to dominate may be necessary for God's purpose, but it is not sufficient. Most parents and teachers understand the distinction implied here between the power to dominate and the power of truth. The superior strength and experience of a parent is legitimate and necessary for the care of growing children. And the authority of the teacher to evaluate and direct the progress of students is legitimate and necessary to achieve an educated citizenry. But it is axiomatic that the power to control children and students is not enough. It is limited as soon as one asks about truth, as in, "What is it to be a true parent? What is it to teach and seek the truth?"

*   *   *   *   *

The source of power is one but the forms are many,[25] and in this chapter we are investigating two forms of power: the power to dominate, coerce, and thus to impose order, and the power of truth, in which alone can there be the unity of the many. There is biblical warrant for claiming that these two forms of power come from God and thus have legitimacy by reason of their source, their author, who is God, and that God communicates, sends, breathes, and bestows all power by the Spirit. If, as with the confrontation between Pilate and Jesus, there is conflict between the power to coerce and the power of truth, we cannot presume that one of the powers lacks legitimacy and must be renounced. Pilate did not believe that Jesus could have any kingship or power precisely for the reason that Jesus gave: his disciples did not fight. But the "failure" of Jesus to qualify as king in Pilate's eyes was the failure of Pilate's limited sight: he could not "see" that there is power in truth, a power that brute force can neither comprehend nor control.

Jesus in turn did not make the foolish claim that Pilate had no power, nor did he renounce the kind of power which Pilate could command, as if Pilate's power came from an evil source. Pilate's power was of the same sort as employed by Joseph in Egypt. It is not far-fetched to suppose that Jesus regarded the power of Pilate as originating in the same source as his own. The source of power is one, but the forms of power are many. The misuse of power is a failure of imagination occurring when those who hold a certain power are as blind as Pilate to other kinds of power, and thus fail to "see" either the limits of their own power or the ultimate source of the power entrusted to them.

UNITY OF THE SPIRIT IN THE BONDS OF PEACE

In practical terms, how can this discussion help us re-imagine the Spirit and thus to relocate the Spirit within the power to impose order and to create unity? In a tumultuous world, there does not seem to be much unity among peoples and nations. Turning to Ephesians 4, one reads a description of a community in which both order and peace are assumed.

> I therefore, a prisoner for the Lord, beg you to lead a life worthy of the calling to which you have been called, with all lowliness and meekness, with patience, forbearing one another in love, eager to maintain the unity of the Spirit in the bond of peace. (vv. 1-3)

The writer assumes unity among his readers and that they are bound together in an ordered community, "no longer . . . tossed to and fro and carried about with every wind of doctrine," because they are to "grow up in every way into him who is the head, into Christ" (vv. 14-15).

The Ephesians do not generate unity and a peaceful order any more than the apostles generate energy for mission (see Acts 1–2). As witnesses to the resurrection of Jesus, the apostles had a great story to publicize. But the risen Christ commanded them to stay in Jerusalem. They were commanded to do nothing but wait and told that "before many days you shall be baptized with the Holy Spirit" (Acts 1:5). They were still impatient to know the scheduled time when Jesus "would restore the kingdom to Israel" (1:6). It was not for them to know, but rather to trust that they would "receive power when the Holy Spirit has come upon you . . ." (1:8). They had the message but did not yet have the power, the Spirit. Words without breath cannot be spoken. Without the Spirit there can be no order or unity.

The claim is that in day-to-day—or secular—experience, intimations of the Spirit's power impose order and create unity. Occasions of order and unity in truth, to the extent that they are found among Christians, are not monopolies, because there are "secular" approximations of the "unity of the Spirit in the bonds of peace." Order and unity are not absent from human experience, even in these latter days of the bloodiest century in human history. Wherever these traits appear, we can call them the ordinary or secular functions of the Spirit of God. *Order* and *unity* are terms that imply connectedness between or among more than one member, unit, or person. Being part of a crowd—at a baseball game or political rally—is a common instance of connectedness in the cause of a shared loyalty and goal. Such a relationship does not deny individuality, because each person is distinguishable from, while locatable among, the others. We can all be picked out from the crowd as individual, unique, and identifiable. The "what" or "who" that reveals both individuality and commonality is an intimation of spirit. "Spirit is that which lies between . . ."[26] and which makes real both the separateness of persons from each other and the conjunction with one another.

The magnitude of hostility among nations and inhabitants of any large city might suggest that there is little of that "Spirit which lies between," and that there is no common ground on which to establish either a peaceful order or unity in shared truth. There seems, in the lethal practice of human interaction, to be only irreducible differences, unbridgeable gaps, and insurmountable barriers between cultures, genders, races, religions, generations, and ideologies. For example, the American motto *e pluribus unum* (from the many, unity) is not a dream but a nightmare for large numbers of African Americans, a nightmare perpetuated by the majority against the minorities.[27]

The Spirit is that power which pervades all power, including the power to impose order, to elicit obedience, to win loyalty. It is that breath which can fire up the many and galvanize them into a disciplined band of loyalists. Such power is necessary for any organization, whether political parties, economic ventures, athletic teams, religious movements, or neighborhood organizations. When a group loses that fire its members withdraw and loyalty diminishes. The group dies. Leaders with the power to dominate are often those able to ignite individuals whose commitments are given to goals which the leaders enunciate, because the individuals are convinced that the goals serve their best interest. When leaders misuse that power or seem to lose it, even if they still hold legitimate office, they lack the power to switch on the current and to win obedience. Outsiders are often dismissive of such leaders as "manipulative," but such an accusation is really a recognition, often mixed with envy, that such is real power—the power to impose order. The critics' suspicion is that the power to impose order is inherently bad. But that suspicion confuses the means (power to dominate) with the ghastly ends to which such power has been put. It is not the means alone that should be isolated for criticism, but the goals for which the power to dominate is used.

Because its source is good, the power to dominate cannot be inherently bad. But the Spirit as source of power does not decide and control how such power is used. As we noted in the case of Pilate, the power to dominate is sharply limited: no person or society can live for long by that use of power alone. The collapse of the Soviet Union is only one—but the most dramatic— of the recent instances of presuming that the power to dominate extends to control of thought, speech, movement, art, and faith. Christian wisdom proposes that the Soviet leaders controlled by none other than the Spirit's power. Their undoing was a failure to acknowledge the source of their power and a presumption that they were not beholden to another, that power was their own doing, and that supplying nothing more than bread was sufficient. Denying the Spirit meant there was no freedom for the Spirit to publicize the Word. Thus the Soviet Union died by its futile effort to live by bread alone.[28]

* * * * *

What are the practical consequences of re-imagining the power of the Spirit as pervasive in all forms of secular power, including power as domination? What are the consequences for leadership in Christian mission? Certainly we begin to question our common habit of demonizing power as domination, which encourages Christians to regard the political realm as godless, or to impugn anyone with economic power as ipso facto greedy and alone responsible for keeping others in poverty. Such re-imagining would require Christians to be honest about social settings in which the church itself has coercive, political, and economic power, and to warn its ecclesiastical leaders against overstepping the limits on coercive power. Churches have too often been guilty of using such power to control thought, speech, movement, art, and expressions of faith. "Secular" forms of power are not inherently wrong. They are forms of the Spirit as power. Thus churches can legitimately acquire such power (owning property or exercising the right of free speech), but the distinctive mission of religious communities does not justify its misuse. We have repeatedly observed that the power to dominate or coerce is sharply limited, but that it is not necessarily demonic. In fact, the power to dominate for the purpose of order is necessary for everything that we call good. The challenge is to discern the point at which domination goes too far. Consider the human capacity to manipulate the natural environment. It is possible, for instance, to fashion an urban garden, in which the human spirit can be nurtured by the beauty devised by a master landscape architect, as surely as both body and spirit have been imperiled by polluting rivers and by constructing cheap, ugly urban housing. Power as domination is not wicked in and of itself. The difference between a child banging noisily on a piano and a pianist is that the latter is able to control with physical precision the manipulation of keys. The difference between the clutter left by the strong men who move your furniture and the designer of a beautiful room is that one is able to direct where furnishings, carpets, paintings, and sculpture will be positioned. The Spirit is not absent from the power to dominate or manipulate, but is as necessary a factor as such power is necessary to achieve things we call good. Discerning the Spirit is not a matter of detecting the absence or presence of Spirit, but requires wisdom concerning limits: What goal should the power of Spirit, considered as power as domination, pursue? The power to dominate is largely physical, external, and observable. As such it can achieve order, but it cannot coerce unity of minds, hearts, wills, commitments. This has been a hard lesson for repressive political regimes to learn.

South Africa in the late 1980s was a model of efficiency, technical advance, productivity, and control. The mechanisms of electronic surveillance and police power made our visits as white Americans to South Africa utterly safe and comfortable. There was order. By the early 1990s, South Africa had embarked on a program to "win the hearts" of the black majority whose lives had been tightly ordered and suppressed. But the black majority, as long as it was externally controlled, was never of one mind or heart with the whites regarding that peculiar order called apartheid.

The power to order the outward features of social life has limits. It cannot achieve unity by sheer force. When those who are excluded from the privileges enjoyed by the dominant order begin to rebel, the limits of the power to dominate are exposed. The release of Nelson Mandela, who more than anyone else symbolized the yearnings of blacks in South Africa, was—at the very least—an admission that the power to dominate is limited. Not long after his release, some groups among the black majority demanded that the majority in a new government have the same unlimited power to dominate under which blacks had long suffered. Their unspeakable suffering at the hands of the white minority understandably drove their demand for a turn at wielding unlimited power, but it did not repeal or nullify the fact that "unlimited" power to dominate is an illusion. Such power can order the external material conditions of society, but it cannot unify the hearts, minds, and wills of the people. No one lives by bread alone, no matter how efficiently or equitably it is delivered.

What, then, is the power of the Spirit to unify the hearts, minds, wills, and commitments of people? The writer of Ephesians assumed that in the Christian community there is "the unity of the Spirit in the bonds of peace," and called on Christian readers to "make every effort to maintain" that unity. The writer listed seven components of such unity: "There is one body, and one Spirit, just as you were called to the one hope of your calling, one Lord, one faith, one baptism, one God and Father of all, who is above all and through all and in all" (4:4-6). It is a straightforward claim. Unity in the Spirit is unity in the faith, specifically faith in Christ. Faith is given by the Spirit, the Spirit of truth. The power of the Spirit to unify is the power of truth.

We are brought back to the close and perilous connection between two forms of power. They are never far from one another: the power to impose a visible, external order and the inward power to unify hearts and minds. The power to dominate is sharply limited. It cannot by force alone unify the hearts, minds, and wills. Yet the unity of one body, one Spirit, one faith is surely hindered in its inward work if people live in constant terror, social disorder, or threat. The missionary expansion of the Christian movement throughout the Roman Empire was possible at the beginning because of the relative safety of Roman highways, the orderly movement of mail, and the possibility of travel on the Mediterranean trade routes. The Christian movement made use of the empire's infrastructure, and never doubted that God had ordained governments. The persecution of Christians was not prompted because believers blew up Roman highways or schemed to overthrow the emperor. The persecutions began because Christians believed in Christ as Lord, and not in Caesar as Lord, that only in Christ can there be one body, one Spirit, one faith. When Caesar, or one of his deputies like Pilate, crossed the legitimate boundaries of the power to dominate and sought to enforce inward unity, loyalty of heart, and commitment of spirit, followers of Christ said, No!

Later, when after Constantine the Christian movement had become the favored religion of the empire, Christians showed that they also were capable of overstepping the boundaries of legitimate use of coercive power. When faced with disagreements about doctrine, which compromised the unity of one body and one Spirit, a bishop like Augustine was quite willing to appeal to the emperor to enforce doctrinal conformity. Augustine was not the last religious leader to make that blunder.

It has been impossible in practice to separate the power to dominate through the machinery of political systems from the power that can unify the minds and wills of people. Given this statement, the separation of church and state is *not* what prevails in the United States. Because the power of each derives from the same source, they cannot be completely separated.

Each serves a distinctive, but not separate, goal. We are re-imagining the Spirit as the one source of such powers. In this view of Spirit, the many forms of power can neither be repudiated as demonic nor can they be isolated and forced into separate spheres. However, we can discern when those given the power to dominate intrude on the inward life of people, in which only the Spirit of truth has legitimate power. And we can discern when that unity of heart, mind, and will which is the property of truth alone is ascribed mistakenly to a political system. That is the beginning of totalitarianism, which places a system above criticism and thus justifies the persecution of those who dissent. We will return to further implications of this re-imagining, especially for the Christian understanding of Christ as the criterion by which to discern God's power to reconcile the world.

What in the world is God doing? is a question driving us to ask about the Spirit of God at work in all forms of power, including the power of force and the power of truth. The misuse of these forms of Spirit-given power is no reason to demonize them nor to despair that they can be instruments of God's will for ultimate reconciliation. The baseline question is, How can the powers of force and truth be used in the Spirit of the one from whom all powers come?

CHAPTER FOUR

THE POWER
OF THE SPIRIT
IN TRAGIC CONFLICT

Before the worldviews of Europe influenced their consciousness, it would have been impossible for Africans to think that the reality of Spirit occupied a different realm than ordinary life. In the traditional African worldview everything is saturated with real but unseen spiritual power,[1] as we now take it for granted that every living thing is saturated with unseen but life-giving oxygen. When I first discussed the design and theme of this book with friends, university lecturers in philosophy and religious studies in Africa, the response was mixed. On the one hand, my friends were interested in differentiating ways of imagining power. Africans live with daily power conflicts that have ravaged Africa for generations. Power is part of their life, their world. On the other hand, my friends thought it curious that a present-day theologian would hold on to a concept like the Spirit, and try to imagine it as the pervasive presence and power of God in the world! It is hardly surprising that all had done graduate studies in British and American universities. In such academic situations power is an empirical and publicly discussed reality, while the Spirit is at best an embarrassing anachronism, and not, in any ordinary sense of the word, real. African intellectuals in postcolonial Africa, like their American contemporaries, often exhibit the same mental split by which they, too, separate spirit from the commonsense meaning of secular—at least they did with me in academic conversation.

What in the world, we are asking, is God doing? We scarcely have an answer to that question unless we entertain—that is, imagine—a different view of the world. The Spirit as the power and presence of God must be relocated within the ordinary experiences of power. Although this century began with confidence in a coming secular era, it is ending as a far more religious century than any might have predicted. These last few decades there have been frequent and much-publicized outbursts of fundamentalist religion. New religions have attracted many adherents. These developments would have been hard to predict. Nonetheless, the Spirit still conjures up—for most people educated in the West—a world apart from the ordinary. For such persons, to speak of the Spirit as the real presence of God in anything, let alone in every conceivable form of power, would be an unaccustomed stretch of the imagination. The Spirit is typically regarded as an exception to ordinary experience and to ordinary manifestations of power.[2]

In the final years of the twentieth century, more theologians have been calling for new images of God's presence and power in the world.[3] Whenever God's power and presence as Spirit are, for practical purposes, denied by Christians, then Christian worship itself is seriously undermined.

> In a secular age, when ordinary life is separated in its self-understanding from its own transcendent ground, sacramental symbols unrelated to the transcendent dimension of our own existence in life become magical or merely traditional. . . . God is already there in our existence as its ultimate ground and its ultimate goal. The role of sacrament and word alike is not so much to insert the divine activity into nature, into the ordinary course of our lives, as it is to bring that prior relation forth into awareness and give it the shape, the power, and form of Jesus Christ.[4]

The present book, in agreement with Gilkey, presents a sustained argument against the widespread habit of preachers, seminary students, and their teachers to speak of God "intervening," "invading," "breaking in," or "inserting" Godself into the ordinary existence of people or history. Such language betrays the preachers' and teachers' assumption that God is absent or removed from the ordinary—except, of course, whenever the church worships or preachers preach. The listener is expected to believe that in those moments the transcendent deity makes the deity's self present and available to those who have the ears to hear, and the transcendent one becomes, for that moment, the immanent one. Apart from such occasions, the Spirit of God is neither present nor efficacious. Those holding this view of the Spirit of God must live in and travel between two realities.

The goal of this book is to counter the split between the secular and the Spirit by examining the ways in which we imagine forms of power, and then to inquire how such forms can be re-imagined in terms of the presence and power of God as Spirit. In the previous chapter I took up the theme of power as domination, either in the form of coercive military or political force, or as the intellectual power to impose unity through authoritative doctrine. It must be granted, as noted, that power as domination and as truth need not be rejected out of hand, but can be, in a qualified fashion, useful for discerning the power of God in the world. Yet too often in such a view, the Spirit of God is taken to be nearly identical with the church as institutional order, and usually can be expected to align itself with conservative political ideologies.

In this chapter, I come to a different mode of imagining the Spirit as the presence and power of God. The emphasis is not on faith as belief in the right doctrine but on faith as a way of life. The real conflicts evident in both nature and human history are not, in this view, neatly reconciled as in a divine comedy. These conflicts persist in an ongoing tragedy that can only be endured, if at all, by the power of the Spirit. It is not mythical theocracy in this view that guides faithful people's discernment of the Spirit, but down-to-earth, pragmatic prophecy.

THE POWER TO VENTURE

The power to venture is of a different sort than the "power to reconcile," which was the focus of the previous chapter. The difference is what distinguishes comedy from tragedy. In comedy the conflicts and predicaments of the actors are not as significant as the harmonious order that somehow reconciles seemingly opposing forces. In tragedy, on the other hand, the focus is on the struggle itself, the struggle for righteousness, and not—as in comedy— on the cosmic order that determines how everything will turn out. In comedy we are aware that the real power behind the scenes is the objective order imposed by the dramatist who is manipulating the characters without their knowing it. Their predicaments and how they deal with them are of no ultimate significance. In this chapter I focus on the power and presence of the Spirit in the struggle itself. Here we honor and value the experience of risk, adventure, pilgrimage, and exploration. Here we draw our attention to the struggle of the actors themselves, because the outcome, rather than being determined by the all-knowing dramatist, turns in large measure on the choices the actors make between competing goods. Here we envision the Spirit as the energy fueling the conflict between the competing goods, and so we do not have to wait for the outcome before we can speak of the Spirit. It is the power and presence of the Spirit that empower every good in conflict with other goods. The struggle between good and good is itself the essence of tragedy, and it is the experience of the power of the Spirit.

To live in the Spirit is to venture. It is to risk a way of life more than to rest on a set of right beliefs. The power of the Spirit is the power to venture without assurance that the encounter with conflicting values will end in a happy resolution. We are dealing here with the tragic elements of history and nature, tragic in that every moment is in some way a life-and-death struggle, a competition among a range of possible outcomes, many of them good. In any conflict of competing goods, not all conceivable outcomes can become the actual outcome. Every good achievement, every good purpose realized, will always be purchased at the expense of other good possibilities that had to be denied. The birth of any actual good means the death, the elimination, of other good possibilities that can never be realized. This way of imagining the power and presence of the Spirit is suspicious of any grand metaphor by which to refer to the Spirit of God, because metaphors always draw our gaze away from what is happening in the present. A metaphor implies that the meaning of the moment must be found somewhere else. According to the tragic vision, however, the meaning is in the moment. The Spirit of God is in the details of this predicament—or it is nowhere.[5] Thus the power and presence of the Spirit of God, in this imaginative construction, are not transferred to a higher order, but are located within the complexities and limitations, however morally serious, of every human decision.[6]

To illustrate, liberal versions of the church and its mission are usually captive to this way of imagining the Spirit. For the liberal, the distinctive activities by which the church makes known the divine will are not first of all its sacraments and rituals. The liberal does not seek to point *beyond* the world to some ideal order. It is by its moral action *in* the world, *in* solidarity with the poor and *in* promoting justice, that the liberal church makes known the will and power of God in the world. The church is not primarily the means by which the invisible divine realm is made sacramentally visible. Instead, the church is a voluntary association of those called and empowered by the Spirit to embody the new humanity in Christ.[7] Sacramental actions and the like empower Christians to act for freedom from oppression and for justice. The controlling image of the church—or, more pointedly, the way one imagines the church—is that of a voluntary association of people empowered for actions calculated to liberate the oppressed and to judge the oppressors. Moral action is primary and sacramental enactment is but a secondary instrument for sustaining the faithful in their public action. Praxis or, more precisely, orthopraxis—as thoughtful action for the sake of the world—takes precedence over orthodoxy, right belief, or doctrinally correct liturgy for the maintenance of the church.

None of this implies that there is no room for a vision, for a hoped-for order not yet realized in the here and now. The power of the Spirit to venture is a call forward into circumstances that cannot be predicted, a call beyond what is familiar. It is not a call upward into a place where there will be no conflict. There is no zone free of the conflict between and among a range of good possibilities straining to become actual. This vision of Christian faith is not otherworldly but empowers people to participate in the human quest for freedom and justice. The vision does not hope for the absence of conflict but for an increase of possibilities for *every* creature, for a social and natural environment in which novelty, diversity, and growth are encouraged and nurtured rather than suppressed. It is a realistic vision because it assumes that choices will become, not simpler, but more complicated. It is a hopeful vision because it believes that increasing diversity and competition can harmonize, that the interaction of the many can be mutually beneficial. In this vision, peace is not achieved by domineering power or authoritative truth. Peace of that sort would deny genuine freedom. It would impose law and order and minimize equal justice for all. When imagination is held captive to fixed notions of power as domineering force or authoritative truth—as in the way of metaphor and comedy—then it is hard to see how there can be genuine growth, novelty, or adventure. Metaphor and comedy trivialize the power to venture and to have a decisive role in determining possible futures. Freedom is sacrificed for the sake of order; justice is sacrificed for the sake of unity. In this chapter I try to imagine power in the form of freedom and justice. Can we imagine freedom or justice as a form of power?[8]

It has often been said that those in bondage accept the pain because they assume it is necessary, that it is their inescapable fate. But when made aware that their condition is not necessary, that it is not predestined and that freedom is a possibility, then the shackles become intolerable. The very possibility of freedom empowers people to struggle against oppression. The same can be said of victims of injustice, who bear a disproportionate share of hardship while receiving a meager share of privilege. Conditioned to accept injustice as necessary, their condition becomes intolerable whenever made aware that justice is a real possibility. The possibility of justice becomes a real power to rise up against the conditions that they no longer accept as necessary.[9]

THE POWER OF FREEDOM AND JUSTICE

Whenever we shift focus from the power to impose order and unity to the power of freedom and justice, something happens to our imagination. Other figures come into view that had previously been eclipsed. The prophet and not the political or ecclesiastical potentates now captures our imagination and reconfigures our sense of power. The power of freedom and justice, in biblical terms, is the power of the prophet. In the prophetic tradition, the rule or kingship of God does not mean that order must preclude novelty. Theocracy—the rule of God—is qualified by prophecy. The biblical narrative of Israel's history presents God's rule through a succession of novel as well as imperfect political orders. God's rule, as depicted in the Bible, does not perpetuate the same political order. The prophets were key actors in this narrative, interpreting the interplay between order and freedom in the religious as well as the civil realm. The prophets' call for justice did not imply chaos or the end of unity for Israel. The restoration of unjustly seized property and redistribution of land would represent a new social order, not social disorder.

The history of Israel is the story of the truth of God working itself out in history. The truth of God, however, is not represented by a fixed order. Rather, the truth of God is God being true to the covenant through a succession of social structures, by which the people of God approximate the covenant of God. The prophets helped interpret the interplay between unity and justice. Not surprisingly, the call for freedom and for justice often placed the prophets in jeopardy to those who saw prophets as enemies of good order and social unity. Opponents of the prophetic vision have no imagination for what a new order might bring. This scenario has played out again and again in history, and throughout Africa since the 1960s. We must not confine our

discernment of the power of freedom and of justice only to the far too frequent, ghastly, and extreme situations of human suffering. Power in its many
forms is not episodic, occasional, or random. The Christian wisdom is that
God's power is everywhere present in all power, including the power of freedom and of justice. It is from God's omnipresent Spirit that freedom and justice as forms of power derive their efficacy. The power of the Spirit in its
many forms extends into every "secular" form of power, a claim that may cut
against the piety of many who claim to have and to know the Spirit.

We can amplify this claim by more conscientious attention to the function
of imagination in a theology of the Spirit as the power and the presence of
God. The power of the Spirit to venture gives the human spirit the virtues of
courage to embrace freedom and *wisdom* to discern the call for and meaning
of justice. Courage and wisdom are gifts of the Spirit before they are achieve-
ments of the human soul. Let us consider how these signs of the Spirit's
power and presence emerge in human ventures both within and removed
from struggles against bondage and injustice.

Previously we had observed that order and unity are the favored images
when theocratic modes of imagination capture thought and language. Preferred images of human action are then drawn from the battleground or the
strong city, and from the academy with its authoritative teaching. The heroes
or preferred figures of leadership are monarchs, bishops, and generals as well
as philosophers, theologians, and other guardians of true belief. What images
suggest themselves when we imagine power in the form of freedom? The
political ruler and general are replaced by the explorer, experimenter, and
entrepreneur, all willing to risk new ventures. The teacher delights in the
intellectual courage of students to challenge authority more than their
appeal to authoritative proof texts. The battleground is replaced by the
uncharted frontier, the expanding marketplace, or the playing field. Such
images evoke the power of freedom, novelty, and courage, and of the lure of
genuine risk. Conflict and tragedy are inevitable. The outcome turns upon
the decisions and actions of those who have received the power of freedom
by the Spirit. Still, the Spirit does not determine how that power will be used
by the empowered.[10]

Similarly, what images does the power of justice evoke? Rarely do the
images include the philosopher and the academic theologian. These images
must give way to peacemakers, who actively seek the right path of life for the
sake of peace—not peace as the absence of conflict, but peace with justice.
Justice is first enacted in the public forum, not in the lecture hall; in the free
and open exchange of ideas in the public media, not in the sanctuary or the
seminar room. It is not to the professor or magistrate to whom peacemakers
must turn but to the prophets, to those who judge rightly, few of whom eat at
the king's table or have tenure.

THE POWER TO VENTURE: BIBLICAL WITNESS

Every reading of scripture is guided by discrete structures of imagination. In this chapter we are investigating how to imagine or "read" power in terms of freedom and justice. The power of the Spirit of God in the world is the power to venture. This structure of imagination, too, can guide the reader of scripture. But reading scripture is like drinking an unfamiliar wine. It is necessary to cleanse the palate so that one can appreciate the fullness of fragrance, taste, and body. We must cleanse our minds of habits that obscure the meaning of terms concerning the power and presence of God as Spirit.

The most extraordinary instance in the Bible of the Spirit as the power to venture is Pentecost. We will return to the New Testament account of Pentecost later in this section. It is not, of course, the first appearance of the power of the Spirit in scripture. Indeed, the New Testament narrative of the presence and work of the Spirit in the mission of Jesus and of the post-Pentecost church presupposes the rich heritage of the Hebrew Scriptures, and most certainly the prophetic tradition. In the Old Testament the Spirit of God is not an isolated or occasional factor of existence. Jürgen Moltmann summarizes the difficulty that Westerners have in understanding the Old Testament.

> If we wish to understand the Old Testament word ruach, we must forget the word "spirit," which belongs to Western culture. The Greek word pneuma, the Latin spiritus and the Germanic Geist/ghost were always conceived as antitheses to matter and body. They mean something immaterial. Whether we are talking Greek, Latin, German or English, by the Spirit of God we mean something disembodied, supersensory, and supernatural. But if we talk in Hebrew about Yahweh's ruach, we are saying: God is a tempest, a storm, a force in body and soul, humanity and nature. The Western cleavage between spirit and body, spirituality and sensuousness is so deeply rooted in our languages that we must have recourse to other translations if we want to arrive at a more or less adequate rendering of the word ruach.[11]

The Old Testament, in short, is a compelling instance of imagining the reality of the Spirit of God as everywhere alive. God is the Lord over good and evil forces. In Judges 9:23, "God sent an evil spirit [ruach] between Abimelech and the men of Shechem." According to 1 Samuel 16:14 it was "an evil ruach from the Lord" which tormented Saul. In short, there is no power or force, no energy, breath, or ruach in the world outside the lordship of God. The Spirit is not an attribute of God but is the very presence of God in the world. Moltmann further points out the close association of the Spirit of God in the Old Testament with the word of God. "Ruach is thought of as the breath of God's voice."[12] Moltmann shows that this very point, at the center of chapter 2 in the present volume, is assumed to be the worldview of Old Testament times.

God's way and presence in the world are the inseparable breath and word of God. The Old Testament understanding of the Spirit of God, then, is akin to my thesis in these chapters. Spirit, to be adequately translated and not confused with Western habits of thought, must include at least three elements. (1) The Spirit of God is God's inescapable and universal presence. Moltmann quotes Psalm 139, "Whither shall I go from thy spirit? Or whither shall I flee from thy presence?" and then refers to Calvin, who said that the presence of God must always be interpreted pneumatologically. (2) The Spirit of God is not only the personal presence of God but also the power of God as the energy by which all existence is sustained. "When we think about the *ruach* we have to say that God is in all things, and all things are in God—though this does not mean making God the same as everything else." (3) The Spirit of God is experienced as the space of freedom, or "breathing room." "Thou hast set my feet in a broad place" (Ps. 31:8).[13]

Surveying the Old Testament literature and relevant scholarship, Moltmann makes the important observation that a shift occurred after the early prophets, who were evidently itinerant preachers possessed by the Spirit. They left no literary traces. It was in roughly that same period, as observed in chapter 3, that Joseph received from the Spirit wisdom and good judgment. Then in the later prophets—Amos, Hosea, Micah, Isaiah, and Jeremiah—who are known by their writings, the prominence of the Spirit is replaced by God's call through the word. Their authority is designated by the formula, "Thus says the Lord." "The 'literary' prophets are molded by the call of God, not by inspiration; by the word of God, not by exceptional ecstasies."[14] Still later, particularly with Ezekiel and Deutero-Isaiah during the exile, the appeal to the *ruach* of God who inspires the prophet with visions and prophecies occurs again.[15] Turning to the wisdom literature, one immediately recognizes the great diversity, yet scholars have argued that wisdom and Spirit are nearly interchangeable. Three great poems, Proverbs 8, Job 28, and Ecclesiasticus 24, present the wisdom (*chokma*) of God "as an ordering power imminent in the world,"[16] in much the same way as the Spirit.

To round out this brief overview of the Old Testament understanding of God's presence in the world, it is necessary to speak briefly of the *shekinah* of God.[17] The idea developed out of cultic language and refers to the tabernacle or tent of God, the divine indwelling. After the deportation of large numbers of people to Babylon, the dwelling place of God had to be dissociated from the temple in Jerusalem. Thus the *shekinah* was thought to be with the worshiping people in their suffering as exiles, in their synagogues, and during their wanderings. The *shekinah* is truly God present, but not in the sense that God is confined to worship settings. Nothing, not even the heavens, can contain God. So *shekinah* indicates the presence of God, but never serves as a name by which God can be placed at the beck and call of human beings. The presence of God is always at God's initiative, and is neither guaranteed by nor dependent on a prescribed structure, ritual, or office.[18]

Walter Brueggemann summarizes the view I am taking here, that the Old Testament prophets represent the paradigm of the Spirit's power to venture into the conflicts of society: "The prophets voice a restlessness about social reality that bespeaks the restless rule of God, and the opening of social reality for God's new possibilities."[19] Brueggemann writes of the prophets that they were "generative personalities" who were "deeply engaged in the socioeconomic, political issues of their day," and that they pronounced "unpopular positions in the conflicts of their communities." They do more than speak as reporters or analysts who simply describe the reality of these conflicts. They are "artists who re-describe reality and who construe social experience in new and venturesome categories" that "require imaginative reception by the hearers." Brueggemann makes clear that the prophets were not antitraditional. Even when they would rail against the injustice of the status quo and conventional religious practices, they were rooted in the traditions of Moses, were informed by and shared the priestly tradition's concern for true sacrifice, and drew on imagery of the wisdom tradition's affirmation of creation under the rule of God. As rooted as they were in old traditions, and as open as they were to the new possibilities of God's future, the prophets nevertheless focused on commitment to the belief that "the present moment of life is a critical moment when life-and-death decisions must be made that bespeak loyalty to God and that impinge upon public power and purpose," a commitment that is frequently "subversive of all that is settled."[20]

In the prophetic books, as elsewhere in the Old Testament, the word of God is inseparable from the power of the breath or Spirit of God, by which all things have their existence. As the Nicene Creed declares, the Holy Spirit is the "Lord, the Giver of [all] life," who also "spoke by the prophets." Even when the prophetic books do not explicitly ascribe the words of the prophet to the Spirit's inspiration, the link between word and Spirit is implicit. Both word and breath come from one source, the mouth of God.[21] *Even God does not speak without breathing.* As for the prophets, their knowledge and inspired insight into the social, political, economic, and religious situation in which they lived was one aspect of their work, but the courage to put their vision into powerful words—to "speak it out"—was another. The words, images, and insightful redescriptions of reality would have gone with them to their graves if the Spirit had not breathed into them, empowering them to speak prophetic words to their contemporaries, many of whom were sure to hear the words as subversive. The life-and-death situations in which the prophet is called to speak God's word of judgment and hope are so intimidating that most of us would keep silent. If we speak or write, it would probably be from the safe distance of a secure pulpit or lecture hall. We cannot account for the prophets' power to speak apart from the breath of God, without which the living and powerful word could not be spoken.

The power of the Spirit to venture is a continuous and everywhere present reality, but such power is not everywhere used to sustain freedom and justice.

The Spirit is omnipresent, but prophecy has never been more than an occasional occurrence. Prophecy reappears in the New Testament as one of the gifts of the Spirit. "Now there are varieties of gifts, but the same Spirit; and there are varieties of services, but the same Lord; and there are varieties of activities, but it is the same God who activates all of them in everyone" (1 Cor. 12:4-6). To the gifts of wisdom, knowledge, faith, healing, and miracles Paul adds the gifts of prophecy, spirit discernment, tongues, and interpretation. "All these are activated by one and the same Spirit, who allots to each one individually just as the Spirit chooses" (12:11). Whatever the gift, it is just that—a gift given by the Spirit and not a self-generated ability, a self-created power. The Spirit chooses which gifts are given, but the Spirit does not control or determine the purpose to which that gift is put. Not all who have the gifts of prophecy, wisdom, knowledge, and so forth use them "for the common good" (12:7). Obviously the believers at Corinth had not been doing so, or Paul would have had no reason to make this point. Paul reminds them that all gifts come from the same source, and then gives his well-known criterion for settling disputes concerning gifts: How are they being used? To what end? Does a group use its gifts to puff themselves up or to build up the church? Are they used to create discord and party spirit or in such a manner "that there be no dissension within the body" (12:25)?

At the beginning of this section we looked ahead to the story of Pentecost. In an introduction to Luke's second volume, the Acts of the Apostles, Bruce Metzger comments: "In fact, the book might appropriately be entitled, 'The Acts of the Holy Spirit,' for the dominating theme is the power of the Spirit manifested in and through the members of the early church."[22] Luke opens his narrative, addressed to Theophilus, with a reminder that in the first volume he had written "about all that Jesus did and taught from the beginning until the day when he was taken up to heaven, after giving instructions through the Holy Spirit to the apostles whom he had chosen" (1:1-2). In the next verses the resurrected Jesus speaks to the apostles "about the kingdom of God" (1:3), and then gives them instructions. He "ordered them not to leave Jerusalem, but to wait there for the promise of the Father" (1:4). They were to stay put and do nothing. They were told to wait until they would "be baptized with the Holy Spirit not many days from now" (1:5). It should be stressed that these disciples were now well instructed and had "many convincing proofs" (1:3) of the resurrection. They were eager to broadcast the great story, supposing that this was the time when Jesus "will restore the kingdom to Israel" (1:6). They had the word, the whole story with necessary proof, and were well prepared with forty days' worth of instructions. Yet Jesus cautioned them, "It is not for you to know the times or periods that the Father has set by his own authority" (1:7). They had the word but they did not have the power or breath for speaking the word. For that they had to wait. "But you will receive power when the Holy Spirit has come upon you; and you will be my witnesses in Jerusalem . . . and to the ends of the earth" (1:8).

So the apostles waited in Jerusalem and did not venture forth with the story of the resurrection as they evidently were eager to do. But they were not inactive. They devoted themselves to prayer (1:14), and they attended to replacing the traitor, Judas, with Matthias, who was then "added to the eleven apostles" (1:26). What happened next is well known among Christians as the Day of Pentecost. The Jews would have been celebrating the day as the anniversary of God's gift of the law. Ever since that particular Pentecost, Christians have remembered it as the day when God poured out the gift of the Holy Spirit in a special way. The apostles—well instructed in the message of the resurrection—received the Spirit (breath), the courage to venture beyond Jerusalem as witnesses. Indeed they received the same Spirit that had descended on Jesus at his baptism, which had driven Jesus into the wilderness to be tempted, which had filled Jesus with power when he preached in his home synagogue, and which Jesus had promised to send after his death. In Luke's telling, the acts of the apostles cannot be separated from the acts of the Spirit. The "witness" (*martyrios*) for which Jesus had instructed them, and for which the Spirit had given them power, came to imply readiness to go into the world and the courage to die, if necessary, for the sake of the gospel.

In brief, the apostles receive the power of the Spirit to venture beyond the boundaries of the Jewish tradition into the broader Gentile world for the sake of the Christian witness. The apostle Paul is the chief exemplar of the Spirit-induced drive to tell others what he has to say. On his way from Macedonia to Jerusalem, where he will be the target of a conspiracy to kill him and from where he will be sent to Rome as a prisoner, Paul speaks with great passion to the elders of the church at Ephesus:

> I did not shrink from doing anything helpful, proclaiming the message to you and teaching you publicly and from house to house, as I testified to both Jews and Greeks. . . . And now, as a captive to the Spirit, I am on my way to Jerusalem, not knowing what will happen to me there, except that the Holy Spirit testifies to me in every city that imprisonment and persecutions are waiting for me. (Acts 20:20-23)

Paul, with the other apostles, now stands in the line of the prophets, empowered by the Spirit to venture forth and speak out. Apostles are now linked with prophets as the foundational witness upon which the Christian movement is based (cf. Eph. 2:20; 3:5; 4:11).

What distinguishes Paul's writing on the Spirit from an Old Testament prophet's is that, for Paul, the Spirit is none other than the Spirit of Christ. In Paul's epistles, far more clearly than in Acts or the Synoptic Gospels, writes Heron, the "Spirit as the active and transforming presence of God cannot be divorced from the crucified and risen Christ." The Old Testament *ruach* of God is none other than the Spirit who raised Jesus from the dead, none other than the Spirit of Christ. "[T]he active divine presence, the 'Spirit,' took on Christian shape. . . ."[23]

DISCERNING THE SPIRIT
IN THE WINDS OF CHANGE

With Africa as the social location in which much of this book was written, it will continue to influence the discussion. Early in the 1960s, the prime minister of England spoke in Cape Town to the then all-white parliament of South Africa. Looking northward across the continent he spoke of the "winds of change" that had begun to stir the peoples of Africa for what was to be more than thirty years of struggle for freedom from European colonial rule. The "winds of change" have now brought majority rule to South Africa, the continent's last stronghold of white political supremacy.[24]

One can assume that the prime minister, Harold Macmillan, was speaking figuratively when he prophesied change. The purpose of this section is to show how we might re-imagine the power of change as the power of the Spirit throughout history, as well as in Africa today. A commonplace way of thinking would be to trace changes in Africa to a multiplicity of factors, social, economic, cultural, and political, with total disregard for Spirit. These factors have all been accompanied by the horror of historical and social conditions—atrocities, corruption, mismanagement, poverty, racism, starvation, disease, civil disorder. These bloody conditions then themselves become causes for the next wave of human misery. Such misery has come to symbolize Africa in the imagination of many Americans and Europeans.

If we are to follow my thesis, we must infer that the Spirit's power in the form of the struggle for freedom has loosed the winds of change—for good and ill—across Africa and in much of the so-called developing world.[25] Theologians in North America like myself need to be cautious when speaking about liberative actions, lest we sound as if the Spirit of God empowers only the struggle for freedom, but is absent among those concerned for order. The power of the Spirit to venture beyond established order is indeed the power of freedom, but freedom is meaningless and can be used murderously when the power of order, or the power to impose order and unity, is cast aside.[26] The Spirit of God remains the source by which all powers are activated. To attend, as we are doing in this section, to the Spirit in the winds of change is not to forget that the Spirit also empowers forces that seek to establish order and unity.

The Spirit is God's power and presence in the world. The Spirit is God as the one who rules, governs, provides for, and sustains the world. Christians have prayed for nearly two millennia: "Thy kingdom come, thy will be done, on earth . . ." This prayer seems to imply both that God rules over the world as sovereign power, but also that God's human creatures are free to be willing subjects or to refuse. It is God who is sovereign. It is God's rule or kingship which is prayed for, implying that it might not come exactly as, or when, expected. The debate among theologians has always been over the "might not." Is the contingency—the "might not"—ultimately because it is up to God's will alone to determine whether or not, or when, the kingdom comes? In that case, human beings exercise no influence on whether or how or when the kingdom comes. Their freedom may be real but of no consequence for God's "kingdom . . . on earth." On the other hand, if God has given human beings genuine freedom, does that not mean that God's sovereignty is compromised?

Such questions have been debated whenever the theme of God's rule in the world is taken up. When Christians pray, "Thy kingdom come . . .," they pray to God. The prayer is not an exhortation to themselves or to fellow humans to change things that will bring in the kingdom. Who are the agents who govern? Who is in control of change? God alone? Humans and other creatures? God and humans together? The position in this reconstruction is that the originating agent of change is the Spirit dwelling within every creature. The Spirit of God in human beings is, among other forms of power, the power of freedom and the power to venture. The Spirit of God is the power without which there is no freedom. Therefore the Spirit is necessary for freedom and change, but the Spirit is not a sufficient guarantee that the outcome of freedom will be constructive rather than destructive. When Paul scolded the Christians at Corinth for their disorder and lack of unity, he acknowledged that they were all activated by the same Spirit, but Paul blamed them and not the Spirit for their sorry condition. When the Spirit as the power of freedom becomes the occasion for bloody excess, the fault must lie with those who have misused the power and not with the Spirit.

The twentieth century, contrary to Erich Fromm's indictment, has not been a time of "escape from freedom" but of the misuse of freedom. Foremost among the abusers of freedom are those who by reason of gender, race, or class have claimed privilege, thus assuming the means of political, economic, and military domination by which to be cruel and unjust to their perceived inferiors. At the close of the century, abuse of power had passed to a different sector of humanity. The postmodern rejection of every presumption of privilege based on inheritance, gender, race, or European custom has given rise to postcolonial regimes, which have grasped the instruments of power once the monopoly of the colonial interests that perfected them. These are the so-called neocolonialists. The ferocity of their resentment toward the racist colonial regimes that had for so long oppressed them is matched only by the ruthlessness of abuses against their own countrymen. Most of their victims are too impoverished by their new oppressors to resist, while the remainder, because they are of the wrong tribe, region, or political party, are systematically denied any share of power.[27]

This scenario presents a challenge to any effort, such as this one, to discern, or to infer, the Spirit in the winds of change. Postmodern thinkers like Michel Foucault have a thorough suspicion of philosophical or religious notions that there is a hidden truth, divine being, or universal purpose working itself out in conflicts among human beings. What is usually referred to as history Foucault regards as "the endless play of dominations" and "the staging of meticulously repeated scenes of violence." There is—in what is usually called history—no meaning by which to unify or schematize these repetitions of violence. There is no plot. "Humanity does not gradually progress from combat to combat until it arrives at universal reciprocity, where the rule of law finally replaces warfare; humanity installs each of its violences in a system of rules and thus proceeds from domination to domination." To our argument that the Spirit of God is the power and presence by which God rules, Foucault, in agreement with other postmodern thinkers, would assert that the "world of actual history knows only one kingdom, without providence or final cause, where there is only the 'iron hand of necessity shaking the dice-box of chance.' "[28]

This postmodern conclusion might seem a plausible way to read reports from Africa, the Middle East, or from the many republics of the former Soviet Union. In this bleak reading the Spirit of God has been deleted, freedom has been renamed "chance," and the only rule or kingdom is "the iron hand of necessity." God's Spirit is not present, nor is any universal power. "[T]he dominant experience of postmodernism is the absence of such presence."[29]

It is instructive to review how the presence of the Spirit came to be "the absence of such presence." Prior to the so-called postmodern era was the modern period, which began roughly in the middle of the 1600s. Modernity came to imply an increasing confidence that the rule of God's Spirit had been displaced by nature and history, a nearly perfect, complex machine whose principles of operation could be described by the natural, social, and historical sciences. Most theologians tended to accept this view of nature and history and to retreat into pietism, in which religion is a matter of inner experience and spiritual feeling; dogmatism, in which the truth of faith differs totally from scientific theories; or confessionalism, in which the certitude of faith alone, rather than philosophy and science, justifies the sinner. Thus most theologians accepted modernity and did not make direct challenges. They tried to preserve a place for theology by separating the truth-claims of faith from the realm of nature and "secular" history. Among modern theologians, Karl Barth has been the great antimodern exception. He resolutely opposed any attempt to let modern academic disciplines influence the content of theology.[30]

Stretching from shortly after the first centuries of the Christian movement through the Renaissance and Reformation, the classical/medieval period offered a still-earlier stage of Christian thought about God's power. During this period intellects such as Augustine, Aquinas, Calvin, and Luther shaped the prevailing views of God's sovereignty in history. For all the differences, their theologies share several features. First, all Christian thought of this era accepted the biblical view that God is both Lord over history and present in history in order to redeem humanity. In addition, the dominant ideas concerning God's rule were drawn primarily from imperial politics, and were reinforced by the church's own imitation of the Roman Empire in organizing structures of churchly authority. Ecclesiastical authority from early in the history of the church owed more to the politics of empire than to the power of the Spirit of God in the world and in the community of faith.[31]

The classical/medieval heritage concerning the Spirit as God's power and presence has bequeathed on Christians an enduring tension. On the one hand this heritage favors the image of God as the overpowering, imperialistic monarch who rules human experience without being affected by what happens in history. Augustine, Aquinas, Calvin, and Luther all argued that God's imperial rule did not eliminate human freedom. Sin indeed goes against divine will, but God knows how to use for redemptive purpose the very sin and evil that goes against God's will. Luther, for example, was consoled by the assurance that the "bondage of the will" relieved him, freed him, of anxiety lest he misuse freedom of the will. One cannot abuse what one does not have. It is unbelief to claim freedom of the will. In fact, belief in divine sovereignty was preferable to the dreadful suspicion that our lives are ruled by "the iron hand of necessity shaking the dice-box of chance" or to the foolish belief that our salvation was determined by sinful creatures such as our "selves."[32] On the other hand, while this seemingly unambiguous view of divine sovereignty does afford some consolation—"The gospel is just this: you are elected by divine decree. Period, full stop, ask no questions"—this view of divine sovereignty has ambiguous and even dangerous consequences. When this view of God's power and rule has been applied uncritically—I emphasize *uncritically*—it has contributed to Christians accepting religious totalitarian nationalism in South Africa from 1948 until 1994 and in Nazi Germany from 1932 until the close of World War II.

THE FUTURE AND WHAT GOD, AND WE OURSELVES, MAKE OF IT

I have been proposing a view of the Spirit as the power of freedom, the power to venture beyond classical views of the presence and power of God and beyond the grim postmodern view of the world as devoid of spirits, gods, purpose, center, or ground.[33] I offer this as a revisionist view in the sense that, like many Christians in the postmodern world, I do not find it possible to accept a view of power that is totally absent of the Spirit. But I do not believe that in order to infer the Spirit within all forms of power one must look at the human situation from the view of Christian faith.[34] The triune character of Christian faith will surely contribute to the multiple ways one can read history, but Christians can no longer control or alone preside over discussions of the Spirit. The challenge of the postmodern reading must be taken seriously in light of the horrors of twentieth-century history, but my revisionist conviction is that the "absence of presence" must also be examined critically. It is one—but only one—of the plausible ways to read the human condition at the end of this millennium. The power of the Spirit as the power to venture implies the possibility of venturing beyond the reductionist, confining, bleak, and finally nihilistic rendering of the human story.[35]

The re-visioning of the Spirit proposed throughout takes seriously but does not cave in to the postmodern challenge as if it were an irrefutable denial of presence. At the same time this re-visioning of the Spirit does not seek to repristinate views of the Spirit that dominated the classical/medieval period. To re-vision is neither to deny the tradition nor to pretend that we can be contemporaries of Luther or Calvin, let alone Augustine or Thomas Aquinas.[36] The view of the power of the Spirit in tragic conflict, I believe, avoids an uncritical, exclusivistic claim that the God of Jesus Christ through the Spirit is the only agent by whom the changes which make up history happen. The view also avoids the other extreme of removing the power and presence of God from all earthly events and powers. Nor have I accepted the mediating position dear to many theologians, namely to assume the absence of God from the secular realm and to proclaim God's presence and power as a now-and-then intervention.

No event can be adequately explained by reducing its origins to one cause. The Spirit as the power and presence of God is the only agent necessary for every event, but the Spirit of God is never the only cause. The power of the Spirit as freedom is impossible without other forms of power, especially the power of the Spirit wielded by "secular" agencies of order and unity. What in the world is God doing? God is not doing everything, but God is doing what only God can do within and among all creatures to cajole, persuade, lure, entice, and inspire them to use the power of their God-given freedom for the sake of justice, to the end that the kingdom of God come on earth.

CHAPTER FIVE

THE POWER
OF THE SPIRIT
IN VICTORY OVER EVIL

If we were to ask, with the following emphasis, "What in the world is God doing?" it would betray desperation about the world, a belief that the scope of misery and evil is so vast and unyielding that one cannot imagine the world saving itself, even with technical wizardry. But if the emphasis shifts to "What in the world is God doing?" we would have to re-imagine—that is, change our minds about—what the power of God as Spirit means. The way we think about power is killing us. We must liberate the way we think from idolatrous forms of trust, and this is the hardest thing in the world to change. Salvation of the world must begin with faith rightly understood. When people invest their faith in deadly misconceptions and poisonous misuses of power, evil threatens the emergence of the good.

Most people have no difficulty identifying power when they see it in operation, and have no problem seeing differences in degrees of power. One can point to a corporation's value on the New York Stock Exchange, to a football team's standing at the end of the season, or to the number of weapons and soldiers in a country's armed forces. Even something as difficult to calculate as scholarly ability can be quantified by an IQ score, books published, degrees earned, and awards and grants conferred.

But we have also been claiming that just as the Spirit implies power, power derives from Spirit. Such a biblically based claim will seem implausible to those who think that power is little more than stock-market reports, or the size of an army. The problem in failing to see the relationship between power and Spirit is not a lack of intelligence, but a failure or deficiency of imagination. The failure is what some have called "secular consciousness," a totalistic way of thinking which supposes that the fully rational person can dispense with imagination as illusion or wishful, rather than properly educated, thinking.

I join with Northrop Frye in naming the "educated imagination" a crucial component in the next millennium. It is the task of understanding or reasoning—that is, the educated imagination—to prevent notions of the actual and the ideal society from being separated. The "fundamental job of the imagination in ordinary life [is] . . . to produce, out of the society we have to live in, a vision of the society we want to live in."[1] But before we can try to understand the relation between the two societies, we have to challenge the so-called secular consciousness, the assumption that the world of ordinary experience is all. This assumption conceals how trapped we are in modern consciousness. The spectacular technological advances of modernity have often numbed us to its negative aspects. Among these negative aspects is the difficulty "moderns" have in imagining power except in terms that can be quantified. Although modernity includes values and beliefs that few want to relinquish, it also includes assumptions that make it difficult to imagine that power, in all its forms, derives from spirit. In short, our failure of imagination makes belief in the Spirit extremely difficult, if not impossible.

FROM PROPHETIC
TO MEDITATIVE IMAGINATION

Two contemporary theologians have proposed alternatives to what I have called our failure of imagination. Each offers a fine example of what might be termed "prophetic imagination," by which to discern the person and work of the Spirit in the world.

> Our problem is that we sophisticated Westerners really cannot believe in such a thing as the Holy Spirit, cannot believe that a Paraclete is at work in the world, or that the world will attain its consummation in God. Perhaps then it is not surprising that it is among the powerless, oppressed, and marginalized that the Spirit is pouring itself out afresh—upon those for whom authentically liberating power can come only from God, not from humanity. The Spirit is arising for us today from the underside of history.[2]

The second challenge comes from Michael Welker, professor of systematic theology at Heidelberg, who observes that "the secular common sense of the West has great difficulty in gaining even a distant perception of anything approaching God's Spirit."[3] Even so, Welker notes that great numbers in the West have chosen to embrace one among several alternatives: (1) the classical pentecostal movement, which erupted at the beginning of the twentieth century; (2) the charismatic movement, which emerged in the early 1960s; (3) neo-Pentecostalism's fundamentalist opposition to the charismatic renewal; and (4) the so-called Third Wave of the 1980s. Together, these movements constitute what Welker calls the largest religious movement of our time. A theology of the Holy Spirit in a worldwide context must be constructed, says Welker, in the "charged field" between the secular consciousness of God's distance still dominant in large areas of the world, such as Welker's Germany, and the testimony of millions who experience God's nearness.

As the references from Hodgson and Welker make clear, they are writing as accomplished, scholarly theologians in well-endowed universities in the northern hemisphere. Both are aware that the economic and political power concentrated in their homelands, the United States and Germany, continue to impoverish and disenfranchise the governments and economies of the southern hemisphere. They are both impressed with the vitality of the "powerless, oppressed, and marginalized," a power that Hodgson wants to believe derives from the Holy Spirit. Both theologians rethink the doctrine of the Holy Spirit, drawing in Welker's case on a fresh reading of the Bible, in Hodgson's case on a proposed "revisionist" theology. Both are concerned to release the beliefs of the Christian faith from inherited and discredited forms of thought and action. The point of these two theologies of the Holy Spirit is to restore the power of the Christian message so that it again can serve as a "potential for redemptive transformation" of the world (Hodgson), which is "self-endangered" (Welker) by oppression, ecological disaster, and destructive interreligious conflict.

One fact is clear about these two fresh proposals for a theology of the Holy Spirit. Neither Hodgson's nor Welker's thinking is in bondage to secular consciousness, which typically is unable to conceive of the Holy Spirit with real power. They both propose new and prophetic ways of imagining the Spirit in the world. Welker suggests conceiving of the Spirit as a "force field" that does not exercise power for its own sake, but that manifests a selfless power "for the benefit of others." Jesus Christ is the exemplar of that force field, which alone can overcome the self-endangerment of the world. Hodgson shows his emancipation from modernity by keying his "revisionist" proposal on the decline of modernity and on the emptiness of secular consciousness. He believes that the Spirit, in fact, is the most retrievable symbol for speaking of God in the postmodern age because of the Spirit's "etymological associations with natural forces—breath, wind, light, fire, water—forces that themselves are vital and that give life. . . . But spirit is also what is rational and conscious in the Hebraic and Christian traditions[,] . . . closely associated with the figures of Wisdom . . . and Word." Furthermore, "Spirit gives us a way of naming God that is not patriarchal and gender-specific."[4] These are two brilliant—and imaginative!—suggestions for retrieving the power of the Spirit in the world,[5] and judgments in the following paragraphs should not minimize this appraisal.

Both proposals—however free from the dogmas of modernity—are nonetheless examples of a particular *structure of imagination*. They fit readily into the scheme for imagining the Spirit examined in the previous chapter. The history of the Spirit, Hodgson and Welker would say, is a tragedy, comprised of endless conflicts between partial goods and limited values. The call of the Spirit is a summons to the human spirit of sacrifice, courage, wisdom, and most important, of freedom and justice. Life in the Spirit means an ongoing search for genuinely new forms of life in which the radical plurality of individuals does not hinder peace, but enriches community. That these two proposals fit into what might be called a stock structure of imagination does not detract from their radicality, or prophetic urgency. Indeed, prophetic radicality is one of the enduring characteristics of this way of imagining the power of the Spirit. Hodgson and Welker discern the power of the Spirit as a radical, prophetic critique of the social location, in North America and Europe, within which they think, teach, and write.

But when Africa, not North America or Europe, is the social location in which one reads these two magisterial books, one cannot ignore a feature of global history that is muted. One too easily gets the sense from Euro-American theologians that liberation, or more precisely the liberating work of the Spirit, has no negative or destructive side. Yet African liberation struggles, which began more than thirty years ago and culminated in the release of Nelson Mandela and his election to the presidency of South Africa, are complex. Any account of the liberation movements in Africa must include the working of the Spirit, mixed as it is with pools of human blood. One can mention the blood of warring tribal groups as well as the atrocities of European settlers against guerrilla armies, and of horrors perpetrated by liberation fighters against the whites who, let it also be said, were the exact counterparts of Europeans who had settled North America. Like European homesteaders on the Great Plains struggling to live in America in their new identity as Americans, whites believed they were fighting for the right to live in Africa as Africans. If Europeans can become Americans, Europeans in Africa, though radically different from those whose lives they had interrupted and forcefully displaced, believed that they could become and have a right to be regarded as Africans. As Native Americans have insisted that the Spirit of God was alive in their land before settlers and missionaries told the story of Jesus Christ, indigenous Africans have made the same claim. It was that same Spirit who not only gave life and veracity to the gospel, but who also urged on the freedom fighters in their struggle against European domination.

In trying to imagine how the power of Spirit can take so many forms, we ask how the Spirit could supply faith in Christ, energize missionaries, and encourage freedom from oppressive colonialism. To live, think, write, and teach in Africa is to rethink what liberation by the Spirit means and to reconsider the price of that liberation, because when such power energizes wars for liberation it often takes a gruesome toll.[6] The hideousness does not stop when liberation comes. Liberation in Africa by the power of the Spirit has not yet brought—and can never of itself bring—a new society to the once-colonized nations carved out by Europeans a little more than a century ago. No one should trivialize the high cost of liberation struggle, but the hard part in the long haul is the conquest of evil in the human heart that continues after liberation wars are won.

The "tragic" rendering of a theology of the Holy Spirit for the postmodern world, à la Hodgson and Welker, is a helpful and indeed necessary imaginative alternative to the theology that led colonizers and missionaries in their conquest of the "dark continent" in the first place.[7] As radical as such prophetic and liberationist readings are, they are not radical enough because, finally, what Africa needs is something other than, and in addition to, its more than thirty-year turn away from European domination. Africa needs a vision of the Spirit's power to conquer evil as it infects all human beings, regardless of color or the culture of one's birth. What sort of power might we imagine? It will require different ideas from what we have considered if we are to imagine the power of the Spirit in victory over evil.

Let us be clear. The foregoing discussion of Hodgson's and Welker's work does not dismiss their prophetic reading of the power and presence of the Spirit in the contemporary world. Rather it reminds us that theirs are but two among many possible readings, and that there can be no single, final, unambiguous, or innocent way of imagining how the Spirit of God might be active in the world. This entire book is written from the view that no theology can escape ambiguity and plurality.[8] Every attempt to read the Bible or to assess our place and time in history in light of the Bible will be partial and far from innocent. This reminder applies as well to the present writer. I take a decidedly postmodern approach to the topic of the Spirit.

If modern theology has assumed the possibility of moving beyond the negative and ambiguous qualities of the various Christian traditions and— by being clear-headed and "objective"—of attaining a position that is faithful, intelligible, and effective, then postmodern theology cannot in good conscience claim to achieve the goal which modernity failed to realize. In this book, one white, American, male, revisionist, Lutheran theologian lays out many ways of re-imagining the Spirit as the power and presence of God. It would be self-deluding, as David Tracy has written, for theologians today to think that we can "leave this ambiguous modern scene and begin anew in innocence. . . . There is no single innocent reading of any tradition, including this postmodern reading of the . . . profound ambiguities of modernity."[9]

Chapters 3 through 6 bring to the foreground how a structure of imagination allows one to focus on certain features of the power and presence of spirit. We have already noted how theocratic themes favor the power of the Spirit as domination and truth (chapter 3), and how prophetic themes, as in Hodgson's work, favor the power of the Spirit as freedom and justice (chapter 4). These chapters and the forms of power they discuss correspond with two modes of "emplotment": the comic and the tragic. In what follows, I will consider a third structure of imagination to focus attention on two other forms of the power and presence of the Spirit, two forms not usually favored by theologians, let alone by philosophers or wielders of political and economic power—the Spirit's power of beauty and the power of love. We will also refer to a third way of plotting the work of the Spirit in the world: the romantic. Popular usage has rendered this word virtually worthless for theology, although some theologians use the term as an adjective to distinguish contemporary from classical theology.[10]

When *romantic* appears in this chapter, however, the reader is urged to regard the term as a designation for the "plot" of a story or of history. The word *romantic* provides one of several ways of identifying what story is being told or what meaning a particular segment of history is thought to have. As a designation of the plot used to organize elements of a story, *romantic* does not refer primarily to the feeling, mood, sentiment, or inner experience of the author.

Northrop Frye is perhaps best known for his *Anatomy of Criticism,* in which he lifts up the theme of plot to give the word *romantic* a distinctive use.[11] In turn, Hayden White's renowned study of nineteenth-century historiography shows how the romantic plot is visible in certain historians, as are the other plots of comedy, tragedy, and satire. In White's view, the Christian reading of history is a romance. "The Romance is fundamentally a drama of self-identification symbolized by the hero's transcendence of the world of experience, his victory over it, and his final liberation from it—the sort of drama associated with the Grail legend or the story of the resurrection of Christ in Christian mythology. It is a drama of the triumph of good over evil . . . light over darkness. . . ."[12]

Perhaps the word *romance* will not be so readily associated with cheap novels, at least in the minds of those who read theology, if one employs the following analogy. When the words *romance* and *tragedy* are used to characterize the plot or meaning of the Christian narrative, *romance* is to the resurrection story what *tragedy* is to the prophetic. When thus applied, the word *romantic* should not arouse notions of swashbuckling male seducers of swooning maidens. *Romance* means victory over evil. But what can victory over evil mean amid the ambiguities that comprise history in an evolving universe?

That question is a stopper, a caution to meditate on this question: How can we re-imagine power so that it can overcome sin, death, and the evil one? Is it possible to imagine any power capable of victory over evil?

MEDITATIVE IMAGININGS ON THE POWER OF LOVE AND BEAUTY

Later I will consider the theological implications—specifically, the pneumatological implications—of love and beauty as forms of power, that is, as the presence and power of God in the world. First it should be helpful to fill in the details of this third structure of imagination. Every mode of imagination is fundamentally a rhetorical strategy. Preachers, teachers, politicians, editorial writers, and policymakers know the truth of this statement even if they have never been instructed in the science of rhetoric. They meditate about the use of language in confidence that it will be persuasive, that the reader or listener will see, perceive, discern, grasp, and indeed understand something that had escaped attention until guided by a different way of seeing or thinking. If Christian imagination is fundamentally romantic, as we have been led to think, then Christians can allow their perceptions of power to be guided by the rhetorical strategy or structure of imagination designated as romantic.

Remembering that Hayden White called *romance* a dramatic plot associated with the resurrection of Christ from the dead, we have turned to what we might call the rhetoric of reversal, in which our normal tragic imagination—by which we recognize that life is always followed by death—is reversed. Resurrection is the great reversal of normal ways of imagining the relation of life and death, and therefore provides theological warrant for reversing the normal way of imagining power. In everyday experience we take for granted that human life is energized by the natural love of power. It is what drives American political and economic life. Power is beautiful. The love and beauty of power pull the human spirit to imagine power itself as beautiful. In the dominant public imagination, "power" is beautiful, lovely, lovable, and attractive; it excites our acquisitive imaginations. Power exists to acquire and, once acquired, is recognized as one's own. In phrases like "love of power" or "beauty of power," the meaning of *power* is self-evident. *Power* means power over others, the power to overpower, having more economic, political, or even physical strength than others.

The close connection between power and imagination becomes obvious when we consider how the love of and beauty of power rule over the popular imagination of contemporary societies. The "love of power" and "beauty of power," as expressions, do not stretch our imaginations, because they conform to what most moderns assume to be the only way of imagining power. The stretch is in trying to imagine the reverse. To do so we must think of utterly neglected forms of power, the power of love and the power of beauty. One need not look far to find lives that can be described by a love of power. Such persons are the most widely celebrated examples of how "leadership" is determined. But one must look elsewhere to find examples of lives that can be described by the power of love and the power of beauty. Living examples are not always close at hand.

Consider what would happen to our understanding of leadership if imaginations were guided by the rhetoric of reversal. If the power of beauty and power of love were brought to the foreground, or were the criteria for discernment, our definitions of the standards of leadership, authority, power, ideology, community, and social order would have to be radically, if not totally, revised. We can imagine, albeit with considerable effort, such a new order. In fact, communities have tried to make such imaginings real. Shaker communities, monastic orders, Amish and Mennonite societies, the counterculture movement of the 1960s, and many charismatic and pentecostal churches have all been guided by visions of leadership, authority, and community that reversed the status quo.[13] They imagined everything differently from the society around them. Their rhetoric of Spirit and power was the rhetoric of radical difference, what I call the rhetoric of reversal.[14]

The dramatic "plot" of victory over evil and death—of reversal and resurrection—is related to the rhetorical strategies or figures of speech (tropes) that cause us to reverse our way of seeing. We can imagine, for example, that another form of leadership might be preferable to, or at least might complement, the image of leader as monarch, ruler, philosopher-king, prophet, or judge. The authority of these leaders can be replaced by the authority of the author, poet, storyteller, artist, or—supremely—by Christ, who reverses our "normal" seeing of the world by telling parables of God's way of living and ruling. Ideology, when one's imagination is controlled by the parables of Jesus, is one of deep suspicion toward so-called authority, whether the authority of professors, magistrates, experts, or specialists, that consigns others to a "lower" class. When one imagines the world revealed in the parables, distinctions by class, gender, or race are radically challenged. "There is neither Jew nor Greek, neither slave nor free, there is neither male nor female; for you are all one in Christ Jesus" (Gal. 3:28). Such ideology is one of virtual *anarchy*, a term implying that the powerful class of leaders, from the Greek *archon*, is not necessary because there are no lower-class servants who need leaders. All are leaders. That is, all lead as servants, comrades, friends. The analogue in social relations is not the competitiveness of the city, academy, law court, or marketplace. The analogue might be the communitarian spirit of the art colony, whose members are bound by their yet widely differing common vision of beauty, or the utopian community that shares a commitment to Paul's radical doctrine of the law of love.

Communities have gathered around such a radically different rhetoric of power, identifying the power as one that is not their own, but that is at work among them. In one way or another they have regarded the power as the power of love and beauty. Few such art communities or utopian societies have survived more than a generation before the spirit of power as love and beauty becomes a hardened sediment of fixed expectations toward each other and of hostility toward outsiders. Yet although their histories are often episodic, brief, and ambiguous, these radical experiments in alternative rhetorical community retain their power to challenge shriveled imaginations of the majority. The majority in such cases might be unaware that their lack of imagination, and not their superior technical intelligence, causes them to dismiss the power of the Spirit as love and beauty. The failure of utopian experiments, including the failure of the apostolic church to sustain its recognition of the Spirit as its true authority,[15] attests to the power of sin among those who have been led by the Spirit to commit themselves to life according to new visions of power. Perhaps the sin among the rest of us is the failure of imagination that prevents us from discerning the Spirit at work among those who have refused, and still refuse, to be cynical about the power of love and the power of beauty. Such is the sin of failure borne of the steadfast refusal to have commonsense notions of power affected by the rhetoric of reversal.

THE SPIRIT IN THE WORLD AS BEAUTY AND LOVE

What in the world is God doing? This book's recurring proposal is that God is an active power as Word—the incarnate Son—and as Spirit. The Word and the breath of God are inseparable, or, put anthropomorphically, even God cannot speak without breathing and the world cannot live without the breath/Spirit of God. God's Spirit is active in the world as the Lord and giver of life, even when the word of God has been denied, rejected, or perhaps drowned out by the distracting noise of humanity's cruelty to nature and to humankind itself. The Bible makes clear that whether or not the explicit word of God is audible, or has not yet been recognized in faith, the created order is sustained by God's breath.[16] In scripture, all creatures that comprise nature or the cosmos are never as "natural" as they seem. Among and within them a transcendent power is at work, often manifesting itself as mystery[17] and as a demand whether or not Christians witness to the presence of God as Word and Spirit. More theologians, especially those in conversation with the scientific community, are willing to reaffirm that distinctive biblical viewpoint. The awesome power and order of nature—which for most of the modern age has been the domain of modern science—can be seen as the image of God. It is as though nature's life is the power of the Spirit of God coursing through all creatures, including human beings.[18] If theologians are now overcoming a neoorthodox reticence about seeing God in the created order, can they also learn to include—as aspects of the power of God's Spirit—the power of beauty and the power of love?

Western Christianity, Protestantism especially and Roman Catholicism to a lesser degree, has given more attention to the power of God as unqualified omnipotence than as the power of beauty or the power of love. Even when love and beauty are admitted into Christian conversation, the concepts are usually confined to Jesus as the incarnation of the Word, the sole revelation of God's beauty and love. It is too often the Son alone who is the embodiment of God's love and the supreme instance of God's beauty. Karl Barth is one of the few twentieth-century theologians to write of God as beautiful. "[God] is the basis and standard of everything that is beautiful and of all ideas of the beautiful."[19] Yet Barth himself, along with many neoorthodox theologies, would strongly deny similarity between God's Spirit and the human spirit's capacity for love and beauty. Barth's great accomplishment was a theology of the Word which denied continuity between the human spirit and the Holy Spirit.[20]

Barth was not the first to subordinate the Spirit to the Word, as we saw in chapter 2 when reviewing disputes about the *filioque*. That controversial phrase in the Western version of the Nicene Creed had the effect, in the history of European theology, of condoning the subordination of the Spirit to the Son. In practice, the *filioque* has meant that however inspired or "empowered by the Spirit" a deed of love or a creation in nature or in art may seem, it must be discounted theologically if it does not explicitly glorify Jesus Christ. Apart from Christ, human experiences of love and beauty have been widely thought to have minimal theological significance.

The subordination of the Spirit to the Word in this century, as exemplified in a "theology of the Word" like Barth's, has favored so-called theologies of proclamation, or christocentric theologies, and has suppressed theologies that have tried to attend to spirituality, meditation, and the dimension of spirit in art, poetry, music, literature, nature, or human experience. In subordinating the Spirit, these theologies also encourage Christian worshipers to adopt an attitude of superiority toward others whose styles of prayer and worship exhibit archaic energy and power. Ironically, and more to the point, theologies that subordinate the Spirit to the Word are not as biblical as one might expect, because they also suppress, neglect, or minimize portions of the Bible itself, namely the wisdom and meditative forms of writing in the Hebrew and Christian Scriptures.[21]

In any case, the tendency of theologies of the Word to minimize love and beauty as instances of the power of God's Spirit has provoked a critical response.

RE-IMAGINING LOVE AS THE POWER OF THE SPIRIT'S VICTORY OVER EVIL

By far the best twentieth-century study of the power of love as a theological doctrine, measured by the standards of fidelity to biblical witness, careful historical analysis, attention to doctrinal distinctions, and intellectual persuasiveness, is Daniel Day Williams's *The Spirit and the Forms of Love*. In the preface he acknowledges that in claiming so much for the power of love he has undertaken a difficult task.

> We cannot escape the aura of implausibility which surrounds the claims that love is real, that love transforms human life, that it is the key to the foundation of all things. Yet along with the implausibility there is a blunt, solid truth. We live largely by our loves. Even our hates are twisted and frustrated loves. Men fight one another, slaughter in war, and kill in cold blood. Yet often they fight to defend something they love, their land, their families, their view of life.[22]

Williams—whose untimely death in 1973 at age 63 cut short his theological work—was a process theologian for whom the metaphysics of Whitehead and Hartshorne functioned in much the same way as I am using, in this book, the discipline of rhetoric and the language of imagination. Williams, contrary to the suspicion that many have had about process theology, did not try to force the Christian faith into alien metaphysical categories. Instead he took seriously the Christian insight that "love is real, that love transforms human life, that it is the key to the foundation of all things."

That "love is real" is an article of Christian faith, but what we mean by "real" or by "the foundation of all things" can be variously understood. How we think about or try to conceive reality is what has been called metaphysics. It is one thing to believe, as Christians do, that "love is real," but it is another thing to decide which version of "real" is appropriate to love. In this postmodern age we recognize that there are many versions of "reality"—women's reality, African Americans' reality, and so forth. Each version will influence how one interprets the claim that "love is real." Some versions of reality would deny that love is real. Williams, contrary to suspicions that love is not real, insists that an analysis of love should determine how we construct or imagine reality, rather than accepting a loveless or Spirit-less view of reality (that is, an anti-Spirit metaphysic) that would reject the Christian belief that love is real.

"A metaphysical system is an instrument of vision, not a dogmatic statement of final truth," he writes.[23] One could easily substitute "a structure for imagining reality" in the place of "an instrument of vision" in this statement. Some instruments for seeing or imagining the power of love in the world are not very helpful, because they imagine God either as so remote from, or uninvolved with, the world that the relationship of God with the world implied by the word *love* is unintelligible. Any real relationship between God and the world is ruled out as contrary to what God must be. Other ways of imagining God are so fixed on God as overpowering and controlling that the coerciveness of God's power removes love from the relationship between God and world. In short, how we imagine the reality of God, and how we imagine the power of love, will rise or fall together. If our faith is that "love is real" and that God is real, then our faith will be well served by a vision of reality—a metaphysic—that will reflect and not contradict the nature and the power of love. Love is not the renunciation of power or the absence of power or even the power of powerlessness. Love is one of the Spirit's modes of presence in the world. Love is that power which alone can be victorious over sin, death, and evil. Williams writes, "It is the mode of love which does not look for salvation through overriding power, but which allows itself to be 'edged out of the world' on a cross, as Dietrich Bonhoeffer saw."[24] The first and principal source for making this claim is, for Williams, the Bible's witness to God's disclosure of who God is, and what love is, through what God has done in history, beginning with creation and reaching supreme expression in the story of Christ in the Gospels.

The history of God is the history of God's love, and the whole of Williams's theological work on love is, in part, an argument against theologians whose imaginations have been so fixed on the overriding power of God that the history of God's love for the world is obscured. God's power, insists Williams, expresses the love of God; it does not violate that love. What, then, remains absolute in God if not God's power? Is it not true that God is the only and absolute power? No! "What God gives is his absolute faithfulness, his everlastingness in unceasing love. . . . The power of God . . . is *not* that of absolute omnipotence to do *anything*. It is the power to do *everything* that the loving ground of all being *can* do to express and to communicate and fulfill the society of loving beings."[25] The foregoing assertion could really be Williams's gloss on Paul's interpretation of the love of God. The final measure of the power of God is the love of God.

> For I am convinced that neither death, nor life, nor angels, nor rulers, nor things present, nor things to come, nor powers, nor height, nor depth, nor anything else in all creation, will be able to separate us from the love of God in Christ Jesus our Lord. (Rom. 8:38-39)

The victory of the power of love over evil cannot mean the elimination of sinful creatures, even though creatures' misuse of the good is the source of moral evil. Nor can such victory mean the cancellation of creaturely freedom, which is real though limited. Neither would it be a victory for love if all the creatures were stripped of their creaturely power, which is also real and limited.

In sum, any alleged victory over evil cannot be the victory of love if it means closing down history. It is the Spirit's power of love that accepts the risks of sin and evil. It is the Spirit's power of love to be generous—not to hoard power, but to give power to the creatures. It is the Spirit's power to accept others, to the point where acceptance of the other means being changed. The Spirit accepts the freedom of the other to be other, and is impartial in judging how the other uses freedom and power. The victory of love over evil is the power of the Spirit, which does not shut everything down so that evil is no longer possible. Love is the power of the Spirit to create and to keep open the possibilities for increased freedom, reconciliation, and communion.[26]

The victory of the Spirit is encompassed in the reality of forgiveness, which is a necessary step to reconciliation. But if evil with all its dreadful consequences is not obliterated, what happens to it? Is evil somehow "saved" or "redeemed"? In a posthumously published lecture, Williams answered this question:

> I have taken the position here that the Christian faith does not require us to say that every evil is redeemable and must necessarily be brought into some service to the divine purpose. But what we must not overlook in the

Christian understanding of evil is that there are ways in which evil is turned against itself. The supreme example is the way in which the hatred of people against the Christ who brings the love and truth of God into history is turned into the occasion of supreme manifestation of that love on the cross.[27]

It remains for us to add but one brief comment to the implications of Williams's views on evil and the power of love. The doctrine of the Spirit which I am exploring via a distinctive structure of imagination rejects any notion that the Spirit and power of love are absent wherever there is evil. Following Williams, I am proposing that we think of hatred and the evil which flows from it as twisted expressions of love. The power of love can overcome hatred and its evil consequences because the spirit of love is already present, but is being expressed in ways that violate the very drive of love toward communion. Historically, whether we think of Nazi Germany or apartheid South Africa, self-consuming forms of love always energize nationalistic and racist separatism and strategies for justifying hostility to, and isolation from, others. Hatred is not the absence of love, but is a twisted form of love's power. When these twisted forms of love are given unlimited expression, they burn themselves out and, at the same time, bring much that is good and promising to destruction. The spirit of love is violated by these distorted self-consuming expressions of the power of the Spirit.

Lest we revert to an un-Christian, dualistic, Manichaean understanding of good and evil, we must always insist on this clear proposition: Evil never has any power of its own, cannot generate power of its own, and does not have a source of power apart from the Spirit, the Lord and giver of life. This statement differs from what Manichaeanism has always taught. Against such dualisms, the Christian can only imagine the power of evil as parasitically drawn from the good, from the spirit of love from which all creatures draw their lives.[28] What makes sin and evil more hideous is misuse of the Spirit's power of love. Evil cannot generate power of its own, but will use up the Spirit within itself. Depleted, evil will perish. Evil can consume, for its own purposes, as much of the power of love as it can draw into itself, but it can never exhaust that power. That is the foundation of Christian hope for love's victory over evil. The Spirit's power of love is often used for evil purposes, but the Spirit never endorses evil; evil can only receive the Spirit's judgment against evil. Evil avariciously and self-destructively consumes what is necessary for the life of evil, namely the spirit of love, the power of love flowing from the Lord and giver of life. Having consumed the Spirit for its limited ends, evil must forfeit its misused power.

BEAUTY'S CAPACITY
TO SAVE THE WORLD

This book is an invitation to re-imagine the nature of power and especially the power of the Spirit.[29] I conclude this chapter with two sections on how to imagine beauty as the Spirit's power in the world. To do so reverses common understandings of power and of beauty.

Commonly employed rhetoric would immediately dismiss the proposition that beauty has any real power, let alone the power to save the world. It is common in everyday speech for actors, top-ranked athletes, and other rich and famous persons to elicit the term *beautiful*. Beauty is rarely thought to have power, but power is called beautiful. The execution of coercive power is thought beautiful. Short of the exercise of power, the potential for power—as in potency—is thought beautiful, whether in athletics, the military, or the economic realm. The powerfully rich are widely thought to live the "beautiful life" because they can afford the beautiful things of the moment. Beauty is made to serve power, but beauty is wrongly imagined as having no power of its own—except when the powerful use the beauty of power to seduce, charm, or deceive, and thus conceal the misuse of power. Beauty then becomes a disguise, a deceit that those in authority often use to cover their quest for more power. Many envy such power and would gladly have such power if they could. The power to deceive is thought to be "beautiful," and its "beauty" empowers much of contemporary Western existence.

Because beauty, or whatever is considered beautiful, will always be misused for utilitarian and commercial gain, a widespread suspicion exists that beauty is—at best and only—in the eye of the beholder. Its value is for decorative purposes, to enhance the standing of those in power, and to conceal the real uses of power. The study of beauty, known as aesthetics, began in the early Enlightenment as a philosophical discipline concerned with beauty and the arts. It takes its name from the Greek adjective *aisthetikos*, which means "perceptible," and was coined initially to designate the science of perception, befitting the Enlightenment's preoccupation with epistemology, the foundation and nature of knowledge. By the time of Immanuel Kant the word had come to mean "philosophical reflection on the nature of art and beauty and of response to both."[30] As a philosophical discipline, aesthetics was quickly diminished to a specialty—study of the arts—and was no longer a scientific inquiry that, studied, all humans can perceive.

Contemporary views of beauty and art usually follow the dictum of the late Enlightenment, with the effect that no moral or theoretical or religious arguments exist for what is beautiful. Unlike Romantic and Victorian thinkers—William Blake, Samuel Coleridge, or Friedrich Schelling—who "found it easy to utter the words 'art,' 'beauty,' 'religion' together in one breath,"[31] most of us, as modern heirs of the Enlightenment, have adopted the view that beauty is a secular concept. For nonphilosophers, beauty as a secular concept is—as already noted—a useful way to enhance power while concealing the misuse of power. For philosophers of aesthetics, for whom such utilitarian views of beauty are disgusting and even dangerous, it is important to show that the aesthetic has its own nonutilitarian value. Such philosophical arguments follow this course: First, beauty does not depend on a religious or moral message; second, because beauty is a question of tactile, visible form as in sculpture, or of the emotional, inward perception of rhythm, tone, pitch, and harmonics as in music, then its value is not crassly utilitarian, but exists for its own sake; finally, rather than existing in the mind of the beholder and then being projected *onto* an object, beauty is expressed *by* an aesthetic object, and thus can be perceived by the beholder.[32]

Controversies about art and what counts as beautiful have discouraged most theologians from attempting a theology of beauty. They excuse themselves from relating faith to aesthetics, art, and beauty.[33] Yet every theologian and practically every Christian takes for granted that Christian faith should describe how the faith relates to questions of truth and ethics—the question of the good. Questions about truth and ethics have become no less secular than questions about aesthetics, yet Christian reflection on the Greek virtue of beauty has never attracted the same intellectual energy as systematic theology and theological ethics. Every theological seminary invests heavily in these two fields, but no seminary offers as many courses in theological aesthetics.[34]

Many would try to make a virtue of contemporary theologians' hesitancy about, if not outright neglect of, beauty. Western Christianity has always attended more to the power of God than to the beauty of God.[35] Thus, theologians can appeal to authority—that there is no historical warrant for a theology of the beautiful. Eastern Christianity, on the other hand, assumes that holy icons have the power to make present what they show as an image. The beauty of an icon is a spiritual, not an aesthetic— in the Enlightenment sense—phenomenon, and as such it is a means of conveying the real presence of the holy. Because an image can be a spiritual rather than a secular form of beauty, the Orthodox Christian is not as hesitant as the Westerner regarding a theology of the beautiful image.[36] Westerners have preferred the word, in preaching and in sacrament, over the image. It is by or through the word that the holy is present. This mode of thought correlates with the Western tendency to subordinate spirit to word. The neglect of beauty in Western theology goes hand in hand with the neglect of the Spirit. In his magnificent seven-volume study of theological aesthetics, Hans Urs von Balthasar exhibits this same tendency to identify the beauty of God with the Son, and gives only a subsidiary role to the Holy Spirit.[37]

To return to the guiding principle of this study, the Spirit implies power, and all forms of power in creation derive from the Spirit. If one accepts that thesis, then the power of beauty in all its manifestations represents the power of the Spirit at work. This statement would apply not only to beauty in creation but to all that we call art, even when a work of art or music is not immediately grasped as beautiful. Beauty is a spiritual reality, not a secular concept whose value can be established independently of spirit.[38] But like all forms of power ultimately breathed into creatures by the Spirit of God, beauty can be used for ends contrary to the will of God, and thus contrary to what is good for humanity. That the power of beauty derives from the Spirit, yet can be used against the Spirit, does not diminish beauty as a power coming from the Spirit.[39] What Christians in the Orthodox tradition take for granted, that images (icons) have power to make present that which is holy and of ultimate worth, is also taken for granted in a peculiar—even twisted—way by those who use images for commercial and propagandistic purposes. The difference between a holy icon and a propagandistic image is that the latter makes present to the beholder that which is of questionable, and not ultimate, worth. What they have in common is that their power is derived from the same Spirit. As I have been arguing throughout, Christian faith does not have a monopoly on the Spirit, and the presence of beauty in the world is striking evidence of that, even when the power of beauty is used in ways which diminish the human spirit and deplete the earth's resources.

I propose a theology of beauty that does not rush to claim that Christ alone is the image of beauty. The Spirit does proceed from the Father into all the world. As John McIntyre suggests, "I would venture to say that the Holy Spirit is God's imagination let loose and working with all the freedom of God in the world, and in the lives, the words and actions, of the men and women of our time."[40] Both creation and human creativity are expression of God's imagination. Too often Christians are deaf and blind to the link between the Spirit and beauty. They would do well to consider the possibility that the Holy Spirit works through the imagination, but instead they too often depreciate imagination, failing to regard it as one of humanity's most important mental and spiritual powers. Lacking such imagination for the work of the Spirit, Christians out of zealous and thoughtless devotion to Christ can make themselves blind and deaf to the Spirit's power in beauty.

It is an axiom of the Christian understanding of creation that beauty is present in all creation by the power of the Spirit.[41] Beauty speaks of the glory of God. Yet death also is a permanent feature of creation. Beauty is not immune to decay. The most beautiful human figure eventually sags and weakens with age; lush forests turn to deserts; glorious rivers dry up and disappear; great societies decline; architectural wonders are reduced to monumental ruins. And as we have seen, much destruction and death is hastened by wicked uses of the Spirit's power which, through beauty, testifies to the glory of God. This ambiguous role of beauty in the world prompts us to ask, "How can we discern—and speak of—the Spirit's power of beauty saving the world?"

BEAUTY AND RESURRECTION: THE RHETORIC OF REVERSAL

"Theologians of the cross" might regard the above section heading with profound suspicion and warn us not to put a rose on the cross, not to try to "beautify" the death of Christ.[42] There is nothing pretty about death, and any theology that would attempt to soften the horror of the crucifixion is not a Christian theology. A theology of the cross challenges any suggestion that salvation, or anything remotely salvific, can come through the power of beauty instead of the power of the cross.

If one adopts a strictly secular consciousness about beauty, the cross is the epitome of the ugly, the obscene, the unjust—of all that is loathsome and disgusting. The crucifixion did take place on the equivalent of a garbage dump or landfill outside and apart from beautifully landscaped gardens or the grand palisades of the city. Seemingly the power of the cross has nothing to do with the power of beauty. Yet we must ask if followers of the cross are obligated to be despisers of beauty, to love all that is ugly and disgusting. To ask such a question of a Christian is to provoke a negative answer. But the negative reply is not a complete answer to the question concerning beauty and salvation. I propose that the rhetoric of the cross comes closest to the rhetoric of reversal and its corresponding trope, the synecdoche, discussed in note 14 of this chapter.

The apostolic witnesses to Jesus Christ were more than witnesses to the crucifixion. After all, they did not camp at Golgotha and glorify garbage dumps and all that is dirty, ugly, and disgusting. That would have been equivalent to being bound by "the law of sin and of death" (Rom. 8:2), of reveling in life on Golgotha. They did witness to the one crucified by the law of sin and death, but they experienced the crucified Jesus as alive among them, just as they knew that they were alive, and living according to a different law. "For the law of the Spirit of life in Christ Jesus has set you free from the law of sin and of death. . . . For those who live according to the flesh set their minds on the things of the flesh, but those who live according to the Spirit set their minds on the things of the Spirit" (8:2, 5). The same "Spirit of him who raised Jesus from the dead" (8:11) they knew as the Spirit who dwelled in them. Only the most grotesque version of the theology of the cross would commend the Christian life as a life committed to death and ugliness. Even Kierkegaard's most scathing ridicule of Christian aesthetics did not require the Christian to endorse ugliness.

Perhaps the best-known example of commending beauty as the reversal of death is from a sermon by Augustine: "He hung therefore on the cross deformed, but his deformity is our beauty."[43] Augustine does not try to beautify the death of Christ. He is not a mortician applying cosmetics to make a corpse look peacefully asleep, but Augustine challenges his hearer to revise what beauty means in light of this deforming execution. Talk of the beauty of

Christ can never mean the elimination or sentimentalizing of the crucifixion. But Christian beauty must include everything that modern ideas of beauty, controlled by secular consciousness, would reject as unbearably ugly.

A Christian can accept this Augustinian principle as a necessary limit on all discussions of faith and beauty. But if the crucifixion alone controls notions of beauty, then the Christian believer will never leave the ugliness of the cross, but will celebrate it as the only beauty. Against that confining notion of beauty secular views of beauty are a welcome, even liberating, invitation to experience the beauty of creation. The beauty of creation and of human creativity is evidence of the power of the Spirit giving glory to God.

This discussion returns us to the old and still urgent question of how to relate the word (including the Word as the crucified Son) and the Spirit, without subordinating one to the other. For all its rhetorical power, Augustine's synecdoche, "his deformity is our beauty," exhibits the problems of the Western view. It leaves no room for the beauty of the Spirit according to which composer Igor Stravinsky could remark, "Music comes to reveal itself as a form of communion with our fellow man—and with the Supreme Being."[44] Simone Weil wrote that the beauty of the world is "the sign of an exchange of love between the Creator and creation."[45] It remains for us to comment briefly on how the beauty of the Son, who was crucified, is distinct from but not contradictory to the Spirit's power of beauty glimpsed in these remarks by Stravinsky and Weil. We seek not to reject Augustine's synecdoche but to amplify it.

The beauty of the Spirit of God witnesses to the glory, the *kabod*, of God. It was the glory of God that transfigured Jesus when he was to set his face toward Jerusalem (Matt. 17:1-8; Mark 9:2-8; Luke 9:28-36). The three disciples who witnessed the transfiguration also received visions of Moses, who represented the authority of the law, and the prophet Elijah, whose appearance would signal the coming of the Messiah. Six days earlier at Caesarea Philippi, Peter, who was with Jesus on the mountain, had confessed that Jesus was the Messiah, but then had protested when Jesus said that the Messiah would be crucified. In Peter's theology of the glory and beauty of the Messiah, there was no room for the cross. Confronted with the transfiguration, he and his companions exposed the serious nature of their failure to grasp fully the true character of that glory. Although "they saw his glory" (Luke 9:32), they had yet to learn that such physical manifestations of glory and beauty do not last; they cannot be frozen in time. Their ignorance of true glory is shown in their desire to build lasting memorials on the mountain.

While the death of Christ cannot be counted as beautiful in itself, it surely is clear evidence of what happens to all beauty, even the glorious beauty of the transfiguration. As much as we, like the three disciples, would wish otherwise, glory and beauty are not timeless. Yet neither is the Spirit-given power of beauty and glory destroyed by the crucifixion. The cross demonstrates with finality that no physical, historical manifestation of beauty endures.

The cross gives the lie to Faust's yearning that the beautiful Helen might be his forever: "Stay, thou art so fair!" Manifestations of beauty are gifts of the Spirit, but none is enduring. They can be no more preserved and hoarded than the bread from heaven that came in the wilderness. The transfiguration, which takes on more importance in the Eastern church, is the chief manifestation of the beauty and glory of Christ, while the cross is the stunning reminder that even divine beauty cannot be rendered timeless.

No manifestation of beauty endures. The most ecstatic dance must end; the symphony that transports our spirits to heights of emotion must have its finale; the city decays; and every earthly life is overtaken by death. Only the Spirit is eternal. The Spirit, by whose power beauty enriches our lives as surely as bread from heaven sustains us, is the same Spirit who raised Jesus from the dead. True beauty does not deny death and conceal its wounds. True beauty bears witness to the Spirit, because its source is the Spirit. Beauty, when true to itself, is true to the Spirit in that it never calls attention to itself, but reveals more than itself. For Christians, that "more" revealed by the Spirit is the suffering love of God acted out in the death of Christ. The suffering is neither beautiful nor deserved, but the same Spirit who raised Jesus from the dead continues to make beauty manifest in created order and in the creativity of the human spirit.

What in the world is God doing? The victory of the Spirit of God over evil can only happen through the reversal, or conversion, of the human heart and mind from twisted forms of love that consume the good, misrepresent the truth, and use beauty to mask abuses of power.

CHAPTER SIX

THE POWER OF THE SPIRIT
IN DESTABILIZING LAUGHTER

eading the New Testament, especially the letters of the Apostle
Paul to the churches he founded in Corinth and Galatia, is the
best antidote for any lingering illusions that the beginning of
Christianity was a time of unity and harmony. Several years after
he established the church in Corinth—"a large and prosperous urban center
with an ethnically, culturally, and religiously diverse population"[1]—Paul
learned that his church there had become divided over a number of issues,
and that several groups were battling for power. His letter begins with com-
mendation to these people as "sanctified in Christ," "enriched . . . in speech
and knowledge of every kind . . . not lacking in any spiritual gift . . ." (1 Cor.
1:2ff.). What more could a missionary hope for among his converts? But then
he gets down to the business of addressing their fractious competition for
power. He contrasts the power of human wisdom, of which they boast, with
the power of the cross which, from the perspective of such wisdom, is foolishness. But "God's foolishness is wiser than human wisdom, and God's weak-
ness is stronger than human strength" (1:25). He reminds the Corinthians
that they were not chosen because of their own power or wisdom. The source
and grounding of their life in Christ was that "God chose what is weak in the
world to shame the strong" (1:27). They can boast of nothing except to "boast
in the Lord" (1:31). In short, Paul reminds the Corinthians of their origins in
Paul's coming among them to proclaim "the mystery of God . . ." (2:1). He
remembers his fear; the sophisticated and multicultural city must have made
him anxious about how to declare a seemingly foolish message concerning a
crucified rabbi as savior. So it could not have been any "plausible words of
wisdom" (2:4) that won their faith at the beginning. No such wisdom came
from his mouth or was visible in his manner. The Corinthians' faith at the
beginning was based on "a demonstration of the Spirit and of power, so that
your faith might rest not on human wisdom but on the power of God" (2:4-5).
The Spirit and the power that brought them to faith in Christ in the beginning
had become, within a few years, the occasion for dispute.

Spirit always implies power. While not stated explicitly, this equation in
scripture is nearly undeniable.[2] That link between Spirit and power, evident
in the New Testament, is no longer obvious to people today. In the popular
consciousness of people in the technological societies of the West, power

would rarely be associated with the Spirit as it is in the sacred writings of Jews and Christians. Is it possible to reclaim a dynamic equivalent to the biblical understanding of Spirit and power, and to begin to discern the Spirit in ordinary forms of power that pervade our public lives? That is one of the questions driving this inquiry. Spirit in the popular imagination is usually associated with what is decidedly nonpublic and nonsecular. The powers of the Spirit are thought, by secularists and by many if not most Christians, to exist in a realm apart from the commonsense realm of secular existence—if Spirit is thought to exist at all. Throughout this book I have been drawing on several distinctive and classic structures of imagination, and have brought into view the ways people imagine power and then, based on these ideas, organize their lives. We have looked at power as sheer domination and authoritative truth (chapter 3); as liberation from domination in the name of freedom and justice (chapter 4); and as the power of beauty and love to overcome evil (chapter 5). The argument has been that the failure to discern the forms of power at work in ordinary life is a failure of imagination, and that the failure of imagination in turn exaggerates the difficulty of discerning the Spirit in all forms of power.

The most common failure of popular imagination is to confine discernment of the forms of power to coercion of the weak by the strong. In the following section, I will appeal to American history for other examples, particularly of the power of equality and the power of dissent. I wager that these forms of power can be recognized anew as real, and not beyond the range of ordinary modes of imagination. In view of the difficulty most moderns have in speaking of power except as an overpowering force, it will serve my purpose to revisit events of eighteenth- and nineteenth-century America. Then we can return to the task of this chapter, which is to propose how the Spirit of God can connect with the power of equality and dissent.

FORMS OF POWER IN THE AMERICAN EXPERIENCE

For Americans the most telling illustration that power takes many forms should be their own history. The history of the United States is the history of change in how people have imagined and understood power and authority.[3] In the relatively short span of American history, one can see how power has been imagined as domination (monarchy), as freedom and independence, as love and beauty (republicanism), and as dissent and equality (modern democracy).

Before the establishment of modern democracies, the peoples of Europe simply could not, in the words of Gordon S. Wood, "imagine a civilized society being anything but a hierarchy" or monarchy of some kind (19). Monarchies typically assumed a long line of dependence, or gradations of freedom and servility, "that linked everyone from the king at the top to the bonded laborers and black slaves at the bottom." Authority thus could only be imagined as divinely ordained and as part of the natural order. This natural, divinely ordained structure of power extended into the family. The head of the household was a "miniature king . . . to whom respect and subjection were due." Parents were told that they "should carefully subdue the wills of their children and accustom them to obedience and submission" (49). Governments before the American Revolution were not supposed to do much "beyond carrying out the king's duty to preserve peace and to adjudicate disputes among his subjects" (81). Prerevolutionary imagination could not comprehend power and authority except as coming from the monarch.

Monarchy's hold on popular imagination was destroyed by the republican principles embraced by the so-called Founding Fathers, but the destruction did not happen at once. By challenging "the assumptions and practices of monarchy—its hierarchy, its inequality, its devotion to [the royal] kinship, its patriarchy, its patronage, and its dependency," republicanism—as exemplified in Jefferson, Madison, and others—presented alternative ways of organizing society. Monarchists loved peace and order, while republicans like Thomas Jefferson loved liberty and independence. The republicanism of the American Revolution was "in every way a radical ideology—as radical for the eighteenth century as Marxism was to be for the nineteenth century."[4]

Republicanism was not yet the modern democracy of the late twentieth century, but was a radical departure from monarchy. Monarchy had assumed a structure of divinely ordained, vertical relationships among people, characterized by degrees of dependency. In a monarchy, a person was a "subject" to those set above him; those below were in turn his "subjects," and owed him obedience and servility. Civil *power* thus flowed downward, while civic *duty* was to be expressed upward, toward the one above who, naturally, had greater power. The new republic, in sharp contrast to monarchy, taught a radical doctrine—namely, that a person is not subject to the monarch but is a citizen. Because republicanism locates power and authority in the free citizen, it destroys a system derived from dependence. Wood reminds us that Jefferson had equated citizenship with ownership of property, and was so keen on this equation that in 1776 he proposed that in Virginia every man without property should receive fifty acres. "Without having property and will of his own—without having independence—a man could have no public spirit; there could be no republic" (179). The emergence of free, property-owning citizens meant that the very conception of power was radically altered. In a republic rulers can lose their personal rights and no longer command the allegiance of their subjects. The consent of the people—of free, property-owning citizens—became the only justification for anyone exercising public power and authority. Although Jefferson's generation of republicans did not abolish the dependence of their slaves, in the ethos of republicanism even the institution of slavery would soon became "excruciatingly conspicuous" in a way that could never have happened in a monarchical society. The American Revolution, based on republican understandings of power, "set in motion ideological and social forces that doomed the institution of slavery in the North and led inexorably to the Civil War" (186).

Republican imagination was an enlightened imagination, and required that a new world be created because of the change in nature of power and authority. Even the "glue" or the social adhesives binding people had to be changed. In the traditional monarchy these adhesives were principally fear, and the need to curry the favor of those of higher rank and authority. In the new republic, these adhesives needed to be replaced by civic virtues that could no longer be commanded from above but could and must be learned through appropriate education.

> Pure monarchists might still define aristocrats exclusively by the pride of their families . . . and the haughtiness of their bearing. . . . [But the] enlightened [republican] age emphasized man-made criteria of gentility—politeness, grace, taste, learning and character. . . . It implied being reasonable, tolerant, honest, virtuous . . . free of prejudices, parochialism, and religious enthusiasm of the vulgar. . . . It meant . . . all those characteristics that we today sum up in the idea of a liberal arts education. (195)

A society in which free subjects would no longer look to the monarchy for direction on how to order their lives required a system for inculcating civic virtues appropriate to a self-governing people. Wood argues that the importance of this "domestication of virtue" for the new American culture cannot be exaggerated. It was the necessary foundation for all later reform movements and for the growth of American industry and commerce. For the enlightened and educated American, caught up in optimism for the new republic, the domestication of virtue meant nothing less than a secular form of Christian love, indeed a "scientific imperative for loving one's neighbor as oneself" (218). Without such an imperative the American republic could not endure. These were to be the republican substitutes for "the artificial monarchical connectives of . . . patronage, dependency and the arrogance, mortification and fear that they had bred" (220). The new republic effectively abolished dependence on a hierarchical system of power, but could only endure if the old connectives—driven by fear— could be replaced by civic virtues freely adopted among all citizens, and by leaders whose only interest was the public welfare.

From the perspective of the late 1990s, this early revolutionary hope seems impossible and utopian simply because public virtue in the United States is said to be in short supply. Selfless leaders are thought to be nonexistent or rare. But in fact, writes Wood, from the beginning of the republic there were doubts, even among the revolutionaries, about the prospects for this new order. Before the ink on the Declaration of Independence was dry, "many of the revolutionary leaders began expressing doubts about the possibility of realizing these high hopes. The American people seemed incapable of the degree of virtue needed for republicanism," which, instead of fostering a new order, was "breeding social competitiveness and individualism. . . . The Revolution was the source of its own contradictions" (230). The revolutionary break from monarchy toward republicanism, instead of guaranteeing new republican order, let loose forces in American society that the signers of the Declaration and the writers of the Constitution could not have foreseen. For men like Jefferson and Adams, the results were not always welcome. No one could have seen how the power of equality would change society. The old revolutionaries thought they were asserting the power of freedom and independence against the domineering power of a monarchical state and an authoritarian church. They thought that once they were rid of the arbitrary monarchical restraints on the careers of talented men like themselves, there could be greater mobility and freedom for the pursuit of fortune. They intended to establish a "level playing field" on which disinterested public servants (as they imagined themselves) would preside over equality of opportunity among free citizens. Every citizen would be properly schooled in and motivated by republican virtues, not by fear. They sought a new republican order whose power would replace that of the monarchy. They asserted the power of freedom and justice over the power of domination and authoritarianism. What the revolutionaries failed to anticipate was the power of equality. As Wood writes, by "adopting the title of citizens for members of their new republics, the revolutionaries thereby threatened the distinctive status of 'gentleman' and put more egalitarian pressure on their society than they meant to." A radical explosion, fueled by the idea of equality, was "the most radical and most powerful ideological force let loose in the Revolution. Its appeal was far more potent than any of the revolutionaries realized."[5]

This extended historical discussion has been necessary to make the point that the power of equality, together with the power of dissent against restraints on equality, is part of American memory. No one should find it difficult to imagine power in the forms of equality and dissent. They have had real effects in American history. To declare, and to dare to imagine, that "all men are created equal" is indeed far more potent than those who endorsed the formative documents of the United States realized. Following the revolution there was what Wood calls a sustained "assault on aristocracy." The visions of republican order had always assumed that the monarchy would be replaced by selfless, landed, aristocratic gentry who had both the leisure and the disinterest to govern a society of free men no longer dependent on and controlled by a monarchy. What happened instead, Wood asserts, is that "in this destruction of aristocracy, including Jefferson's 'natural aristocracy,' was the real American Revolution—a radical alteration in the nature of American society whose effects are still being felt today."[6]

THE POWER OF THE SPIRIT
AS A HUGE JOKE

Religious institutions and especially their theologians, teachers, clerics, and bishops are not known for their openness to the Spirit.[7] Neither are they known for their openness to jokes aimed at exposing their pretensions of power and authority. Can we imagine that the power of the joke is another form of the power of the Spirit, in this case the power to deflate academic and ecclesiastical authoritarianism? When we, or our preferred theological or political "authorities," are not the butt of a joke, we can be cool and philosophical about how jokes, cartoons, and satires exist as important forms of rhetoric, exposing the pretentiousness or false airs of someone else. But when our own certainties—religious, political, intellectual, or moral—are the target of satire, and the contradictions of our most cherished doctrines are laid open to examination and ridicule, we may be moved not to laughter but to vengeance against those who blaspheme. The vengeful reaction to Salman Rushdie's *Satanic Verses* is only one of the most recent in a history of religio-political vendettas against anyone who would dare satirize what is held to be a sacred foundation of life.

Irony and satire are the rhetorical means by which a story, even a favorite episode of history, can be retold to bring out the contradictions in what is otherwise a cherished and familiar narrative. We can return to early American history to illustrate the point. From the vantage of the late twentieth century we can more easily spot the contradictions in the arguments of heroic revolutionaries like Franklin and Jefferson, who were certain that they were free of monarchical pretense, even as they argued for a new republic in which a natural rather than a hereditary aristocracy would govern—a high calling for which they thought themselves and their peers manifestly qualified. Many of those revolutionaries eventually lost faith in the revolution, and before their death they often bewailed "the democratic fact that their fate now rested on the opinions and votes of small-souled and largely unreflective ordinary people."[8] Gordon Wood allows that Jefferson himself, who had put much faith in the common people, lived too long, and came to see that the coming generations were not what he expected, not more enlightened and genteel. Instead they were becoming more religious, which Jefferson equated with superstition and bigotry. In the same passage, Wood writes of Jefferson: "As late as 1822 he still believed that there was not a young man now alive who would not eventually die a Unitarian!"

The Founding Fathers indeed were radical revolutionaries because they fervently believed that the new republican order would be victorious over the evils of monarchy. Furthermore, they believed that citizens, who were no longer servile "subjects" of the monarch, were created equal. So, united in their dissent from monarchy, they believed rightly that their cause was powerful enough to win. But these revolutionaries, by the very way they construed (or emplotted) the historical drama in which they were chief players, showed themselves as romantics at best, or as players in a classic comedy at worst. But the "plot" of American history in which they were indeed major players was neither a pure comedy, tragedy, nor romance, at least not in the sense that we have come to understand these modes of arranging a narrative. Jefferson's belief in the ultimate victory of Unitarianism—and of a new rational republic—is its own satire. When the narrative of American history is told in the ironic mode, so that the events constitute a satire, what is satirized is not the players themselves but their expectations. The spirit of satire, and its power, comes from the frustration of our normal expectations. In the case of early American history, the expectations of the revolutionaries were frustrated by the radical forces of equality and dissent that they had set loose. "Satire," writes Hayden White, "presupposes the ultimate inadequacy of the visions of the world dramatically represented in the genres of Romance, Comedy and Tragedy alike."[9] Who can read about Jefferson's frustrated expectations and not smile at the satirical turn of his career?

The power of satire to destabilize, disorient, decenter, and undermine all attempts to give a total interpretation—historical, natural, religious, political—is more daunting in our own time, when most people already have a pervasive sense of contradiction and dislocation. None of the preferred "plots"—including the "American dream"—seem to be working in our life and time. Few of us, least of all the average Christian, can be comfortable with satire aimed at our hopes and expectations, which we already feel are under attack. The Christian community, as noted, has rarely taken kindly to satire directed at its Bible, creeds, sacraments, and sacred symbols, yet few thoughtful Christians today would deny the ambiguity of Christian texts, practices, or symbols. Any attempt to deny such an ambiguity by appeals to an alleged and unassailable authority would invite even greater satirical dismissal.

In *Rhetoric, Power, and Community,* David Jasper proposes that the Christian community stop its defensive "weary retreat into the pseudo-authorities of traditionalism" and claim the power of satire for itself. Jasper cites a letter written by Flaubert: "When will people begin to write down the facts as if it were all a divine joke *(une blague superieure)*, that is to say, as the Lord sees them, from above." Jasper goes on to suggest that "this huge, unstable and destabilizing joke . . . must lie at the very heart of all theology."[10] This book argues that the Christian community would do far better if, instead of dismissing as "unspiritual" the various forms of secular power, including the power of satire, it brought these forms into the center of Christian thought about the Spirit of God. In this chapter I ask, "Is the laughter we hear, perhaps, the sound of the Spirit, and is it not a joke that is simply divine?"

The Spirit is a huge joke and has immense power, in particular the power to destabilize all forms of institutional authority in the church, particularly when these authorities seek to shut out the ironic mode of discourse.[11] Our task is to explore how such power can be called the power of the Spirit. In the next section, I will consider forces in the church that many faithful people regard as dangerous. I refer especially to the voices of women, who claim they have been empowered to speak with equal authority as men, and who therefore insist on their right of dissent from much that has been held sacred for most of the church's history.

THE POWER OF EQUALITY AND DISSENT

The first draft of this chapter was written not in Africa but during a stay in the United States in 1995. It was the seventy-fifth anniversary of women's suffrage in the United States, and the year when history's largest and arguably most powerful global assembly of women occurred in Beijing under the auspices of the United Nations. The power of the women's movement is now a fact of life in the world, including the two-thirds underdeveloped world. For example, in Africa it is now widely recognized that the role of women, as in all developing parts of the world, is important to the economy and the future of the continent. This fact is visible in the crowded cities and throughout the countryside in every part of Africa, where women carry immense burdens of wood, water, food, luggage, or produce on their heads and swaddled infants on their backs while their hands knit an article of clothing for their family. The irony appears in the posturing of the male leadership, whose only visible symbol of power is often ubiquitous caravans of Mercedes-Benz automobiles.

In American society and in its churches the women's movement has been resisted on all sides. The power of the movement is evident by the immense powers employed to repel it. Women active in the movement are still ridiculed as "women's libbers," and there are still many men—and women—puzzled that *American* women should think they need to be liberated. This puzzlement may be a clue to an important and largely unacknowledged fact, namely that the movement is not only about liberation but, more significantly, is about the power of equality and the right to dissent. Large numbers of women in America do have broad liberties, among them the freedom of assembly, the freedom of speech, the freedom to publish, and certainly the freedom to vote. Affluent women have access to cars and credit cards and can enjoy, for example, the freedom of travel without depending on a male escort. American women enjoy a broad range of freedom, but do not yet have equality. They do not have equal representation in legislatures, in Congress, on faculties of major universities, or in the boardrooms of major corporations. They are free to speak, but their voices are not given equal weight, and are often dismissed or tuned out. Even in sectors of the economy where they are close to achieving equal pay for equal work, women do not have equal voice or authority in matters of policy or decision making. The seemingly insurmountable opposition to the Equal Rights Amendment supports the contention that what its opponents fear most about women's liberation is not the freedom of women, but the prospect of women's equality and the force of their dissent from the status quo.

The power of equality will always threaten anyone whose power and authority derive from the obedience and acquiescence of those with less power, and over whom they exercise that authority. The spirit of equality challenges all authority structures. This is the ironic lesson that the aristocratic leadership in the American Revolution had to accept. The precept that "all men are created equal" had power they could neither imagine nor control, and consequences they neither anticipated nor could bring themselves to embrace. In that regard the revolutionaries were indistinguishable from authoritarian theologians, bishops, and clerics who have always resisted the Spirit, especially when their presumption of superior status was challenged.

It is now common to read women theologians and to hear women preachers address empowerment, usually meaning empowerment to resist oppression and to dissent from hierarchical structures of power. Women more and more are being liberated from the status of enforced silence; they are free to speak and obviously have the power to speak.[12] Much of their scholarship deserves the highest marks, and they often write more persuasively and clearly than their male colleagues. They are among the best preachers, and rarely is their speaking censored, although they are still targets of hurtful and hateful epithets like "femi-Nazi." At the risk of sounding like the familiar, impatient, and exasperated male who wails (or whimpers), "What do these women want?" I raise this question: What is the goal for which women are seeking empowerment? Do women not embody the power of equality that will always provoke resistance from those in authority? Is not the power of equality often missing in the community of Christian faith? I believe the answer is obviously yes, and in the next section I will pull samples from several of the best-known contemporary theologians to amplify that point.

THE RADICALISM OF EQUALITY AMONG THE DISCIPLES OF JESUS

Equality and dissent not only have power, but the power is radically revolutionary in the ironic sense of reordering the structures of power.[13] It is becoming increasingly common for theologians to "read" the plot of the Jesus story in the ironic mode. Jesus acted and spoke in a way that unleashed that revolutionary power in the world of first-century Judaism and throughout the patriarchal empire of the Greco-Roman world. Even so, for centuries the power of equality has been thwarted by the authoritative structures of church and society. This fact is now coming to light among North American Christians through the work of scholars who have studied the New Testament and the history of its interpretation, and then published their findings "from the underside" of society. Hispanic theologians like Justo L. González, Latin American theologians like Juan Luis Segundo, Native American theologians like George E. Tinker, African theologians like Mercy Amba Oduyoye, African Americans like James Cone, and a host of first-rank American women theologians—Rosemary Radford Ruether, Susan Thistlethwaite, Carter Heyward, Delores Williams, and Letty Russell—have revolutionized biblical and theological studies by reversing the viewpoint from which to read the narrative of Jesus and the writings of Paul. They accuse scholarly organizations and ecclesiastical authorities of practicing a continuing form of imperialism, as though revelation from God will most naturally be revealed first to privileged authorities at the top, and will then trickle down through their authorized pronouncement to the people on the ground. These new voices are saying, to the contrary, that "God is not an idea removed from the social realities of daily concrete existence, or an idea which is designed to answer academic questions about the existence of God or about the proper understanding of the Trinity."[14]

Every aspect of Christian faith and life would be radically redefined if one were to begin, not from the privileged status of those who benefit from the present order, but from those who are excluded and kept at the bottom. The previously mentioned theologians do not begin their theology, their God-talk, with ideas from on high. They begin with the Christian claim that God lives and acts in the world—in all the world. Their emphasis on the world of the poor, homeless, and outcast is not driven by politically correct ideology. They attend to the world in its most ugly places, because that is precisely the kind of world in which Jesus was born and died. He began his life in the filth of a stable, wrapped in the only fabric available, menstrual rags, and his life ended by execution in the trash heaps, where the poorest were forced to live from garbage. His life began among the homeless, and he died homeless. *The radical power of equality originates with Jesus.* The religious authorities who conspired to kill him regarded him as a dissenting blasphemer without credentials or power—he was not regarded as their "equal."

The narrative concerning Jesus, primarily the canonical New Testament writings, is a matter of record, and it is a matter of historical record that the narrative has not always been read as satire. How a reader might construe or "emplot" the narrative will vary with the rhetorical commitments she brings to the reading. Elisabeth Schüssler Fiorenza is foremost among contemporary scholars who discern the satirical plot and ironic mode throughout the Jesus narrative.[15] In her scholarly study of Christian origins, Schüssler Fiorenza follows and accepts the standard methods and results of biblical scholarship: historical-critical exegesis, two-source theory concerning the synoptics, form-critical analysis, and so forth. By her own self-description she differs from other scholars in her reading of these texts and traditions. "The difference is methodological," she writes.[16] What she means is that the difference is deeper than scholarly methods and techniques. Where other scholars have usually used these specialized techniques to uncover what many would call the "message" of the Bible, she focuses on the narrative. She is straightforward about her reason for doing so. It is because "women are found in the story of Jesus and his movement."[17] The standard scholarly practice of focusing on the message or the revealed word misses something radically important. Such scholarship usually fails to recognize how radical it was, at the time of the New Testament, to describe the important role of women in the story of Jesus. In Schüssler Fiorenza's reading, it is not enough to acknowledge the fact that Jesus was a Jew. She does not minimize his Jewishness as many Christians have done, but what is crucial for Schüssler Fiorenza is how Jesus the Jew differed from the *typical* Jew in his society. Any reader familiar with the culture of first-century Palestine would notice immediately that Jesus' way of relating to women was radical. He did not treat them as marginalized and unequal. By noticing Jesus' behavior with women, which contrasted with the dictates of his Jewish heritage, one can read the narrative of Jesus in a way that matches that radical difference.

> Only when we place the Jesus stories about women into the overall story of Jesus and his movement in Palestine are we able to recognize their subversive character. In the discipleship of equals the "role" of women is not peripheral or trivial, but at the center, and thus of utmost importance to the praxis of "solidarity from below."[18]

To read the Jesus story with special attention to women gives the story a subversive character. Without saying it explicitly, Schüssler Fiorenza argues that the place of women pushes us to read the gospel narrative in the ironic mode. The gospel narrative, when read ironically, has the effect of satire, and therefore will frustrate the expectations of those trying to find meaning, a grand word, or a "message from on high." When we read the narrative as Schüssler Fiorenza does, we understand that the plot frustrates the expectations of all sectors of authority—of the several Jewish parties, of the Romans who occupied Palestine, and even of the disciples themselves. They all thought they had a handle on who Jesus was, according to their own reading of the received scriptures or according to the imperial policies governing Roman occupation forces. In Schüssler Fiorenza's reading of the New Testament, there is an unmistakable clue by which to discern what happens in the narrative. Anyone whose social location is at the margins, and who views history from this perspective, should be able to read the plot as Schüssler Fiorenza does. By implication, anyone from a higher social location, or with an imagination limited to romantic or tragic modes, "will not get it." What triggers the release of the reader's imagination for other dimensions in the Jesus narrative, and especially for discerning the power of equality, is the role of women. *The women in the story of Jesus are the hermeneutical key for re-imagining the power of the Spirit as the power of equality.*

As Schüssler Fiorenza points out, what distinguished Jesus and his movement from other groups during his time was his vision of the kingdom (*basileia*) of God. The whole Jewish community was caught up in the expectation of a renewal of the *basileia*, and there were many visions of what the rule of God would mean. Most Jews in the time of Jesus had a vision of the promised reign of God. When this vision of God's rule was then told as the story of the Jesus movement it became a radically different reading from all other expectations. According to some other readings, the *basileia* was centered in the holiness of the Temple and of the law, the Torah. Jesus did not reject what the Temple and law meant to the Jewish community. However, what is different about Jesus' vision of the *basileia* is that, instead of occurring in precincts removed from the ordinary, the kingdom becomes actual, present and experiential, in everyday life. This fact is especially evident when he tells parables about the lost who are found, about the uninvited guests who now are the invited, or about the last who will be first. The *basileia* in Jesus' telling is most fully realized in the table community, when all those who "do not belong"—tax collectors, prostitutes, the poor, sinners—are transformed into a discipleship of equals. "Women as well as men, prostitutes as well as Pharisees. . . . Not the holiness of the elect but the wholeness of *all* is the central vision of Jesus."[19]

Schüssler Fiorenza's proposal for reading the narrative of Jesus obliges the reader not only to focus on the person of Jesus, without whom there would have been no movement called Christianity, but also to recognize that we cannot know the early Jesus movement without paying attention to people who comprised that movement. Sinners, prostitutes, the socially unacceptable, and "the ritually polluted, the crippled, and the impoverished—in short the scum of Palestinian society—constituted the majority of Jesus' followers" (129). As such they were in tension with the dominant patriarchal culture. Schüssler Fiorenza does not wish to represent the Jesus movement as opposed to Judaism, but there were tensions between his movement and the dominant Jewish culture, just as that culture was often in tension with the prophets and certainly with John the Baptizer. She points out that it was the radical and distinctive inclusiveness of this "discipleship of equals" which "ran counter to everything thought to be the will of God revealed in the Torah and Temple." As such the Jesus movement gave expression to a "quite different understanding of God," because those included in the movement were not "the righteous and pious ones of Israel but its religiously deficient and its social underdogs."[20]

In order to give dramatic expression to this different understanding of God, Schüssler Fiorenza selects Jesus' parable of the laborers in the vineyard. The typical first-century householder would often try to save money by hiring hourly laborers as needed, much like present-day employers who hire temporary workers and thus avoid the cost of mandated benefits for full-time staff. By contrast, the householder in the parable offers an unusually generous wage for the unemployed workers, who quickly accept the offer. At the end of the day he pays this same generous wage to those hired only for a few hours. The workers glad of his generosity when they signed on at the beginning of the day then accuse the householder of being unjust. They did not think that all should be treated as equals. Schüssler Fiorenza writes, "Jesus' parable thus startles his hearers into the recognition that God's gracious goodness establishes equality among all of us, righteous and sinner, rich and poor, men and women, Pharisees and Jesus' disciples." This understanding of equality set forth in Jesus' parable is similar, she believes, to that of the contemporary women's movement (132).

Christianity began as the Jesus movement, and later became a missionary movement. To trace that transition, Schüssler Fiorenza turns from the Gospels to an extended inquiry about the earliest period of the missionary movement and the beginnings of church theology. Her argument, as I have summarized it, is that in the originating "Jesus movement" of the Gospels the fundamental experience was of "God's gracious goodness in the ministry and life of Jesus." In the presence of such splendid and generous goodness, human gradations of dependence are flattened as everyone experiences the power of equality contrary to conventional practices of rank. But consider what happened to that original but short-lived equality in the missionary movement following the end of Jesus' earthly life. Schüssler Fiorenza marshals considerable evidence to support her contention that, in the first generation of that movement, women were "among the most prominent missionaries and leaders"; they were apostles, ministers, teachers, preachers, founders of house churches. This early missionary movement, Schüssler Fiorenza argues, was not "structured after the Greco-Roman patriarchal household." It was only later that church structures were adapted to structures of broader society, and eventually those hierarchical adaptations were introduced into the church and sanctioned by the all-male powers-that-be (183f.).

For our purposes the most striking proposal Schüssler Fiorenza makes is that the early missionary movement understood itself theologically as a continuing discipleship of equals. The movement could not have been sustained as a continuing mission if all that was available after the crucifixion was the memory of experiences with Jesus. If this missionary movement were to continue *it could not live on memory alone.* Its memories concerning Jesus, as essential as they were, were not enough. As Schüssler Fiorenza writes, "The experience of the power of the Spirit is basic for the Christian missionary movement." And that power is what the disciples received.

> The God of this movement is the God who did not leave Jesus in the power of death but raised him "in power" so that he becomes "a life-giving Spirit" (1 Cor. 15:45, pneuma zoopoioun). Christ is preached to Jews and Greeks as "the power of God" and the "sophia of God" (1 Cor. 1:24). Therefore he is the Lord of glory, the Lord is the Spirit (Sophia) and the liberator (wherever the Spirit of the Lord is, there is freedom; cf. 2 Cor. 3:17). (184)

Anyone who was part of the earliest missionary movement understood themselves to be "in Christ" and as such were "filled with the Holy Spirit" and "full of grace and power." To be called into the mission was to live by the Spirit (Gal. 5:25); this was true of both women and men. In the missionary community was the power of equality in the Spirit, which can be described as a palpable "force field" that liberated the disciples and set them free "to share in the glorious freedom of the children of God" (Rom. 8:21).

By peeling away centuries of interpretation, which pictured the first generations of the Christian community along the lines of Greco-Roman patriarchal society, and by retrieving the image of "equality in the power of the Spirit," Schüssler Fiorenza uses that image in her reconstructed picture of the Christian movement. The movement gathers in house churches, its members are Spirit-filled, and, like other associative groups in the Greco-Roman society, their gatherings culminate at table fellowship. Christian table fellowship would include hearing and meditating on the promises of God in scripture, and singing new songs to Christ the Lord. They were a diverse lot: "Jews, pagans, women, men, slaves, free, poor, rich, those with high status and those who are 'nothing' in the eyes of the world." But Schüssler Fiorenza emphasizes their equality in the Spirit. All are called, elected, sanctified, and justified. Her reading of the early Christian movement as a discipleship of equals subverts subsequent efforts to impose a hierarchical order on the Christian church. In that community "there is no longer Jew or Greek, . . . there is no longer male or female; for all of you are one in Christ Jesus" (Gal. 3:28). But instead of reading this much-quoted text as a "theological breakthrough achieved by Paul," she reads it as a key expression of how the Christian missionary movement understood itself. Even Paul's reputation as first among equals is qualified in Schüssler Fiorenza's reading of this classic text on equality. She does not commend the apostle for hitting on an inspired "peak formulation," which he then holds up as a timeless ideal for the church. She does not give Paul the credit that belongs to the Spirit of Christ, in whom there is the discipleship of equals. Equality in the power of the Spirit is not a praiseworthy insight by Paul, but an inspired description of the Christian community in the missionary environment. If this text by Paul is "inspired," it is so because it reflects the community that had been given the power of equality in the Spirit (199). Paul is the author, but he could not have written the words apart from his own experiences in the community in which equality in the power of the Spirit was manifest.

THE POWER OF EQUALITY, THE POWER OF THE OTHER

The irony of Christianity—for Schüssler Fiorenza and for all who read its history from the margins or from below—is the long story of failure to sustain the discipleship of equals in the church or to be open to dissent from the marginalized.[21] The Christian movement began in the Greco-Roman world, and because of its egalitarian nature, based on its experience of the Spirit of the risen Christ, executed by crucifixion, it was perceived as a subversive decentering, destabilizing alternative to the structures of hierarchical power. By worshiping the one whom the authorities had crucified, this Christian movement mocked and defied the power of the empire to suppress dissent.

The equality in the power of the Spirit characteristic of the early Christian movement, which provoked Rome, was eventually replaced by an authoritarian structure much like that of imperial Rome itself. The spirit of equality would no longer be welcome in the hierarchical church after Constantine. Because the power of the Jesus story as irony or satire will unmask the pretensions of religious authority, the satirical power of story would eventually be directed away from church structures and redirected primarily against others—other religions, other faiths, other cultures. Equality among those in Christ—male and female, free and slave—would be reinterpreted in the church as a harmless, spiritualized sentimentality camouflaging the real disparities and misuses of power in the Christian community. The power of equality in the Spirit, which arouses opposition from those anxious to protect their authority, would have to find its outlet in protest movements. Protest among Christians usually took place outside official church channels, and eventually most struggles for equality would take place outside the church altogether.[22]

The Reformation of the sixteenth century, while more a recovery of the word than a renewal of the Spirit, was one such protest movement. In particular, Luther's protest, based on the word in scriptural form and carried out by the word in preached form, stressed the equality of all believers in their baptism and Christian calling. The reformers refused to regard the priesthood and the religious life in monasteries and convents as higher callings than other vocations. As a consequence, authoritative church structures based on the elevated status of priests, established through the sacrament of ordination, were permanently destabilized by Luther's doctrines of vocation and of the priesthood of all believers.

In the centuries since the Reformation there have been several so-called Great Awakenings, or revivals in the power of the Spirit. These post-Reformation movements gave rise to enthusiasm for foreign missions and led to the twentieth-century ecumenical movement. The organizational efforts involved in mounting the foreign mission programs fell to mission societies throughout Europe and North America. These societies, like pre-Reformation protest movements, had to go outside the structure of denominational authorities for financial support, and many volunteers were drawn from the ranks of lay people, with little or no theological education. To a great extent, the modern missionary movement was egalitarian and was thought to be Spirit-led. It was not thought to be dependent on hierarchical authority. Its adherents would claim similarities between their own missionary movements and primitive Christianity. What Schüssler Fiorenza calls "equality in the power of the Spirit" was very much the spirit of the eighteenth-, nineteenth-, and early-twentieth-century missionary movements, and informed their internal practices. Within the missionary societies the Spirit's power of equality prevailed, but the attitude or consciousness of missionaries toward people they encountered in overseas cultures was often quite different.[23] One prominent African church leader told us that when visiting a fellow pastor, who was European, he would be instructed to call at the servants' entrance at the back of the house. In spite of the cultural bias of missionaries toward the receiving cultures, they did immerse themselves in the languages, translate the Bible, and let loose among African people the Jesus story. The Jesus story became the basis of revolution against colonialism in many places, often to the missionaries' chagrin.

The irony is obvious. The missionary goal was salvation for Africans. But revolution? Salvation as revolution was not the scenario that European and American mission boards had in mind for the people of Africa. African Christians, in catching the spirit of life in Christ,[24] caught the spirit of equality. The Spirit not only destabilized the authority of missionaries and of the boards of mission societies, but led many native residents to participate in the struggle for political liberation across Africa. The irony continues in postcolonial Africa. Purged of European influence, the new governments in Africa, whose people benefited from the revolutionary rhetoric of equality, have been unable to establish systems that can guarantee equality of rights for their citizens. During struggles for independence from colonial rule, some revolutionary leaders had been effective in winning ideological and material support from Scandinavian governments or from the World Council of Churches in the West, while others turned to the Soviet bloc, pleading the rightness of their cause in overthrowing colonialism from below.[25]

The powerful rhetoric of irony, which could destabilize colonial oppressors and win support from abroad, was no basis for a positive worldview because, as Hayden White writes, irony "dissolves all beliefs in the possibility of positive political action."[26] In one new African political regime after another, the leaders that demanded and fought for equality of their nation in the global community have shown themselves unable to create stable democracies as replacements for colonial systems. More than forty years after independence movements began, inequalities of wealth and power were as great or—as in Zaire—far greater under neocolonial leaders than when the countries were ruled by Europeans. The consequence is gross injustice and political instability, putting sustainable economic development seemingly beyond reach. A major obstacle to democracies of equality is the inability of postcolonial leaders to treat others, especially their opponents, as equals, with the result that free and fair elections are often nearly impossible. The irony is complete. During the struggles for liberation against white minorities, black leaders were able to use the power of equality against the power of the "other," whose otherness was manifestly visible as the ruling white minority. Now the disparity of wealth and power favors a minority of black leaders who, having enriched themselves at the expense of the people, are in the ironic position of having to confront fellow blacks, who are demanding equality, as the "other." The rhetorical power of equality (anticolonialism, anticapitalism, antiracism) worked well to propel leaders into positions in the new "ruling party," but is powerless to construct a system that can safeguard the very equality of opportunity for which the wars of liberation were fought.[27]

This brief rehearsal of the unintended contribution of Protestant missions to revolution against colonialism is offered to illustrate what has become of the New Testament experience of the power of the Spirit. At the end of the twentieth century, we have a come a long way since such notions of equality were introduced into the ancient Mediterranean world through the Christian movement. In this postmodern world it is more difficult to retrieve that experience of power in the Spirit. It also appears that nothing of that power remains for most people, except the power of the rhetoric of equality, stripped of reference to the power of the Spirit.[28] In the United States as in Africa that rhetoric has been used with great destabilizing force. What sort of power is it? At the least, the bare rhetorical assertion of equality does have the power to destabilize systems of authority, because it dissents from all forms of social, racial, political, and economic inequality. Yet the mere assertion of equality is powerless by itself to construct a social system or to bring together a community that can sustain equality.

Satire and irony are not strategies for construction. They are strategies of deconstruction, of showing how every version of reality is a human and social construction, not a divinely revealed, self-evident, undeniable, and authoritative rendition of the way things are. Thus, in satire, no version of reality is reality for everyone; it is reality for some, but not for others. There are as many versions of reality as those who hold them. Satire and irony lead to radical relativism for which there can be no universally accepted view of what is real.

Those who engage in assertions and counterassertions about equality rarely suppose that the power of equality they assert is the power of the Spirit. There is scarcely a thought or conception of the power of the Spirit when so-called special-interest groups press for equality. Contemporary power struggles for equality and freedom of dissent are real. Such power comes by the rhetorical assertion of equality.

When equality derives its power from the deconstructing force of irony and satire alone, without reference to a source or spirit beyond the one making assertions of equality, we are far from the biblical vision of equality in the power of the Spirit. We are in present-day America, or in a social location in which special-interest groups have turned up the volume on demands for equality. The rhetoric of equality sounds like what some have called "culture wars." Discourse in the public square has been replaced by groups speaking past one another, lobbing rhetorical explosives from behind walls.[29] When the power of equality and the right of dissent are not based on a common understanding or vision, then prospects for a community of assent are dim.

Anxiety and fear induced by the clamor for equal rights have provoked many Christians to adopt one of two tactics regarding the "other." The first is to engage in campaigns against equality for gays, lesbians, foreign religions, and so forth. The fear has led to demands that those in authority exclude the influence of these "others" from the Christian community. The second tactic is flight. When the other becomes many, representing multiple and competing versions of reality, it leads to retreat. This impulse can easily overtake communities of Christians and drive them into ghettos. But the second impulse of escape is blocked by the missionary character of the Christian movement.

The command to "go into the world and teach all nations" becomes more daunting when it requires the Christian to cross cultural boundaries and to be among others asserting their own equality. The requirement involves more than being in the presence of, but involves engaging the other. Christians cannot simply assume a ready-made knowledge, and that "others" are the same as we are. To be "other" is not to be "same." Christians cannot, on Christian grounds, excuse themselves from relating to the other. Were it not for the missionary mandate, Christians could sigh with relief and argue for a policy of isolation, segregation, or apartheid. The mandate, however, makes it impossible for the Christian to strike a pose of nonchalant or even benevolent indifference. Equality in the power of the Spirit is no warrant for either Christian arrogance toward the other or a laissez-faire opinion that belief systems, while different, are already equal in principle, and therefore that equality in the Spirit of Christ should not be a goal in our relation with others.

Christians are not alone in their unease about engaging the world, an unease occasioned by the many others asserting equality under the rubric of multiculturalism. Debates about multiculturalism are but the feverish symptoms indicating how much others with whom we share limited space and resources "disturb our being at home with ourselves."[30] Christians, in fact, can be disturbed by the prospect of engaging the other for three reasons. First, the other does make it more difficult to feel at home with ourselves. Second, as part of a missionary movement, Christians are sent into all the world, every neighborhood. That means crossing boundaries and engaging others whose otherness can be disturbingly unfamiliar. Third, because the Christian missionary mandate implies a vision of unity in the Spirit of Christ, that vision itself can easily arouse understandable opposition from those who perceive the mission as a rationale for another wave of imperialism aimed at sweeping all cultures under the triumphal banner of "civilization" in the name of Christ.

This threefold unease has led to an array of responses. Christians have responded to their sense of discomfort with a threefold strategy. We have hinted at all three: (1) a ghettoized Christian community that seeks homogeneity of values and practices, a response which can still be found in Christian missionary compounds in Africa or in walled suburbs across the United States; (2) a triumphalistic Christian campaign that can sometimes resemble a present-day version of the medieval crusades;[31] or (3) a bland, uncritically liberal, relativistic, and modernist Christianity that might encourage foreign aid in order to relieve physical suffering among people overseas, but will not engage their religious and cultural beliefs with any message about redemption centered in the Christian Scriptures.

THE POWER OF THE OTHER AS THE POWER OF THE SPIRIT

The previous section underscored the point that the other has power to disturb our sense of being at home, especially as the other presses for equality and dissents from the inequalities of power and privilege which some of us enjoy. The power of the other disturbs our sense of commonality and community, because the other exposes how our community excludes and marginalizes those not thought to be "our equals." The title for this section announces an equation, namely that the "secular" power of the other's pressure for equality is in fact the power of the Spirit, destabilizing and decentering our sense of community.

By now we should have no difficulty recognizing that the "power of equality" is real power. Equality as power should not stretch our imagination, especially as it confronts us in the presence of, and through the demands of, many others. There is power in equality. Can we also imagine that the power of the other pressing for equality is the power of the Spirit? We can do so without baptizing the multicultural movement as an unambiguously Christian cause, or without embracing multiculturalism as identical with the kingdom of God. To claim the power of equality as *one* form of the power of the Spirit does not oblige us to conclude that it is the *only* form of such power. This should be clear at this late point in our consideration of the diverse forms of the secular power of the Spirit.[32]

The power of the other asserting her equality can destabilize a community, family, or marriage. Yet by itself the power of equality can do nothing to construct a society or a community capable of sustaining the equality of all. We have observed the same limitation in the rhetorical powers of satire and irony. They can expose the instability and contradictions of all systems but are powerless to propose a positive course of action that can sustain a community. A family, marriage, political order, economic system, or congregation can endure as a community of assent only if built on a sufficient supply of social capital or trust. Every community is based on a belief or value that is held in common, a sense of the commonwealth. These beliefs must be conserved for the sake of the community's political stability and economic viability.[33] They must be taught to each member as necessary for the well-being of all.

Communities of assent are by necessity conservative in the sense of upholding common beliefs. Therefore, a community must resist any who would satirize, deconstruct, or destabilize confidence in what is thought to be foundational. The power of equality cannot easily destabilize a hierarchical community when all assent to what is thought to be foundational, and when all dissenters are excluded. Exclusive communities are possible only if totalitarian measures can be enforced behind iron curtains, bamboo walls, or ecclesiastical systems of discipline. But no community can any longer live B.C.—before CNN. Prior to the whole world being linked by more affordable travel and instant communication, equality was simply "being one of us." More important, before the rise of democratic movements that displaced monarchical and republican systems and modes of thought, there had been no effective challenge to the dogma that a community was organized vertically. Power and authority moved down, while duty moved up toward the monarch. Along that vertical line of dependence everyone was equal only in the curious sense of being one of the group. When community is rigidly imagined as a vertical arrangement, then the power of equality in the sense of radical democracy is unimaginable. But the persuasive power of equality now spans the earth. There is no place beyond the lines of communication and travel. Even the strangest of others can be brought into the range of awareness, into the privacy of home. Claims for equal access to the finite resources of the earth can be resisted, but there is no way to prevent their claims being dinned into our ears and displayed before our eyes.

The power of equality and dissent to destabilize communities has spread to virtually every society linked by travel and electronic communication. The necessarily conservative impulse of communities, which drives them to maintain belief systems, must now contend with the power of equality and dissent, forcing every community to redefine what it means to be British or Japanese or South African or American. Religious communities are not exempt. The question for all communities of assent is not *whether* to admit the power of equality; the question is *how* there can be stability when a community welcomes a power that will destabilize the sense of being "at home." Communities of assent can no longer exclude the voices of irony and satire, because it is physically impossible to be shielded from this power. Instant communication has turned the globe into a village in which everyone hears about the power of equality.[34]

Christian communities of faith—by the power of the Spirit—are being forced along with communities of assent to admit the power of equality into the heart of their thinking and living. The proposal for Christians is that they acknowledge this power as the work of the Spirit and stop the centuries-long error of insisting that the Spirit's power be confined to ecclesiastically sanctioned modes. The power of the other *is* the power of the Spirit. What does that require of Christians in their engagement with the other? First, the equation would make it impossible to demonize the other, and by doing so to justify lynchings, racial cleansings, "final solutions," or dehumanizing with labels. Second, Christians could not trivialize or sentimentalize the other's demand for equality, as though the power of the Spirit were a "spiritual narcotic" or "opiate" by which to suppress demands for equality and to hold onto privileges for ourselves. Such tactics are unacceptable because they do not affirm the integrity of the other. The only acceptable option for the Christian community is to pursue a more difficult question: What is the power of equality good for? By itself the power of equality cannot propose a goal and a structure of community by which to serve that goal. How can the power of equality and dissent, which always destabilizes, serve a community of assent without dissolving or betraying everything to which the community holds?

THE POWER OF THE SPIRIT AS THE SPIRIT OF CHRIST

The history of humanity is strewn with communities that confused their need for assent with totalitarian demands for literalistic and absolute allegiance to king, codes, or texts. By denying the infusion of the power of equality and dissent, which the other brings, a community welcomes and embraces its own demise. The power of equality is the power of the Spirit and—as Christians confess—the Spirit is "the Lord, the giver of life." Where there is no equality in community, life is diminished. No Spirit, no vitality. Only dry bones and relics remain of communities that closed themselves off from the power of equality. While the power of equality implies no program or structure for community, it does more than destabilize. Only if a community is first destabilized by the power of the other, which is the power of the Spirit, can a community also be revitalized and restored. Christians should not be surprised by this fact, yet they have been sadly resistant, clinging too often to literalisms, legalisms, moralisms, and nationalistic patriotisms. I will touch only on literalism to illustrate that the power of the Spirit is the Spirit of Christ,

who, though he was in the form of God
did not count equality with God
as something to be exploited,
but emptied himself,
taking the form of a slave,
being born in human likeness.
And being found in human form,
he humbled himself
and became obedient to the point of death—
even death on a cross. (Phil. 2:6-8)

The irony in this passage should—but typically does not—knock us off balance. Its familiarity lulls us into inattention, like droning our way through the Nicene Creed. In what follows we will have to work at catching the irony that can release us from our customary dead-letter literalism, which infects even the most scholarly interpreters.

The steadfast obedience of Jesus, which led to his criminal execution, was his determination to live a life that irritated the authorities. He refused to cave in and accept the common wisdom about others, the despised ones on the margins of society. We can only account for his death by the way he lived. The way he lived can be accounted for by his obedience to the Spirit, the same Spirit that drove him even into temptation. The way he was determined to live did not equal conventional standards, else why the crucifixion? He did not measure up as the equal of human authorities, enraged by his presumption to forgive sinners and the like. He was not the equal of anyone's notion of God, having been born in a stinking stable, homeless, having consorted with riffraff, and then having been nailed upright to a cross on a refuse heap. The irony is that he was not equal as a human being, and certainly not equal to what one would suppose of God. The literalist misses this irony. The literalist wants to freeze the text into a dead creed containing abstract definitions of true humanity and divinity, and then use the creed for exercising power. When treated as a dead letter, the Nicene Creed becomes a conceptual tool by which we can take the measure of someone: "Do you believe that Jesus was true God and true man?" If not you are excluded; if so you are one of us. The unbelieving "intellectual" form of literalism will use the same question to conclude that, if you believe it, you must be feeble-minded.

The irony is that Jesus as depicted in this text or in Mark's Gospel is *not* "one of us." He was crucified because, unlike us, he associated with others, and thus forfeited his right to be equal. The way God is depicted in the life of Jesus is not in accordance with a proper God. If we miss the irony and freeze the text into a literal statement, we can easily sanitize the birth of Jesus on Christmas cards, and neutralize the political and religious motivation of his execution with a theory of atonement. The literalist in us removes the Jesus episode from our comfortable existence, and offers a handy means by which to exclude from the church others not willing to be literalists. The literalist reading misses the point. Literalistic readings of the texts can only be enlivened by the decentering, disarming power of irony.[35]

Literalism deadens the text and seeks a lifeless formula for excluding others. Irony enlivens the text and gives it the fire of the Spirit that can ignite faith. We are bowled over with this ironic, decentering claim: God is not what we thought God had to be if God were God. God is not like Caesar or the czar or the majestic sovereign or the unmoved mover, but *God is like Christ.* Can you believe it? Jesus' "equality with God" is the power of the Spirit, who anointed Jesus to bring good news to the poor (Luke 4:18-19). The way of Jesus, who was *not* thought equal to his accusers, is nevertheless equal with God.

If the irony gets through, if it breaks the dead literalism of doctrinal formulations, then we have to look again at the "power of equality with God" which Jesus did not exploit. His equality with God means his identity—his identification—with the ones we are inclined to exclude. His equality with God is his identity with others, with those disturbing us with their claim to be equals. It is these others who must be regarded as showing us the Spirit of God in Jesus. To exclude them or to assume that they have nothing to show us of God is—irony of ironies—to exploit and exclude God by whose Spirit they are the power of equality confronting us, disturbing us, and destabilizing our understanding of Jesus' equality with God.

The equality of Jesus with God is a vision received in faith. The vision of equality should not be confused with various understandings of that vision. But our understanding of that equality should be disturbed when others point out how a literalistic formula can exclude the ones with whom Jesus would have identified, precisely because of his equality with God. Faith in Jesus' equality with God cannot be undone by ironic readings of the texts, but certain understandings of that equality (for example, when notions of equality are used to wield power) can be undone by satire and irony. When the irony of the texts breaks through dead literalism, and Jesus' equality with God, by the power of the Spirit, is re-imagined and reignited, literalism's beguiling power to exclude others is subverted by fresh outbursts of renewed faith no longer captive to old understandings.

The power of equality and dissent as the power of the Spirit will always disturb communities of assent, and certainly Christian communities of faith.[36] It is no longer possible for communities to shut their gates, doors, and windows to prevent the energies of the Spirit from entering, nor can they long silence those who have caught the Spirit. For example, as the texts of the Bible eventually ignited the fires of liberation in Africa, it is conceivable that Bible readers in China will catch on to the texts' subversive power, and the power of the Spirit will sweep across that nation like never before.

The new technologies of communication make it nearly impossible to contain the power of equality. Among the largest portion of the world's population—those born after 1950—the most contagious and effective language of communication across culture is rock music. "The Power of Equality" is the title of a song by the rock group Red Hot Chili Peppers. It may well have been heard around the globe. Christians should get used to the fact that rock music is the sound of the Spirit.[37] The chorus: "The power of equality is not yet what it ought to be. . . ."

CHAPTER SEVEN

DISCERNING THE SPIRIT
IN THE WORLD
AND THE CHURCH

The poet William Blake—mystic, nonconformist, eccentric—may have been the first modern writer to call attention to the link between Christian faith and imagination, a basic assumption of this book. Nearly two centuries ago, in his poem Jerusalem, he wrote, "I know of no other Christianity and of no other Gospel than the liberty of body & mind to exercise the Divine Acts of Imagination."[1] By the time this poem was written in 1804, modern rationality had already, following Descartes, torn asunder the mind (or spirit) from the body (or matter) and it was Blake's vision—or should we say his inspired imagination disciplined by faith?—that joined and kept them together. Only recently have theologians in increasing number begun to recognize the inescapable role of imagination in constructing theology or interpreting scripture. Imagination is not the abandonment of thought but it is thought renewed, provoked, and guided by images. Images, for example, "tongues of fire," have power to captivate and move the mind as well as to energize the human spirit far more readily than abstractions of the philosopher. Furthermore, religious imagination moves the human heart and spirit toward ways of seeing and depths of insight that are universal in scope. Spiritus creator calls to the mind's eye nothing less than the power of God who is creator of heaven and earth.

Three decades ago Susan Sontag observed that, even though modern people no longer use religious vocabulary easily when speaking, they often retain a certain secular piety or respect for the grand "emotions that went into that vocabulary." She continues with this striking observation: "The religious imagination survives for most people as not just the primary but *virtually the only* credible instance of an imagination working in a total way."[2] The modern imagination—unable to embrace the "total way" of religious imagination even while respecting its power—is fragmented into disconnected and often incompatible modes of imagining reality. This fragmentation is reflected in the modern university, which for a long time has had no unified frame of reference. Its proliferating academic specialties find it difficult to communicate with one another. Just as universities today are "pluriversities," the broader multicultural societies, in the absence of pre-modern religious or cultural worldviews, have become fragmented into competing special-interest groups. Some of these interest groups do indeed have a controlling "imagination working in a total way." Religious imagination by definition cannot be other than total in its outlook, but there is more than one such outlook in the world claiming to be total. And so the modern observer of the plurality of religions—however respectful of the universal scope of religious imagination—is not able to embrace religious vocabulary precisely because each "total way" has a history marred by the cruelties of religious totalitarianism.

But the secular totalitarianisms of the twentieth century are no more acceptable than religious ones—especially when any one of them manages to accumulate overpowering force to control populations. When secular imagination presumes to be "total" we are presented with the specter of Nazi Germany, its fascist and militaristic partners in Italy and Japan, Stalinist Russia, Maoist China, and Mobutu's Zaire.[3] Ever since the rise and fall of twentieth-century totalitarianisms, Christian imagination has too often retreated into the illusory security of inward, private, and individualistic belief. More Christians find it impossible to imagine what God might be doing about the horrors perpetrated by secular powers. Yet the strategy of retreat finds no support in Christian Scripture, and it rejects all that is implied by the power of the Spirit pervading secular power.

THE SPIRIT AND THE SECULAR FORMS OF POWER

The four previous chapters have been devoted to eight distinct forms of secular power, some of which can escape notice if our minds are captured by the widespread notion that there is only one form of secular power, the coercive power that dominates by force. Because we Americans are reminded repeatedly that we live in the only "superpower" nation, it is little wonder that power as domination seems the only way to imagine power. Before the collapse of the Soviet Union as a competing superpower, this single-minded way of imagining power convinced most Americans that there was no alternative to building a massive arsenal of nuclear weapons capable of obliterating the enemy many times over. Opponents regarded the policy of a nuclear arms buildup as insane, and then often took what they regarded as the moral high ground, verging on the suggestion that the power of force had no legitimacy, and that the use of force was always bad. When power is imagined exclusively as physical force, the result is a useless argument between those who favor power and those who favor powerlessness. The proponents of power too easily fall into a mind-set that cannot imagine power as anything except the power to dominate the enemy by force, and their opponents cannot seem to imagine—or remember—occasions when force is the only way to restrain evildoers and to protect the innocent. Both sides of this largely useless debate could benefit from a short lesson in rhetoric aimed at exploring the structures of imagination. There are other ways to imagine power, but we may all need training in the discipline of re-imagination. A lack of imagination is dangerous, and the twentieth century offers evidence.[4] Power can be re-imagined to include power to subdue and dominate by superior force, but there is no good reason to restrict the meaning of power to such images. There are practical—not to mention biblical and theological—reasons for expanding our imaginations concerning power.

It should be obvious on reflection that spirit is always associated with power. One need only recall that as Americans—with awareness that we as a nation have enough power to subdue others—we are both fascinated by and repulsed by violence. It is not hard for Americans to sense that violence occurs when the power to subdue is carried out in a certain spirit. Thus Americans are divided about the power to subdue. We cannot simply renounce the power to subdue, but we should ask, "With what spirit can and should that power be best—if ever—used?" That question haunts us as we approach the end of the millennium, and it is urgent that Christians in America learn quickly to re-imagine power—not to renounce America's power to subdue, but to recognize spirit in the powers of the world, especially in secular power. Christians can play a role in helping America understand that the Spirit is incarnate in all forms of power. Contrary to some theories concerning power, this book proposes that there is nothing inherently wrong with the power to subdue and to dominate, but there is no warrant for claiming that such power is the *only* form of power. There is much warrant for re-imagining other forms of power in which to discern the Spirit.

Truth is surely a form of power. We must resist every attempt to isolate the power of secular truth from so-called spiritual truth. One aid is to remember that the Spirit is associated with every form of power, and certainly with the power of truth. In the Fourth Gospel, the Spirit whom Jesus promises to send is the spirit of truth who comes from the Father. One can argue that the power of physical force to enforce social order depends on the Spirit. Likewise, the power of truth to unify the differentiated minds of the many depends on the Spirit. The link between the Spirit and the human spirit is never perfect or unambiguous, so that the secular power given by the Spirit for imposing civil order is carried out in ways that inevitably reflect the heights and depths of the human spirit. The power for imposing social order is given by the Spirit, but *how* that power is used depends on the spirit of those who use it. We are no longer surprised to observe how power can be seized and then dispensed in a mean and selfish spirit, often apparent during political campaigns. Politics does not represent the absence of the power of Spirit. Political power is always discharged as a mixture of a spirit of service toward all and a spirit of meanness in support of the few. Likewise with the secular power of truth. The search for truth is always empowered by the Spirit and can be celebrated as such. The search for truth has often been carried out in a spirit of wonder and gratitude. On the other hand, we need look no further than modern universities and colleges to observe how the power of truth that comes *from* the Spirit can be used to serve the privileges of the few *against* the Spirit, whom believers know as the Spirit of Christ.

I have also proposed *freedom* and *justice* as two other secular forms of the Spirit's power. Freedom and justice do not lend themselves to simplistic definitions. There are few concepts that generate more controversy in religious and political circles than perspectives on freedom and justice. They have considerable power to stir emotions and to fuel action, evidenced by the French and American revolutions. Theologians have been tempted to drive a wedge between secular struggles on behalf of liberation against *political* tyranny, while religious struggles like the Reformation have opposed the *spiritual* tyranny of the papacy. The antithesis violates the integrity of the power of the Spirit, who energizes all movements for freedom—civil and spiritual. Such energy resists every attempt to split freedom movements into separate categories of secular and spiritual.

Who can question the power of freedom and justice to energize transformative events? The great power of America is not only in its economic and military force. America continues to attract millions of people. Changing metaphors, the power of freedom and justice, however imperfectly realized in the United States, still blows the winds of the Spirit's power, stirring the oppressed to action. The only question concerning the power of freedom and justice arises when one tries to imagine the Spirit as the power behind *all* such movements. Freedom and justice are secular forms of the power of the Spirit. It is in the exercise of those powers that they can be used either for or against the Spirit from which these powers flow. The widespread misuse of freedom's power gives no cause for supposing the Spirit's absence among those who use freedom irresponsibly. Freedom remains a secular form of the Spirit's power even when that power is used in a spirit of hostility against God, who is the source. Freedom does not generate its own power. It is the father's generosity that empowers the freedom of the prodigal son, despite his irresponsible use of that freedom. The power behind all freedom is the power of the Spirit. The gift of freedom can be used to puff up special interests or to build up communities of freedom and justice.

Theories of justice abound, and there is deep postmodern suspicion that every theory of justice will favor the interests of the powerful, who presume to be arbiters of justice. Is not justice another secular form of the power of the Spirit? Confidence in the Spirit allows us to resist romantic idealism about justice, as well as cynicism that follows from the denial of Spirit common in secular society. The power of justice still works its way in the human spirit, especially where there is neither romanticism nor cynicism about the possibility of justice in the real world. The misuse of law has become commonplace in these litigious times, and yet it is still possible to identify such misuse in the judicial system. Justice is another secular form of the Spirit's power, and as such can be used in meanness of spirit or in a way that lets "justice roll down like waters, and righteousness like an ever-flowing stream" (Amos 5:24). Christians of all people should advocate justice as a form of the Spirit's power.

The power of the Spirit has two other seemingly cherished dimensions in secular life: *love* and *beauty*. There is no difficulty in imagining how love and power, or beauty and power, can be associated in the popular mind. The power that comes with wealth, prestige, or political influence is an attractive force in American life. The love of power drives much of our economy and political system. There is also the beauty of power. To have power can be thought beautiful. Athletes and film stars are said to live the beautiful life. The love of and beauty of power are ready-made explanations for how people are motivated to become famous. The love of power can account for loyalty to political tyrants; the beauty of power can account for the uncritical adoration showered on celebrities. These connections among love, beauty, and power pose no difficulty, and require little imagination, because the media daily confront us with lives driven by the love of power and by a fascination for the beauty of being powerful.

It is much more difficult to re-imagine power in the reverse, and to speak of the power of love and of beauty as secular forms of the power of the Spirit—that is, the Spirit of Christ. The difficulty in taking seriously the power of love and of beauty as secular forms of the Spirit's power lies in the history of religious movements like Christianity. Their history is one of neglect of the power of love and indifference to the power of beauty. Religious communities can become so preoccupied with the power of the truth of doctrine that they feel justified in being ruthless toward those who question the authority of their teachings. Likewise, the history of liberation movements is one of becoming preoccupied with liberation from old oppressors. Liberation movements then become oppressively intolerant of dissent in their own ranks. Not only has the power of truth and of freedom been exercised by religious and political groups in a loveless spirit, which in the end destroys communities, but the world is also strewn with examples of what happens when the power of truth and of freedom overwhelms the power of love and of beauty.

Honesty compels us also to recognize two sides to the history of love and of beauty. The history of the power of the Spirit is the history of societies being transformed by the Spirit, but it is also the history of the *mis*use of love and beauty. The rhetoric of love and beauty has been used for seductive and abusive purposes, as well as to sentimentalize the crucifixion and to soften the scandal of the cross. Love and beauty as secular forms of the power of the Spirit have, nonetheless, been used repeatedly in a loveless spirit.

One of the permanent challenges for Christians is to interpret the horror of the crucifixion of Jesus in terms of beauty and love. Augustine said of the crucifixion: "[Jesus] hung therefore on the cross deformed, but his deformity is our beauty." How can the ugliness of Christ's deformity be regarded as beautiful?

There is also vigorous debate today about how the crucifixion can serve the will of God and disclose the love of God. The antinomies expressed in these questions are permanent features of the life of faith. They can never be eliminated, but they can be transposed into a different key, that is, into the logic of Spirit.

Beauty and love are forms of the Spirit's power. We can cling to bare existence without beauty and love but we cannot live well without them. A life without love and beauty is a life nearly desolate of Spirit. To insist that beauty is a form of the Spirit's power is not the same as putting a rose on the cross to make it pretty. Rather, the power of the Spirit as beauty does not call attention to itself. Beauty is not religious kitsch. As beauty the power of the Spirit reveals more than beauty itself. That is why the Spirit's power of beauty is closely related to the Spirit's power of love. The power of beauty resembles the power of love in that neither beauty nor love is "envious or boastful or arrogant or rude. It does not insist on its own way; it is not irritable or resentful; it does not rejoice in wrongdoing, but rejoices in the truth" (1 Cor. 13:4b-6).

At the close of the millennium, there are two forms of secular power that cannot be ignored: the power of *equality* and of *dissent*. I have made extensive use of Gordon S. Wood's *The Radicalism of the American Revolution* in order to drive home that point. Prior to the American democratic experiment, the mind-set of Europeans was stuck imagining that monarchy was divinely ordered and that power was vertically organized, flowing from top to bottom, so that all members of society were subject to those on the rung above them. The American experiment radically changed the conception of power with two simple principles. The first is that power flows from the consent of citizens, who no longer must obey the king. The second is the equality of all people. Eventually the principle of equality meant that slavery in America would be abolished, and that the vote could not be denied to women. The right to dissent has replaced the absolute power of monarchy. Americans appeal to the power of equality and of the people's right to dissent as secular forms of power. Are they not as well secular forms of the Spirit's power?

Some churches continue to be among the last defenders of the divine right of hierarchical power, embedded in their ecclesiastical structures. Wherever that defense is mounted, it is a lost cause. Still, many women in the church have become casualties in the ongoing struggle for equality. But as the Declaration of Independence established the principle of equality that would later doom slavery, the Reformation's doctrine of the priesthood of all believers will eventually defeat every attempt to maintain a priestly hierarchy. Those of us men who have enjoyed the dubious privilege of superior status have had to revise our understanding of power because of feminist readings of the Jesus tradition. The radical power of equality originates with Jesus. Whenever someone learns—usually from women—to read the Bible differently and to pay attention to the role of women in the Jesus story, he must also re-imagine the power of the Spirit as the power of equality, rather than the power of privilege.

The power of the Spirit is experienced everywhere where there is pressure to pay attention to the "other," to those who are different. They disturb our sense of commonality and community. This secular power of equality, which we feel as pressure from those others, is in fact the power of the Spirit refusing to blow only where we want the Spirit to blow; instead, the Spirit is destabilizing and decentering us. The "other" is simply not like us, and does not live according to customary standards. It is hard to imagine the other as our equal. It is a strain on our imaginations to think that the Spirit pressures us through someone other than "one of our own." But it helps to remember that the Spirit is the Spirit of Christ, who himself was never treated as an equal. He was certainly not considered equal to anyone's notion of God. In fact, he forfeited his right to be treated like an equal by associating with the marginalized. He did not claim equality with God but "emptied himself, taking the form of a slave" (Phil. 2:7), an unequal form of humanity.[5]

In this inventory of the forms of secular power, which are the forms of power that the Spirit takes in the world, the challenge becomes urgent for the churches in the twenty-first century to be able to discern the power of the Spirit. The inventory serves as a mandate to churches to re-imagine the secular forms of power as the power of the Spirit, transforming the world.

THE CHURCH IN
THE POWER OF THE SPIRIT

The Spirit is everywhere, existing in the omnipresent secular forms of the Spirit's power.[6] There is no place in the world where the Spirit is not. We cannot say the same thing about the church—simply because there are still many places in the world where the church is not. Wherever they are, churches make claims about how the Spirit relates to churches, usually to the neglect of how the Spirit exists as the power of God in the world. For some the Spirit is closely identified with structures, orders, or priestly hierarchy and sacraments. In the Eastern tradition, for example, when the priest invokes the Spirit on the bread and wine, the earthly substances become the body and blood of Christ. The peril is that the Spirit is subordinated to the church as the institutional embodiment of Christ.

In churches of the Reformation, the Spirit is closely identified with preaching and teaching that are true to the gospel, as interpreted in the churches' confessional documents. The peril is that the Spirit is subordinated to the word of Christ, rightly preached and correctly taught, which tempts preachers and teachers in those churches to think the Spirit is captured in words and doctrines. They are tempted to neglect the Spirit as the power that alone makes words live. In some churches it is by speaking the right words that the bread and wine become the body and blood.

A third group of churches does not think *they* have captured the Spirit in structure or in doctrine but that the Spirit has captured *them.* The peril in the third group is to praise gifts bestowed by the Spirit, and then to insist that the Spirit exists only among those who possess the gifts of the Spirit.

Thus, while every type of church makes a claim for how the Spirit calls and empowers it, it is still rare for churches to pay attention to how the Spirit is present in secular powers—in those places where the church is not visible. That shortcoming can be called a failure of imagination—the failure to imagine what in the world God is doing. The overall effect is to confine the Spirit to churches and to encourage the impression that the world—because it is not the church—is a Spirit-forsaken, and therefore God-forsaken, place. It is as though the question, "What in the world is God doing?" has only one answer: "Nothing."

I can only agree with Moltmann's insistence that the church is in the power of the Spirit. Otherwise there would be no church. In *The Spirit of Life: A Universal Affirmation,* Moltmann developed a view that could have been called "*creation* in the power of the spirit."[7] Without the presence of the power of the Spirit in the created order, *everything* would cease to exist. It is clear that all churches, in one way or another, acknowledge the necessity of the Spirit for their life as churches. Not all churches have been as clear in acknowledging the necessity of the Spirit for the life of world. Instead they have often been forceful in rejecting all forms of life in the Spirit as satanic, if not under the church's control. Such extreme reactions only serve to underscore the ambivalence of Christian churches toward any view of the power of the Spirit.

CALLED BY THE SPIRIT TO WITNESS TO THE SPIRIT OF CHRIST

What practical difference can this discussion make in the life of churches? How would churches change were they to acknowledge that the Spirit of God exists within all forms of secular power—the proposal set forth in this book? Churches would have to expand their understanding of the Spirit to match the understanding of scripture, and then to abandon any notion that the Spirit of God is alive only in the structures of the church, in teaching and preaching, or in those churches with special gifts of the Spirit, such as speaking in tongues. Churches would witness to the Spirit in all the world, but churches would not be the only place where the Spirit is at work in the world.[8] To witness to the Spirit does not mean taking the Spirit into the world but discerning and witnessing to the Spirit of God already there, pervasive in the powers that sustain and preserve the world, even when those powers are used against God and against good. Such action would represent a radical reversal of much thought and practice.

What would be the practical consequence of this reversal in the churches' faith and order, and in their life and work? I list four headings for this discussion, corresponding to the customary four marks of the church ("One, Holy, Catholic, and Apostolic"). For the purpose of these concluding paragraphs, the headings will be listed in unconventional sequence: apostolic, catholic, one, and holy. What follows, then, is a modest proposal to re-imagine ecclesiology, to change the way we think about the reality of the church.

1. *Evangelism in a world of many faiths: the church as apostolic.* The Christian church is a missionary movement by definition. Gathering for worship always entails a sending forth, the apostolic mandate. How to carry out that mission is a never-ending topic of theological debate. To locate the Spirit in the world of power—as we have been proposing—means that no religious faith or secular commitment, including atheism, draws vitality solely from itself, nor is it self-generating. The Christian witness assumes that the presence and the power of the Spirit of God already exist in all forms of life. This assumption requires Christian witnesses to learn what has been long neglected, to learn how to discern the signs of the Spirit in the other. That step will induce modesty and openness toward others' commitments regarding the powers of the Spirit in their search for truth and in their struggle for justice, equality, and freedom. This course does not require that the Christian be silent or play down the distinctiveness of the Christian witness, but it does eliminate a basis for arrogance toward the religious faith, or the atheistic denials, of others, who all live by the power and in the presence of the same Spirit. What distinguishes the Christian witness to the Spirit is that—for the Christian—the Spirit of God has been supremely, but not exclusively, manifested in the life and death of Jesus.

Christians bring an announcement that is good news or gospel. It is this announcement or news that is distinctive. In their engagement with people of other faiths, Christians bring a name for the Spirit. Jesus is the Spirit of God in person. It is the name, or more precisely the story of the life and death of Jesus, that for Christians focuses questions about the Spirit. The question to other faiths is *not,* "Is the Spirit of God among you?" The chief question that the witness to Jesus raises is, "*How* are the powers of the Spirit among you being used?" Witness to Jesus as the Christ cannot proceed until Christians open themselves to how others witness to the power of the Spirit in times and places in which the name of Jesus has not yet been proclaimed. The power of the Spirit is universal, but something new happens when the powers of Spirit are manifest and focused in the reality of the one named and identified as Jesus. The powers are transformed and redirected in service to God's mission, to the end that all the world will be renewed and redeemed. In that sense the name of Jesus saves, because Jesus embodies God's way of saving the world.

2. *Ecological concern for our threatened globe: the church ascatholic.* The mission of the church is worldwide. Until recently the global mission was

pursued with nearly complete indifference to the welfare of the globe itself. The churches of the northern hemisphere have for the past several centuries come to accept a great and deadly illusion. That illusion has controlled the imagination of most movers in the political and economic realms, namely the illusion that the Spirit is only found—if anywhere—in the privacy of human souls and, maybe, in the sacraments and structures of churches. According to this deadly illusion, the earth does not live by the power of the Spirit. Therefore, the earth's resources can be used for whatever goal pleases human beings without regard for the sustainability of that use. The churches have passively accepted this untruth, and only in the past generation or so have many Christians, but not all, repented. There are still pockets of resistance to what some have called "creation spirituality" and the like, and there is still fear of talk of the Spirit living in and breathing life into creation. For some the talk smacks of pantheism, nature worship, spiritism, or a return to so-called animism.

But much biblical scholarship, and an awakening of trinitarian speech about God, have warned us that we had better be "suspicious of our suspicions" of the Spirit in creation. The awesomeness of God's transcendence and the fearful mystery of God's hiddenness notwithstanding, God has not been banished from the earth, but is present and active in all things by the energizing powers of the Spirit. If the witness of churches to the powers of the Spirit were taken seriously, the witness would bring a thoroughgoing change in attitude and practice. Christians would become more steadfast, vocal, and visible in their concern for the earth, and not be put off by the insinuation that political correctness or liberal ideology is replacing the gospel. Concern for the earth is a profound, direct, and urgent implication of the Christian commitment to the Spirit of Christ. Following Christ means being concerned for the least of the brothers and sisters of Jesus. There is no way of showing that concern out of obedience to Christ without also participating in political and social action designed for renewing the earth, whose devastation in cities and in the countryside hurts all creatures, great and small.

3. *Ecumenism for a fractured Christian community: the church as one.* It is widely acknowledged that the ecumenical movement of the twentieth century began in response to the concern of missionaries that the witness of churches in India, Africa, the Orient, and Latin America was being compromised by denominational divisions. Ever since, the ecumenical "problem" is often, and understandably, formulated as an organizational problem: how to get all the churches into one structure. Unity characterized in terms of one structure is still a tempting goal for ecumenism, especially because a structure that many regard as the best model for that unity is already in place. The model dates to Peter. Its successors sit as the chief bishops in Rome. It is no surprise that that model of unity as a catholic structure grates on those for whom unity is "the unity of the Spirit" (see Ephesians 4).

The debate—Spirit versus structure—will probably never end, and is guaranteed to multiply and deepen the divisions among Christian believers as long as it is cast in terms of *either* Spirit *or* structure. The powers of the Spirit are found in structure. Spirit blows where it wills but, by its very nature, the Spirit never blows independently of discernible structures. And structures—whether sociohistorical or physical or natural aggregates—are always embodiments of Spirit. In ecumenical discussions it is, finally, pointless to debate how churches can guarantee for themselves the *gifts* of the Spirit. No structure or practice can guarantee that the gifts of the Spirit, whether apostolic succession or speaking in tongues, are safely confined within its borders. Ecumenical dialogue will fail when it focuses on the gifts of the Spirit. Debates about gifts of the Spirit end up creating "enmities, strife, jealousy, anger, quarrels, dissensions, factions . . ." (Gal. 5:20). Churches require gifts of the Spirit for mission in the world, but the gifts can never be the basis for unity in structure and in Spirit. As soon as churches try to regulate these gifts with laws of institutional governance, they undermine unity.

Church unity itself will not occur until churches stop worrying about how to organize and regulate the gifts and begin paying attention to the "fruits of the Spirit." "There is no law against such things," writes Paul (Gal. 5:23b). Indeed, there can be no law regulating or guaranteeing "love, joy, peace, patience, kindness, generosity, faithfulness, gentleness, and self-control" (5:22). When churches are too anxious about unity, they tend to turn inward, spend money on official dialogues, and end up with "works of the flesh" such as jealousy, enmity, and strife. If churches were to cease being anxious about organizational unity, and instead were to become clearer witnesses to the Spirit, they would have to look outside themselves to discover where—in the economy of God called the world—the fruits of the Spirit such as "love, joy, peace, patience, kindness," and so forth exist. These fruits can and often do appear outside churches. An aid to ecumenism would be for churches to witness to what the Spirit is doing in the world, and not to be scornful when fruits of the Spirit grow in surprising places, even among those who do not "name the name." There can be no law against the fruits of the Spirit, against churches encouraging them, or against Christians working to nurture those fruits regardless of who joins in the work.

Unity in the Spirit is possible only when churches repent—turn away from their anxiety about regulating the gifts of the Spirit, turn around, look around, and witness to the fruits of the Spirit wherever they are happening in the world.

4. *Equipping the faithful for Christian witness: the church as holy.* The word *holy,* when applied to communities of flesh-and-blood human beings like churches, is sure to arouse suspicion. There is no way to prevent someone from taking the word *holy* to mean moral perfection, spotless character, lack of blemish, and the like, so that *holy* finally means having no worldly traits. It is no wonder that, when that meaning is applied, no church qualifies as holy.

Here Luther's catechism is a great help. It is not the worthiness of Christians that makes the church holy. The church is holy because it is the Holy Spirit who calls, gathers, enlightens, and sanctifies the church. To be holy or sanctified does not resemble earning merit badges or academic degrees, which will qualify one for high rank in the church or for a tenure track on a theological faculty. To be holy is more like being drafted, being called for service, being lured or drawn with others into a company for a job that none would seek on their own. What makes the Christian church holy has little—or perhaps nothing—to do with the gifts of the Spirit. Every human community has most of the same gifts as the church. What makes the Christian church holy is that the Spirit has called people, drafted them, drawn them together, and then sworn them to the duties of their office. Even when the church does its duty, it is not the doing of duty that makes the church holy. It is being called by God through the Spirit for that duty, not the duty itself, which makes the church holy.

What makes the church holy, then, is not gifts of the Spirit but that it is drafted and empowered by the Spirit for a duty or mission, for distinctive activity in the world. The church is holy because the church has been drafted by the Spirit. It is distinctive because the church believes and acts on the belief that only God can save the world, and Jesus is God's way of doing that. Even when the church proclaims the gospel of Jesus Christ, it is not the proclamation itself that makes the church holy. The church is holy because it has been drafted by the Spirit to make known God's way of saving the world. But God's way of saving the world is not done apart from the Spirit. Without the Spirit, there would be no story of Jesus to tell. Jesus was conceived by the power of the Spirit, baptized by the Spirit through John, driven into temptation by the Spirit, and led by the Spirit to preach good news to the captives and recovery of sight to the blind. When he was crucified, it was by the Spirit of the one who raised Jesus from the dead that the Spirit of Christ remained alive as the body of Christ, the church.

What are we to say of the gifts of the Spirit, if the gifts do not make the church holy? The church is holy by the calling of the Spirit, and the church is equipped for its calling by the gifts. The distinction is utterly important. It is the calling of the Spirit by which the church can be holy, dedicated and pledged to God's mission in the world. But the gifts of the Spirit are indeed used for equipping the saints—those drafted for service—"for the work of ministry, for building up the body of Christ, until all of us come to the unity of the faith and of the knowledge of the Son of God . . ." (Eph. 4:12-13). There is one ministry with a diversity of gifts of the Spirit.

By taking another look at the four marks of the church, we can see how recovering the pervasiveness of the Spirit as the power and presence of God serves as a mandate for change into the next millennium. First, the apostolic witness of the church assumes the presence and power of God's Spirit in all those who have not yet heard the name of Jesus. Evangelism among people of other faiths or no faith will be respectful, nonintrusive, and open to discern the work of the Spirit who precedes those committed to telling the story of Jesus as God's way of saving the world.

Second, the mission of the church is catholic, universal, and global, for it is the purpose of God that all creatures be reconciled. Any mission that does not include care of the earth in its scope is, by definition, not catholic. At the close of the twentieth century, perhaps the most visible evidence of fragmentation is the devastation that has been done to the earth itself, which takes its toll on the poor in American cities and impoverished rural areas, in ecological wreckage left by the failed economy of the Soviet Union, and among marginalized peoples of the southern hemisphere. The church catholic embraces and engages in a ministry of reconciliation with all suffering creatures of God. The mission of the church catholic is an ecological mission in the fullest sense.

Third, gifts of the Spirit are not the exclusive property of Christians. They can never be a sign of unity. Those who want to believe that the church is one will never find that unity by looking for ways to regulate or stipulate the gifts of the Spirit—asking what they are, who has them, where are they, and when do they happen. Such questions will lead to endless debate and not to unity. Unity can never be attained by law, only by attending to the fruits of the Spirit against which there is no law. These fruits can be discerned in the world. There is no law against Christians joining others in works that provide "love, joy, peace, patience, kindness, generosity, faithfulness, gentleness, and self-control." The fruits of the Spirit are urgently sought. Christians can help nurture these fruits for the benefit of the world.

Fourth, the power of the Spirit—who is the Spirit of Christ—is everywhere, but the name of Jesus as the Christ is not known everywhere. The church is holy in the sense of being called, drafted, selected, and set aside by the Spirit for the job of making the Jesus story known. Why should the news be broadcast? Because for Christians Jesus means salvation. His name literally means "God saves." Yet that equation, which defines the distinctiveness of the Christian church, provokes this question: Does it mean that there is no salvation for those who have not heard the name of Jesus? A Christology of Spirit or a Spirit Christology would respond by affirming that only God can save the world, and Jesus is indeed God's way of saving. There are ways of presenting a Jesus-centered message that contradict the Spirit of Christ, who is the Spirit of God. Churches must remember that the Spirit of God drafts and calls the church into service. A Spirit Christology serves as a check on the impulse to carry out that mission in unholy ways, a glaring example of which is to insist that *our way* is the way of Christ, and therefore the *only* way. It is not the church's life or witness that is holy. It is through the enlistment or call of the Spirit to be witnesses to the Spirit of Christ that the church is holy. This call makes the church holy, but does not minimize the importance of the church's way of life. *How* the church presents the name of Jesus in word and deed can frustrate, hinder, and perhaps act as blasphemy against the Holy Spirit.

THEOLOGY OF THE SPIRIT MADE PRACTICAL

Countless efforts have been undertaken to make Christianity more practical, to overcome the gap between Christian faith—born of Word and Spirit— and daily life. Nothing is more practical and down-to-earth than power. No one has ever thought power to be such an abstract idea that it does not relate to anything practical. Power is neither an abstraction nor is power a simple idea, but no one should conclude that the complexities of power make it unreal or something that does not exist. Spirit is not a simple idea, either, but its existence is problematic to many people. To others Spirit can be easily classified as (1) a superstition; (2) an inner mood, feeling, or sensibility; or (3) a public reality, but only in religious communities and therefore of a different realm from human bodies, political systems, economic transactions, scientific experiments, and so forth. My own Christian faith and my lifetime as a Christian pastor and teacher have put me at odds with these and other dismissals and diminishments of Spirit. The theological tradition of the church and the Bible's narrative and teaching would not endorse such a dismissal. Perhaps I could have lived for the rest of my life with the dichotomy between the secular powers and the Spirit; perhaps I would have continued pushing the question about their relationship into my unconscious. That I did not continue doing so is in large measure this American theologian's response to Africa.

Others might disagree, but I am satisfied that I have succeeded in what I set out to do. First, I did not try to defend a dogmatic prescription of the Spirit. There is no "dogma" of the Spirit comparable to the Chalcedonian Formula and its doctrine of the incarnation. Rather, I have used structures of imagination as a device for uncovering what is often overlooked in the Bible or suppressed in the churches. I have attempted a more ample description of the Spirit as pervasive of all powers.

Second, I was aware at every point that to describe every power as a form of the Spirit's power and presence would draw objections about the power of evil. Repeatedly I have tried to make clear that evil involves the misuse of powers which evil does not itself generate. God is generous in giving power to creatures, who all too often use it against the one from whom it flows. I believe my position both honors God as omnipotent in the sense of being the source of all power, and remains realistic about the suffering unleashed in the world by the "powers" who wrongly imagine that they are self-made.[9]

Third, I have tried to show that faith in the presence and power of God's Spirit can free our imaginations so that we can both honor God as the supreme agent in all creation and also call human beings to respond to the Spirit of God within them. The indwelling Spirit calls humans, not only to faith as trust and confidence in God—that God is as good as God's own Word incarnate in Jesus—but also calls our spirits to respond with words and deeds that serve God's will. The indwelling Spirit of God can empower the human spirit to live in hope and not to despair. Hope is not simply a mood; it is a form of action. Hope is the Spirit energizing our spirits to persevere in the conviction that human beings can learn to live in unity with one another and with creation, that truth will prevail in the long-term, that freedom and justice for all will increase, that beauty and love can turn aside ugliness and triumph over evil, that dissent from a partial good can clear the way for a larger good, and that in the Spirit there is a splendid equality of the many, each enriching the life of all.

NOTES

INTRODUCTION

1. After this book was accepted for publication, I was directed to another constructive proposal for a pneumatology that departs from common understandings of power. Nancy Victorin-Vangeruud contrasts two kinds of power arrangements that shape communities and households. She calls them "economies of domination," expressed in a trinitarian model as a patriarchy in which the Father rules the Son and the Spirit hierarchically, and "economies of recognition," in which the Trinity is modeled as the intersubjectivity of mutual recognition ("From Economies of Domination to Economies of Recognition: A Feminist Pneumatology," Ph.D. diss., Vanderbilt University, 1995).

2. Which is the title of the first of Hall's three volumes on theology in North America (Minneapolis: Fortress Press, 1989).

3. "I believe that by my own reason or strength I cannot come to believe in Jesus Christ, my Lord, or come to him. But the Holy Spirit has called me through the Gospel, enlightened me with his gifts, and sanctified and preserved me in true faith . . ." (*The Book of Concord*, translated and edited by Theodore Tappert [Philadelphia: Fortress Press, 1959, 345]).

4. This mind-set, which might be called "despiritualized," has been well analyzed by Joel Kovel in his book *History and Spirit* (Boston: Beacon Press, 1991) in response to what he calls a "profound spiritual crisis." Like others he thinks the American culture is one of individualism. When people try "to rescue their own spirituality" they only do so by splitting themselves off, a process that "spares the individual spirit, but at the cost of fragmenting reality and dehumanizing social production." In the resulting atmosphere, everyone "is free to pursue spirituality under capitalism, and almost everybody does. But none of it matters to the order of things" (11).

5. I would have to allow many exceptions to this large generality about theological seminaries in the American context. A significant example would be Peter Hodgson's recent *The Winds of the Spirit* (Louisville: Westminster/John Knox Press, 1994).

6. "There are no words of God without human experiences of God's Spirit. . . . But this is only possible if Word and Spirit are seen as existing in a *mutual relationship*, not as a one-way street. . . . To bind the experience of the Spirit solely to the Word is one-sided. . . . [T]he Word is bound to the Spirit, but . . . the Spirit is not bound to the Word, and . . . Spirit and Word belong in a mutual relationship which must not be conceived exclusively, or in merely intellectual terms" (Jürgen Moltmann, *The Spirit of Life: A Universal Affirmation* [Minneapolis: Fortress Press, 1992, 3]. In a more recent book, Moltmann writes of God the Spirit, similarly, as source (*The Source of Life: The Holy Spirit and the Theology of Life* [Minneapolis: Fortress Press, 1997].

7. Regarding the influence of cultural ethos on theological discourse and personal formation, see Jackson W. Carrol et al., *Being There: Culture and Formation in Two Theological Schools* (New York: Oxford University Press, 1997). As for the impact of missionaries on theology and church cultures, the missionary history that I know best is that of Zimbabwe. That knowledge has been enhanced greatly by the comprehensive

study of a colleague, C. J. M. Zvobgo, *A History of Christian Missions in Zimbabwe, 1890–1939* (Harare, Zimbabwe: Mambo Press, 1996).

8. Harvey Cox, *Fire from Heaven: The Rise of Pentecostal Spirituality and the Reshaping of Religion in the Twenty-first Century* (Reading, Mass.: Addison-Wesley, 1995), 252.

9. Ibid., 255. The medical research on the relation between health and spirituality, or spirit, is expanding rapidly. See the resources cited in Dean Ornish, *Love and Survival* (New York: HarperCollins, 1998).

10. This is Cox's way of giving the "broad outlines of the vast historical metamorphosis we are living through." See *Fire from Heaven*, 301.

11. For a brief summary in support of this point see Alasdair I. C. Heron, *The Holy Spirit: The Holy Spirit in the Bible, the History of Christian Thought, and Recent Theology* (Philadelphia: Westminster Press, 1983), especially pt. 1, "The Spirit in Scripture."

12. If it were easy to see the world in biblical imagery, to imagine the Spirit of God in all forms of secular power, there would be no need for this book. We cannot simply go back to pre-Enlightenment readings of the Bible, but we must go back and reread the Bible. Michael Welker's recent book is a careful rereading of the Bible with a view to re-imagining the Spirit in ways that take into account new forms of thought. His own proposal is to use the concept of *force field* in order to make the biblical understanding of Spirit available today. See *God the Spirit* (Minneapolis: Fortress Press, 1994).

13. As I began the final revision of this book, *Newsweek* published a cover story, "Science Finds God," which reported on the convergence of theology and cosmology over the past years. The story asked how—after the long war between science and religion—we could speak of what God is doing in the *cosmos*. "To most worshippers, a sense of the divine as an unseen presence . . . is all well and good, but what they yearn for is a God who acts in the world" (July 20, 1998, 49).

14. *Luther's Works*, ed. Jaroslav Pelikan, vol. 24 (Saint Louis: Concordia), 364f.

15. *Experience* is a notoriously difficult term in both philosophy and theology. Scientific method in the modern sense began when Galileo studied the sky with a telescope and saw celestial bodies that are not revealed in the Bible or other traditional authorities. Whatever else is meant by "scientific method," the concept relies on experience, but also curtails and limits the scope of the uses of experience. In this book the notion of *experience* is expanded to include all dimensions of reality, both subjective and objective, both immanent and transcendent, both finite and infinite, temporal and eternal, mental and physical. What follows is intended to show how one might reasonably think of, conceive of, or imagine spirit as a factor in all experiences. I am following Moltmann and others here in rejecting the "antithesis between revelation and experience," which always seems to conclude with "revelation that cannot be experienced and experiences without revelation." See J. Moltmann, *The Spirit of Life: A Universal Affirmation* (Minneapolis: Fortress Press, 1992), 2.

16. See Peter Hodgson, *Revisioning the Church* (Minneapolis: Fortress Press, 1988), who proposes an ecclesiology for postmodern America.

CHAPTER 1

1. Elizabeth A. Johnson, *She Who Is: The Mystery of God in Feminist Theological Discourse* (New York: Crossroad, 1992), esp. "Forgetting the Spirit," 128ff.

2. Pierre Pradervand, *Listening to Africa: Developing Africa from the Grassroots* (New York: Prager, 1989), esp. "Learning from Africa," 208–13.

3. Peter Berger, *The Social Construction of Reality* (Garden City, N.Y.: Doubleday, 1966), and M. F. C. Bourdillon, *Religion and Society: A Text for Africa* (Gweru, Zimbabwe: Mambo Press, 1990).

4. Walter Rodney, *How Europe Underdeveloped Africa* (London: Bogle-L'Ouverture, 1972).

5. *Postmodernism* has been variously defined, but roughly it rejects the claims of the Enlightenment, especially the notion that cultures can be graded or evaluated against an objective view of what is rational, verifiably true, and universal. A postmodernist might say, with Michel Foucault, that what is rational or true depends on who has power, or what those in power say about truth. See Michel Foucault, *Power/Knowledge: Selected Interviews and Other Writings,* ed. and trans. Colin Gordon et al. (New York: Pantheon Books, 1980). For a discussion of the question whether universal truth claims are possible, see David J. Krieger, *The New Universalism* (Maryknoll, N.Y.: Orbis Books, 1991).

6. Rosemary Radford Ruether, *Gaia and God: An Ecofeminist Theology of Earth Healing* (San Francisco: HarperSanFrancisco, 1992), is among those who have analyzed aspects of Western cultures that have resulted in destruction of the environment.

7. Robert Wuthnow, *The Struggle for America's Soul: Evangelicals, Liberals, and Secularism* (Grand Rapids, Mich.: Eerdmans, 1989). *Secularism, secularity,* and like terms also have a wide range of meanings in modern discourse. In the medieval church and until fairly recently, a parish cleric was distinguished from monastic priests and was called a secular priest. *Secular priest* in current idiom is an oxymoron. Among many theologians *pluralism* has almost replaced *secularism* as a one-word description of the dominant culture. See William C. Placher, *Unapologetic Theology: A Christian Voice in a Pluralistic Conversation* (Louisville: Westminister/John Knox Press, 1989).

8. Jean Comaroff, *Body of Power, Spirit of Resistance: The Culture and History of a South African People* (Chicago: University of Chicago Press, 1985); Jean Comaroff and John Comaroff, *Of Revelation and Revolution: Christianity, Colonialism, and Consciousness in South Africa* (Chicago: University of Chicago Press, 1991).

9. In 1971, Shona stone sculpture from Zimbabwe attracted the attention of the world art scene with an exhibition at the Rodin Museum in Paris. The exhibit presented pieces that moved beyond the stereotypes of African artifacts and so-called airport or marketplace curios. The Shona items were truly "contemporary" sculpture, yet challenged the assumptions of modern sensibility because the artists were able to "see" in the hard raw stone shapes saturated with spirit. One French critic remarked that "the shape seems to struggle to emerge out of matter . . . as parts of the rough stone become testimony to the sculptors' endeavors to free the shape from the rock, as

with Michelangelo or Rodin" (Olivier Sultan, *Life in Stone: Zimbabwean Sculpture, Birth of a Contemporary Art Form* [Harare, Zimbabwe: Baobab Books, 1992, 13].

10. See Lois Snook, *Spirit in Stone*, photographed and edited by Frederick H. Gonnerman (St. Paul, Minn.: Luther Northwestern Theological Seminary, 1990), an illustrated catalog of Zimbabwe stone sculpture.

11. Allan Anderson, *Moya: The Holy Spirit in an African Context* (Pretoria: University of South Africa Press, 1991); John S. Mbiti, *African Religions and Philosophy* (London: Heinemann, 1969).

12. Prominent among theologians in this regard is Jürgen Moltmann, especially his more recent books, *God in Creation* (San Francisco: HarperSanFrancisco, 1991) and *The Spirit of Life* (Minneapolis: Fortress Press, 1992). Thomas C. Oden, *Life in the Spirit: Systematic Theology*, vol. 3 (San Francisco: HarperSanFrancisco, 1992), is especially informative in organizing and summarizing the person and work of the Spirit in both scripture and in what Oden calls the classic consensual teaching of the church. Oden would likely not think a book like this one is necessary for reclaiming life in the Spirit. All that is necessary for Oden is to honor the scriptures and ecumenical teaching. He is especially critical of theological efforts to translate the "consensual reliable formularies" into new terms that might be acceptable to moderns. This effort is based on the "arrogant" assumption of "modern chauvinism" (2). But surely new "formularies" can be both reverent toward the classic consensus and relevant to culture, so that persons who now live at a great remove from both the age of scripture and of classical theology can reasonably and faithfully re-imagine the Spirit in the world of power.

13. The privatization of religious faith, as well as moral conviction, has been much noted in the twentieth century. See, for example, Richard John Neuhaus, *The Naked Public Square* (Grand Rapids, Mich.: Eerdmans, 1984.)

14. This sentiment is indeed a common opinion among moderns, if the research of Robert Bellah and associates can be taken at face value. See Robert Bellah et al., *Habits of the Heart: Individualism and Commitment in American Life* (Berkeley: University of California Press, 1985), and *The Good Society* (New York: Alfred Knopf, 1991).

15. Michael E. Lodahl, *Shekhinah/Spirit: Divine Presence in Jewish and Christian Religion* (New York: Paulist Press, 1992). See also Blair Reynolds, *Toward a Process Pneumatology* (Cranbury, N.J.: Associated University Presses, 1990).

16. Among the earliest American theologians to begin shaping a new Christian consciousness toward the earth, beginning with his New Delhi address to the World Council of Churches in 1961, was the late Joseph Sittler. He spoke of "the realm of nature as a theatre of grace," a theme he later elaborated in *Essays on Nature and Grace* (Philadelphia: Fortress Press, 1972). John B. Cobb Jr. was also an especially articulate early champion of a theology of ecology. For a recent study, see John B. Cobb and Herman Daly, *For the Common Good: Redirecting the Economy toward Community, the Environment, and a Sustainable Future* (Boston: Beacon Press, 1989).

17. Summarizing Michel Foucault's understanding of power, Kyle Pasewark writes, "Foucault . . . demonstrates the possibilities and limits of confining a discus-

sion of power to a political model." Pasewark introduces his analysis of power in the thought of Foucault, Tillich, and Luther under the heading "The Ubiquity of Power" (*A Theology of Power: Being beyond Domination* [Minneapolis: Fortress Press, 1993, 5]. *Power* is not an occasional phenomenon in Pasewark's terms, but "saturates being" while not dominating or obliterating being.

18. Anna Case-Winters, *God's Power: Traditional Understandings and Contemporary Challenges* (Louisville: Westminster/John Knox Press, 1990); Pasewark, *Theology of Power*; James Newton Poling, *The Abuse of Power: A Theological Problem* (Nashville: Abingdon Press, 1991).

19. Process theologians are usually the first to be identified with this position, but others have come to regard it as warranted by scripture and by worldviews influenced by modern science. Moltmann explicitly adopts the position in his *God in Creation* and *The Spirit of Life*.

20. In *God's Power*, Anna Case-Winters demonstrates that the answer to this question is affirmative. Her book refers to the relevant literature by Hartshorne and others regarding dipolar theism and panentheism.

21. Joseph Haroutunion, "The Church, the Spirit, and the Hands of God," *Journal of Religion* 54, no. 2: 154–65, 1974.

22. For the history of the doctrine of the Holy Spirit, controversies surrounding it, and contemporary discussion, the reader can consult the following standard works: Hendrikus Berkhof, *The Doctrine of the Holy Spirit* (Richmond: John Knox Press, 1964); Frederick Dale Bruner, *A Theology of the Holy Spirit* (Grand Rapids, Mich.: Eerdmans, 1970), a study of twentieth-century Pentecostalism; Stanley M. Burgess, *The Spirit and the Church: Antiquity* (Peabody, Mass.: Hendrickson, 1984), including annotated excerpts of the relevant writings on the Holy Spirit, from the view of the tension between prophecy and order; José Comblin, *The Holy Spirit and Liberation* (Maryknoll, N.Y.: Orbis Books, 1989), the history of the Holy Spirit doctrine from the view of Latin American theology; Yves M. J. Congar, *I Believe in the Holy Spirit*, vols. 1–3 (New York: Seabury Press, 1983), and *The Word and the Spirit* (San Francisco: Harper and Row, 1986); F. W. Dillistone, *The Holy Spirit in the Life of Today* (Philadelphia: Westminster Press, 1947); Paul Opsahl, ed., *The Holy Spirit in the Life of the Church* (Minneapolis: Augsburg Press, 1978); James D. G. Dunn, *Baptism in the Holy Spirit* (Philadelphia: Westminster Press, 1970), and *Jesus and the Spirit* (Grand Rapids, Mich.: Eerdmans, 1997); Donald L. Gelpi, *The Divine Mother: A Trinitarian Theology of the Holy Spirit* (Lanham, Md.: University Press of America, 1984), which contains a review of the theological history of the Spirit; George S. Hendry, *The Holy Spirit in Christian Theology* (Philadelphia: Westminster Press, 1956), still one of the best studies; Alasdair Heron, *The Holy Spirit* (Philadelphia: Westminster Press, 1983); G. W. F. Lampe, *God as Spirit* (Oxford: Clarendon Press, 1977); Moltmann, *The Spirit of Life*; Oden, *Life in the Spirit*; Alan M. Olson, *Hegel and the Spirit: Philosophy as Pneumatology* (Princeton, N.J.: Princeton University Press, 1992), a careful, lucid study of the philosopher's proposal for locating spirit in history; Regin Prenter, *Spiritus Creator*, trans. John M. Jensen (Philadelphia: Fortress Press, 1953); Blair Reynolds, *Toward a Process Pneumatology* (Cranbury, N.J.: Associated University Presses, 1990), which

incorporates the Spirit and comparative metaphysics as one theme; Eduard Schweizer, *The Holy Spirit* (London: SCM Press, 1978), which discusses the Spirit in the New Testament; John V. Taylor, *The Go-Between God: The Holy Spirit and Christian Mission* (New York: Oxford University Press, 1972); John Thompson, *The Holy Spirit in the Theology of Karl Barth* (Allison Park, Pa.: Pickwick Publications, 1991); Paul Tillich, *Systematic Theology,* vol. 3 (Chicago: University of Chicago Press, 1963); Michael Welker, *The Spirit of God* (Minneapolis: Fortress Press, 1993); Daniel Day Williams, *The Spirit and the Forms of Love* (New York: Harper and Row, 1968; Lanham, Md.: University Press of America, 1981).

CHAPTER 2

1. Elizabeth A. Johnson, *She Who Is: The Mystery of God in Feminist Theological Discourse* (New York: Crossroad, 1992), 132.

2. See especially Frederick Dale Bruner's evenhanded review of the exegetical work on these passages and the relevant sections of Acts in his study of Pentecostalism (*A Theology of the Holy Spirit* [Grand Rapids, Mich.: Eerdmans, 1970], as well as James D. G. Dunn's exhaustive research in *Baptism in the Holy Spirit* (Philadelphia: Westminster Press, 1970). Also see Bengt Holmberg's *Paul and Power* (Minneapolis: Fortress Press, 1980).

3. This antagonism is already evident in the first centuries of Christian history as Stanley M. Burgess documents in *The Spirit and the Church: Antiquity* (Peabody, Mass.: Hendrickson, 1984). See also William G. Rusch, "The Doctrine of the Holy Spirit in the Patristic and Medieval Church," in *The Holy Spirit in the Life of the Church,* ed. Paul Opsahl (Minneapolis: Augsburg Press, 1978). Eduard Schweizer points to the sources of these conflicts in the New Testament ("What Is the Holy Spirit? A Study in Biblical Theology," in *Conflicts about the Holy Spirit,* ed. Hans Küng and Jürgen Moltmann (New York: Seabury Press, 1979).

4. See Hans von Campenhausen, *Ecclesiastical Authority and Spiritual Power in the Church of the First Three Centuries* (Stanford, Calif.: Stanford University Press, 1969).

5. The crucial aspect of narrative for any discussion of revelation has been the major theme of theologians who have come under the influence of Hans Frei. See, for example, William Placher, *Unapologetic Theology* (Louisville: Westminster/John Knox Press, 1989), and Ronald Thiemann, *Revelation and Theology: The Gospel as Narrated Promise* (Notre Dame, Ind.: University of Notre Dame Press, 1985).

6. Ep. 101. *The Later Christian Fathers,* edited and translated by Henry Bettenson, © London Oxford University Press, 1970, p. 108.

7. See two essays by Dietrich Ritschl, "The History of the *Filioque* Controversy," in Küng and Moltmann, *Conflicts about the Holy Spirit,* and "Historical Development and Implications of the Filioque Controversy," in *Spirit of God, Spirit of Christ: Ecumenical Reflections on the Filioque Controversy* (Geneva: World Council of Churches, 1981).

8. For an extensive discussion of the Trinity as God moving into the world of human experience, see Catherine Mowry LaCugna, *God for Us: The Trinity and the Christian Life* (San Francisco: HarperSanFrancisco, 1991).

9. For one of the most thorough discussions of these issues see Jürgen Moltmann,

The Trinity and the Kingdom (San Francisco: Harper and Row, 1981).

10. This perception is nearly universal among the hundreds of students who have enrolled in my courses. Such anecdotal evidence is so prevalent that empirical research would be a case of documenting the obvious.

11. I owe this reference to the trinitarian pattern of prayer to W. Robert Jenson, *The Triune Identity* (Philadelphia: Fortress Press, 1982).

12. Neoorthodox theology early in this century, anxious to assert the centrality of the Word and eager to establish the authority of the Word independent of human experience, philosophy, or reason, verged on heresy at this point; that is, in practice neoorthodoxy subordinated the Spirit to the Word.

13. As Frederick Dale Bruner has demonstrated in *A Theology of the Holy Spirit* (Grand Rapids, Mich.: Eerdmans, 1970), the Pentecostal movement of the twentieth century fits this description exactly. In his *Jesus and the Spirit* (Grand Rapids, Mich.: Eerdmans, 1997), James D. G. Dunn, who acknowledges his own "fairly close acquaintance with and interest in Pentecostalism and the modern charismatic movement" (5), investigates exhaustively the New Testament witness to Jesus as the unsurpassable instance of the Spirit of God; indeed, Jesus is the "yardstick" by which to assess the power of the Spirit of God. In Jesus, "the Spirit has himself taken on the character of Christ" (322). These New Testament witnesses are, for Dunn, sufficient warrant to allege that "the doctrine of the Trinity is grounded in experience. . . . To say that the first Christians experienced the Trinity would be inaccurate; they experienced the Spirit, who made them conscious of their dual relationship as men of spirit" (326).

14. Doctrinal formulations do, of course, function most of the time as rules of discourse for Christian theology, but theology does not exist for its own sake but for the sake of the church's mission in the world, a point which is too easily lost in George A. Lindbeck, *The Nature of Doctrine: Religion and Theology in a Postliberal Age* (Philadelphia: Westminster Press, 1984).

15. This discussion is obviously indebted to the extensive work of Yves Congar, whose four volumes on the Holy Spirit are cited in the bibliography.

16. I decline to enter the discussion about the "immanent" Trinity and the "economic" Trinity, on which much has been written. To the specialists I would say that I do not intend to identify the two. I do recognize that in the order of knowing, the tri-unity of God as "economic" is prior, and that in the order of being, the tri-unity of God as "immanent" is prior. LaCugna, *God for Us*, has reviewed the distinction in great detail. I prefer Douglas John Hall's emphasis, namely that the test of a credible profession of faith (for example, belief in the Trinity) is that the confessor is thrust into the world, where God's beloved creatures are denied the fullness of life breathed into them by the Spirit of God (*Confessing the Faith: Christian Theology in a North American Context* [Minneapolis: Fortress Press, 1997]).

17. Three who have emphasized imagination in theological discourse include Harvard theologian Gordon Kaufman, *The Theological Imagination* (Philadelphia: Westminster Press, 1981); Old Testament scholar Walter Brueggemann, *The Prophetic Imagination* (Philadelphia: Fortress Press, 1978); and New Testament scholar Amos Niven Wilder, *Theopoetic: Theology and the Religious Imagination* (Philadelphia: Fortress Press, 1976). See also Lee E. Snook, "The Human Spirit's Relation to the Holy Spirit" (*Dialog* 23, no. 2 1984: 109–13), in which I attempt to describe the several aspects or disciplines of imagination in theology.

18. Jaroslav Pelikan has shown how Martin Luther's reform movement was a protest against the elevation of ecclesiastical structure above the Spirit. See *Spirit versus Structure: Luther and the Institutions of the Church* (New York: Harper and Row, 1968).

19. The meaning of the word *world* in this exhortation is as ambiguous as the term *secular* became several decades ago with the appearance of books like *The Secular City* by Harvey Cox (New York: Macmillan, 1965); *The Secular Meaning of the Gospel* by Paul van Buren (New York: Macmillan, 1963); and *Honest to God* by Bishop J. A. T. Robin (Philadelphia: Westminster Press, 1963). Those who warn against the world setting the agenda seem to suppose that the word *world* implies an atheistic or secular denial of God. John B. Cobb's *God and the World* (Philadelphia: Westminster Press, 1969) was one of many efforts to restore a balance and avoid a God-denying affirmation of the world and a world-denying belief in God.

20. Harold H. Ditmanson, "The Significance of the Doctrine of the Holy Spirit for Contemporary Theology," in *The Holy Spirit in the Life of the Church*, ed. Paul D. Opsahl (Minneapolis: Augsburg Press, 1978), 203. Emphasis added.

21. Ian Barbour, *Religion in an Age of Science: The Gifford Lectures, 1989–91*, vol. 1 (San Francisco: HarperSanFrancisco, 1990). The discussion that follows is based on chapter 2, "Models and Paradigms." A growing number of books by scientists open to the rapprochement between science and religion have appeared. Philip Hefner, the editor of *Zygon: A Journal of Religion and Science*, in commenting on the work of one such scientist, John Polkinghorne, observes that what is needed are "new paradigms for understanding reality"—that is, imaginative constructs that would honor both science and religion as complementary ways of engaging the world. See Hefner, "Confessions of a Scientist Theologian," *Christian Century*, May 20–27, 1998, 533–39.

22. Barbour, *Religion in an Age of Science*, 34.

23. Ibid., 36.

24. Ibid., 84.

25. Doctrines and theology do not fall out of the sky in completed form, but develop. In this sense, revisionism has been a permanent feature of Christian thought. David Tracy is perhaps the foremost proponent of "revisionist" theology. See his *Blessed Rage for Order: The New Pluralism in Theology* (New York: Seabury Press, 1975), and *The Analogical Imagination: Christian Theology and the Culture of Pluralism* (New York: Crossroad, 1981).

26. Among the more widely discussed proposals in recent years are Peter C. Hodgson's *God in History* (Nashville: Abingdon Press, 1989) and Jürgen Moltmann's *God in Creation* (San Francisco: HarperSanFrancisco, 1991). In the latter work, Moltmann— for the first time to my knowledge—made explicit use of the term *panentheism*.

27. The theological literature on this topic is vast. Two recent works have advanced the discussion significantly: Edward Farley, *Good and Evil: Interpreting a Human Condition* (Minneapolis: Fortress Press, 1990), and Paul Fiddes, *The Creative Suffering of God* (New York: Oxford University Press, 1988).

28. For example, see F. W. Dillistone, *The Power of Symbols in Religion and Culture* (New York: Crossroad, 1986), a theological study; and David Freedberg, *The Power of Images* (Chicago: University of Chicago Press, 1989), written by a historian of art.

29. Deborah Tannen, *You Just Don't Understand* (New York: Morrow, 1990), analyzes differing patterns of communication between men and women. Riane Eisler, *The Chalice and the Blade: Our History, Our Future* (San Francisco: Harper and Row,

1987), offers a popularized view of a once peaceful woman-centered world, overthrown by militaristic males. The book uses powerful images to emphasize the point.

30. Joseph Sittler frequently made the important distinction between *evocative* and *denotative* language. His life and work are a significant inspiration for what I am attempting in this book. See especially *Essays on Nature and Grace* (Philadelphia: Fortress Press, 1972), in which he seeks to "relocate" grace in the realm of nature, and thus to stem the Western habit of "de-naturing" grace and "dis-gracing" nature. I would like to think that I am continuing this program in relocating the Spirit in the world of power.

31. Richard Rorty, *Philosophy and the Mirror of Nature* (Princeton, N.J.: Princeton University Press, 1979), presents one among several analyses of philosophy's failure to realize the Enlightenment ideal of certainty.

32. Charles Davis, *What Is Living, What Is Dead in Christianity Today?* (San Francisco: Harper and Row, 1986), 11.

33. See Hayden White, *Metahistory: The Historical Imagination in Nineteenth-Century Europe* (Baltimore: Johns Hopkins University Press, 1973), and Davis, *What Is Living?*

CHAPTER 3

1. Bernard J. Cooke has documented this claim meticulously in *The Distancing of God: The Ambiguity of Symbol in History and Theology* (Minneapolis: Fortress Press, 1990), 9–257.

2. My indebtedness for format and analytical categories will be obvious to anyone familiar with the work of Hayden White in *Metahistory: The Historical Imagination in Nineteenth-Century Europe* (Baltimore: Johns Hopkins University Press, 1973), and with Charles Davis's use of White's scheme in *What Is Living, What Is Dead in Christianity Today?* (San Francisco: Harper and Row, 1986). White acknowledges his own dependence on two literary theorists, Northrop Frye and Kenneth Burke (p. 2, n. 4). Just as White appropriates literary criticism in order to uncover precritical factors that guide great historians of the nineteenth century, and Davis employs the same scheme to analyze differences in religious imagination, I take a similar tack. Historians produce works which "represent alternative, and seemingly mutually exclusive, conceptions both of the same segments of the historical process and of the tasks of historical thinking" (White, *Metahistory*, 4). There is a plurality of versions of what happened and what it means.

David Tracy writes, "To a non-specialist like myself, the debates among historians of the French Revolution present one of the most compelling examples of the difficulty of interpreting any classic or even any classic text, symbol, ritual or person. . . . [I]f we are to understand ourselves and our postmodern situation, we must risk interpreting that revolution which inaugurated the modern world[,] . . . for that event still affects us" (*Plurality and Ambiguity: Hermeneutics, Religion, Hope* [San Francisco: Harper and Row, 1987, 8]. However theologians may want to claim finality for the Christian revelation, there can never be a final interpretation. Similarly, the person and work (that is, the power and agency) of the Holy Spirit have been variously understood from the beginning of the Christian era. Thus, the Holy Spirit likewise has not been immune from a plurality of interpretations, some of which surely have been misunderstandings. The risks of interpretation are daunting, and can never be eliminated, but our anxieties concerning these risks can be somewhat alleviated if, as interpreters, we can uncover those deep structures of imagination which influence, or even control, our interpretations.

3. Davis, *What Is Living?* 20.

4. Tillich's interpretation of the Fall provides a more ample account of the profound alienation described here. See *Systematic Theology,* vol. 2 (Chicago: University of Chicago Press, 1957). "Man as he exists is not what he essentially is and ought to be. He is estranged from his true being. The profundity of the term 'estrangement' lies in the implication that one belongs essentially to that from which one is estranged. Man is not a stranger to his true being, for he belongs to it. . . . Man's hostility to God proves indisputably that he belongs to him" (45). "The general rule that the negative lives from the distortion of the positive is also valid in this case. . . . Actually even the awareness of estrangement and the desire for salvation are effects of the presence of the saving power . . ." (86).

5. Elsewhere I have argued that the many images of lostness have corollaries in how Christian theologians have depicted Christ as the savior from lostness. See Lee E. Snook, *The Anonymous Christ: Jesus as Savior in Modern Theology* (Minneapolis: Augsburg, 1986).

6. *Metaphor* is one of the four basic tropes both in traditional poetics and in modern language theory, just as comedy is one of the four basic plots by which to organize a narrative. As we shall see in subsequent chapters, the other three tropes are *metonymy, synecdoche,* and *irony,* which are corollaries to tragedy, romance, and satire.

7. The work of Sallie McFague is probably the best known on this topic. See *Metaphorical Theology: Models of God in Religious Language* (Philadelphia: Fortress Press, 1982), and *Models of God: A Theology for an Ecological, Nuclear Age* (Philadelphia: Fortress Press, 1987). See also Elizabeth A. Johnson, *She Who Is* (New York: Crossroad, 1992), as well as Catherine Mowry LaCugna, *God for Us: The Trinity and the Christian Life* (San Francisco: HarperSanFrancisco, 1991).

8. The existence of a canon of authorized writings presents a challenge to any historian who tries to explain why these and not other texts were accepted, how the choice was made, and when they acquired the status of apostolic witness, to which all theology and doctrine must be held accountable. Certain influences can be noted, even passages within the texts themselves. Criteria or tests of canonicity seem apparent. These include authorship, content, and harmony with other canonical books. The editors of the *New Oxford Annotated Bible,* Revised Standard Version, expanded ed. (New York: Oxford University Press, 1977), conclude their discussion of these questions with the following: "In the most basic sense, neither individuals nor councils created the canon, but only came to recognize and acknowledge the self-authenticating quality of these writings, which imposed themselves as canonical upon the church" (1170).

9. Avery Dulles's *Models of the Church* (Garden City, N.Y.: Doubleday, 1974) has become the standard reference for sorting through the plurality of views on this question. Proposals for a doctrine of the church that will affect society without sacrificing the distinctiveness of the church appear quite regularly, and also stir up controversy. See Leonardo Boff, *Church, Charism, and Power: Liberation Theology and the Institutional Church* (New York: Crossroad, 1988), and Peter C. Hodgson, *Revisioning the Church* (Minneapolis: Fortress Press, 1988). Two recently founded journals, *Pro*

Ecclesia and *First Things*, usually present a point of view that opposes Boff, Hodgson, and others.

10. This summary has been widely reported by major news services. Even in Africa there has been no effort to conceal or gloss over the facts. This summary is derived from the African desk of Reuters, printed in the Harare *Herald*, May 7, 1997.

11. For one argument against the ordination of women by a prominent male Catholic theologian, see Michael Novak, "Women, Ordination, and Angels," *First Things*, April 1993, 25–32.

12. "Thus, [even] in nonpolitical contexts, the use of 'power' is itself controlled and dominated by its political analogue" (Kyle A. Pasewark, *A Theology of Power: Being beyond Domination* [Minneapolis: Fortress Press, 1993, 3]. After settling on the general design of this study of the Spirit and power, Pasewark's impressive study became available. His exposition of Foucault, Luther, and Tillich is perceptive and fascinating. To the degree that I understand his effort, I think that I am, with the help of categories gleaned from White, Davis, and others, going further "beyond domination" than Pasewark in these chapters on spirit and power. Using the distinction, prominent in his book, between power as external and its "communication of effects" within the person subjected to power, I am attending more than Pasewark to the effects wrought by forms of power such as novelty, peace, harmony, and community.

13. Davis, *What Is Living?* 23.

14. Albert Nolan summarizes what he takes to be the political theology of those who first brought Christianity to South Africa. "The British never doubted that they were living and acting according to the gospel of Jesus Christ and that God had chosen them to 'civilize' and 'Christianize' vast areas of the world with their empire. Nor did the Boers who trekked further north from the Cape ever doubt that God was on their side and the journey was like the journey of the Israelites to the promised land" (*God in South Africa* [Grand Rapids, Mich.: Eerdmans, 1988, 1].

15. The prime minister of then Southern Rhodesia, Ian Smith, openly declared that in the Rhodesians' efforts to put down the liberation forces under Robert Mugabe and Joshua Nkomo they had "struck a blow for the preservation of justice, civilization and Christianity. . . ." This is part of an oft-quoted passage from the Smith government's Unilateral Declaration of Independence in 1965.

16. The discussion of God and religion in the United States has been extensive. Leading up to the bicentennial in 1976, many books and articles appeared on the topic of civil religion. See Robert Bellah, *The Broken Covenant: American Civil Religion in a Time of Trial* (New York: Seabury Press, 1975), esp. p. 62 on conversion and covenant; Sydney C. Meade, *The Nation with the Soul of a Church* (New York: Harper and Row, 1975); Martin E. Marty, *Righteous Empire* (New York: Dial Press, 1977); Conrad Cherry, ed., *God's New Israel: Religious Interpretation of American Destiny* (Englewood Cliffs, N.J.: Prentice Hall, 1971); E. A. Smith, ed., *The Religion of the Republic* (Philadelphia: Fortress Press, 1971); John F. Wilson, *Public Religion in American Culture* (Philadelphia: Temple University Press, 1979); and Robert Benne and Philip Hefner, *Defining America: A Christian Critique of the American Dream* (Philadelphia: Fortress Press, 1974).

17. See Martin Hengel, *Christ and Power* (Philadelphia: Fortress Press, 1977).

18. Gerhard von Rad, *Old Testament Theology*, vol. 1 (New York: Harper and Brothers, 1962), esp. 129–35; G. E. Mendenhall, "Covenant," in *The Interpreter's Dictionary of the Bible* (New York: Abingdon, 1962), 1:714–23.

19. Gerhard von Rad, "The Story of Joseph," in *God at Work in Israel* (Nashville: Abingdon, 1980), 19–35.

20. Cited in Hengel, *Christ and Power,* 8.

21. Ibid., 9.

22. See Walter Wink, especially *Naming the Powers* (Minneapolis: Fortress Press, 1984) and *Engaging the Powers* (Minneapolis: Fortress Press, 1992). Also Herman Waetjen, *A Reordering of Power* (Minneapolis: Fortress Press, 1989).

23. "It is important to grasp precisely what it was that led Jesus to the conclusion that the eschatological rule of God was already operative. It was *not* present because *he* was present, [as though] 'where Jesus is, there is the kingdom.' . . . This gives to Jesus a uniqueness he did not claim. *The eschatological* kingdom was present for Jesus only because the eschatological Spirit was present in and through him.

"Since it is by the *Spirit of God* that I cast out demons, then has come upon you the *kingdom of God.*

"In other words, it was not so much a case of 'where I am there is the kingdom,' as 'where the Spirit is there is the kingdom.' It was the manifestation of the power of God which was the sign of the kingdom of God" (James D. G. Dunn, *Jesus and the Spirit* [Grand Rapids, Mich: Eerdmans, 1997], 49).

24. "Pilate's famous question . . . is not to be understood psychologically or philo-sophically. It is meant to demonstrate total misunderstanding on the person who counts on and lives by the power of 'this world' alone" (Hengel, *Christ and Power,* 49).

25. "However, according to the religious tradition, both Jewish and Christian, as well as many other religions, God is first of all the Almighty. He is power. He is unrestricted. He is infinite power. He is *the power in all other powers, and he gives them the power to be.* This element of power belongs to the concept of spirit." In these few sentences from a 1962 lecture to students at the University of Chicago, Paul Tillich summarizes the doctrine of the Spirit contained in the third volume of his *Systematic Theology.* This passage (emphasis added) is from his *Perspectives on Nineteenth- and Twentieth-Century Protestant Theology* (New York: Harper and Row, 1967), 120.

26. John V. Taylor uses this phrase to explicate his doctrine of the Holy Spirit in *The Go-Between God: The Holy Spirit and Christian Mission* (New York: Oxford University Press, 1972), 8.

27. James Cone, *Martin and Malcolm and America: A Dream or a Nightmare?* (Maryknoll, N.Y.: Orbis Books, 1991).

28. Dorothee Soelle, *Death by Bread Alone* (Philadelphia: Fortress Press, 1978).

CHAPTER 4

1. See Allan Anderson, *Moya: The Holy Spirit in an African Context* (Pretoria: University of South Africa Press, 1991).

2. I have been greatly encouraged in this project by reading Joel Kovel's *History and Spirit: An Inquiry into the Philosophy of Liberation* (Boston: Beacon Press, 1991). Kovel is a psychiatrist whose experiences in Latin America studying tropical medicine led him to reconsider the role of psychoanalysis in terms of the "prepsychological core in the dynamics of human ontology. . . . The modern crisis of faith has driven many to redefine their relation to the place in culture traditionally occupied by religion" (2–3). In other words, for Kovel, spirit, because of its omnipresence, is too important to be

left to religionists. Kovel writes in response to the crisis which neither conventional religion nor psychoanalysis can reach. "Spirit reaches beyond the material, historical world of economy and technology, yet it is deeply affected by the time and place at which it arises. Thus spirit stands outside history, acts within history, and is acted upon by history. There is always something of the 'beyond' in history with respect to history. It is this very tension which causes the two to act upon each other. And in our time, history has been very hard on spirit" (6).

3. Not surprisingly, women have been prominent among these theologians. Sallie McFague's *The Body of God: An Ecological Theology* (Minneapolis: Fortress Press, 1993) is perhaps her most sustained effort to challenge classical theology's depiction of God's relation to the world. She proposes alternatives appropriate to the Bible, compatible with current scientific views, and helpful in encouraging Christians to participate in the public task of caring for the earth. She prefers to speak of God's power in the world as Spirit. God's power is not the absolute mind controlling the world from another realm. The connection between God and world "is one of *relationship* at the deepest possible level, the level of life, rather than *control* at the level of ordering and directing nature. . . . [T]he metaphor of breath rather than mind might help us to support, rather than control, life in all its forms" (145). As I pointed out in chapter 3, there is biblical warrant for retaining the image of power as control or domination. I am not as ready as McFague seems to be to abandon the language of control, at least in a limited sense.

4. Langdon Gilkey, *Through the Tempest: Theological Voyages in a Pluralistic Culture* (Minneapolis: Fortress Press, 1991), 59f. Emphasis added. The quotation is from "Symbols, Meaning, and Divine Presence," a paper originally published in a Catholic theological journal. Gilkey, who is Protestant, is chiding Catholics who may have separated liturgy from ordinary life, making divine presence a reality that can only refer to another place. Instead, he argues what we have faith in, and "thus to what in the end our worship, trust and commitment respond, is the divine presence throughout the scope of natural and social life" (54). Divine activity in the creative process grounds and establishes special Christian actions like preaching the word and celebrating the sacraments. But these specific activities are not the only places where God, as power and Spirit, is present.

5. The preferred trope or figure of speech, then, is not the *metaphor*, but *metonymy*, literally a name change by which the whole is reduced to a part. Metonymy is an alternative to the metaphor. It breaks to pieces the pretensions of a metaphor. For instance, "the White House" is a metonymy in the sense that the whole of a particular administration is reduced to a specific piece of real estate in Washington, D.C. The administration in power is neither accorded nor does it symbolize some grand metaphorical significance bidding for patriotic loyalty, but is reduced to the machinations of mere human beings associated with that house.

6. Building on Hayden White, Charles Davis writes: "When the Christian myth has been broken up into its elements, the Christian story is predominantly read as a tragedy. If comedy is a presentation of things as they should be and thus of ultimate harmony, tragedy is a disclosure of things as they actually are and of the impossibility of resolving all oppositions. Tragedy tells a story of the conflict between good and good, rather than between good and evil. When the Christian religion is reduced to moral practice, it loses its festive tone and takes on a note of resignation . . ." (*What Is Living, What Is Dead in Christianity Today?* [San Francisco: Harper and Row, 1986], 21).

7. See Leonardo Boff, *Church, Charism, and Power: Liberation Theology and the Institutional Church* (New York: Crossroad, 1988); José Comblin, *The Holy Spirit and Liberation* (Maryknoll, N.Y.: Orbis Books, 1989).

8. Kyle A. Pasewark's *A Theology of Power: Being beyond Domination* (Minneapolis: Fortress Press, 1993) is a masterful analysis of the contemporary discussion of power. His discussion of Michel Foucault is particularly insightful. The entire book is an effort "to establish more firmly the shortcomings of the identification of power and domination and to develop a more persuasive alternative" (10). He draws on both Luther and Tillich in order to construct his own proposal for a geography of power. His treatment of power is subtle and nuanced. His project agrees with mine in the view that power is not an occasional, episodic reality, but "is the fundamental ontological element, and is therefore present in all places where there is anything." He attacks the view that power is domination, and proposes instead that power, while including sovereignty, is better defined as "the communication of efficacy," so that sovereignty is not the end of power (322). I attempt to show that the forms of power, and thus the forms of the presence and power of the Spirit in the world, do include domination, but also truth, freedom, justice, beauty, love, and more.

9. These assertions imply a view of reality akin to process metaphysics. To say that a possibility exists, that it is real, and that it has efficacy—which is to say the power to make a difference—is to argue that past influences (for example, family, race, social status, religious upbringing) *and* envisioned possibilities (any of which could become actual) are among the causal factors behind any emerging event. Reality adds the actual to possibilities appropriate to that moment, but which are not yet actual. When freedom and justice are introduced as real possibilities into an oppresive, unjust system, they have effective power.

10. In this formulation of freedom and power one can ascribe the source of all power—as well as the gift of power in the form of human freedom—to God through the Spirit, *without* excusing God from association with the misuse of power. The power of freedom is a gift from God and is not generated by humans, so we cannot let God off the hook. Nor is the human user of that power excused from culpability when power is misused. Responsibility is laid at the feet of those to whom God, by the Spirit, gives the power of freedom. The generosity of God in giving power to creatures implies the risk, and the tragedy, of freedom. The inheritance the father gave to his younger son is precisely the power of freedom that the son squandered. It was also the memory of (and spirit of?) the father's generosity which, when the son came to his senses, drew him back to the father. Who are we but the begrudging elder son when we want to blame the father for our kid brother's misuse of his inheritance?

11. Jürgen Moltmann, *The Spirit of Life: A Universal Affirmation* (Minneapolis: Fortress Press, 1992), 40.

12. Ibid., 41.

13. Ibid., 42f.

14. Ibid., 45. The call of God cannot be separated utterly from the Spirit of God. Moltmann's contrast between call and inspiration can surely not mean, given Moltmann's thesis, that the call of the literary prophets was not mediated by God's Spirit.

15. See also Alasdair Heron, *The Holy Spirit* (Philadelphia: Westminster, 1983), esp. pt. 1, and Yves M. J. Congar, *The Word and the Spirit* (San Francisco: Harper and Row, 1986), esp. chap. 2, "The Word and the Spirit Are Linked: Scriptural Testimonies."

16. Moltmann, *Spirit of Life*, 47. I am grateful to my colleague, Dr. Dianne Jacob-

son, for her scholarly support for these claims concerning wisdom. In coteaching a seminar, "Spirit and Wisdom in Scripture, Theology, and Experience," I have learned much and have been more and more convinced of the close affinity of the Spirit of God to the wisdom of God.

17. See especially Michael E. Lodahl, *Shekhinah/Spirit: Divine Presence in Jewish and Christian Religion* (New York: Paulist Press, 1992).

18. "The idea of the Shekinah points towards the *kenosis of the Spirit*. In his Shekinah, God renounces his impassibility and becomes able to suffer because he is willing to love. The Spirit is not anthropomorphism, but is made possible through his indwelling in created being" (Moltmann, *Spirit of Life*, 51).

19. Walter Brueggemann, "The Prophetical Books," in *The New Oxford Annotated Bible*, ed. Bruce M. Metzger and Roland E. Murphy, New Revised Standard Version (New York: Oxford University Press, 1991), 862.

20. Ibid., 865.

21. "In the Old Testament, when referring to God, the Mouth is, with hardly more than two exceptions, the organ of the word" (Congar, *Word and the Spirit*, 15). Congar quotes Isaiah 34:16, "For the mouth of the Lord has commanded and his Spirit has commanded them," as well as Psalm 33:6, "By the word of the Lord the heavens were made, and all their host by the breath of his mouth."

22. See the introduction to Acts in Metzger and Murphy, *New Oxford Annotated Bible*, 160NT. Again, for an exhaustive account of this point see James D. G. Dunn, *Jesus and the Spirit* (Grand Rapids, Mich.: Eerdmans, 1997), 95–196.

23. Heron, *Holy Spirit*, 47f.

24. Alan Paton's novels are probably the best literary introduction to the beauty and pathos of South Africa. *Cry the Beloved Country* and perhaps especially *Too Late the Phalarope* disclose how South Africa was governed by a theologically justified theocracy. Apartheid viewed God's rule as a divinely revealed political system. God's presence and power were invoked to justify the established social order, articulated by the Afrikaner theology and executed by the civil authorities. This system was termed state theology in the *Kairos Document*, a declaration of theologians who called for the dismantling of the system on the basis of "prophetic theology." The controversial document was one of the factors that eventually led to the largely peaceful transition from white minority rule to the beginnings of multiracial democracy.

It must be mentioned, however, that as South Africa was conducting its first all-race election, one of the worst outbursts of civil disorder was occurring to the north in East Africa. In the small mountainous country of Rwanda, an estimated 200,000 people have been killed (the Red Cross puts the number at 500,000), and 250,000 have fled into neighboring Tanzania, many swimming across a river covered with floating corpses.

All change derives its awesome power from the blowing Spirit, even when that power is put to demonic use and overwhelms forms of power by which order and unity are established.

25. The inference may sound unconvincing to anyone who wants to discern the Spirit in the world of ordinary experience. Inference seems like a weak form of knowledge, and certainly not scientific. Yet the logic of inference is empirical and not merely speculative. There is evidence. But the move from evidence to conclusion is indirect. The "object" of this study, the Spirit, is never directly captured by the senses. One never stubs one's toe on the Spirit. I might not have used the word *infer* in this

context if I had not, by chance, come across a report in the international edition of *Newsweek* (May 9, 1994) about the "discovery" made by a team of 440 physicists of the long-sought elementary particle called "the top quark," the last of the suspected building blocks of matter. The headline reads, "The great advances now defy the senses. Nothing is actually found: it's inferred." The director of the Brookhaven National Laboratory in New York, physicist Nick Samios, said that "no one looks at the thing itself anymore. . . . We look at what the thing does, at the traces it leaves behind." The process of discovery at the "cutting edge" of all sciences is not a direct sighting, because the object of study is inaccessible to the senses. About the elemental particle called "top," another physicist said, "We never see it. Just its decay products."

26. The struggle for independence in Zimbabwe (formerly Southern Rhodesia) from the early 1960s until 1979 was one of the bloodiest wars against colonial (European) settlers in Africa. The white minority regime under Ian Smith enforced an apartheid policy every bit as oppressive as that of its neighbor South Africa. The black majority in Zimbabwe was far larger than in South Africa, and had tried peaceful means for having their grievances addressed. When they finally turned to guerrilla warfare as a means to gain political freedom and to regain a just portion of land from which indigenous Africans had been forced in the 1890s, their only allies outside Africa were the Soviet Union and China, who supplied them with arms and military training. In Africa itself, neighboring countries Zambia and Mozambique provided staging areas from which to execute the campaign.

It is of particular interest for our discussion of the power of freedom and its conflict with order that the white minority thought of itself as defending Christian order and civilization against the "terrorists" or "terrs," while the Africans referred to the guerrilla forces as "freedom fighters." Both sides of the protracted struggle were guilty of ghastly atrocities. For an account sympathetic to the African majority, which gained power in the 1980 elections, see David Martin and Phyllis Johnson, *The Struggle for Zimbabwe: The Chimurenga War* (New York: Monthly Review Press, 1981).

27. I have been greatly instructed by Peter C. Hodgson's *God in History: Shapes of Freedom* (Nashville: Abingdon Press, 1989). My indebtedness to this book is probably not sufficiently obvious. Hodgson champions freedom as the chief evidence of the Spirit in the postmodern age. But Hodgson's own social location, at a well-endowed private university divinity school in North America, may have made it too easy to neglect other forms of the Spirit's power. His work is a philosophically sophisticated prophecy against the economic, political, and cultural privileges that North American Christians take for granted, privileges implicated in the denial of freedom to most of the world's people.

28. Quotations cited in ibid., 34f. The view that there is no plot to history, but only satire of the pretensions to meaning, will be taken up in more detail in chapter 6.

29. Ibid., 36.

30. Hodgson summarizes Barth's antimodern view of God's rule: "God rules creaturely occurrence by *ordering* it and thereby *controlling* and *directing* it. In agreement with the mainstream Catholic tradition against Calvin, Barth affirmed that creatures use their freedom under divine permission rather than compulsion." Barth was not a strict determinist, according to Hodgson, and came quite close to Hodgson's (and my) revisionist view of the power of the Spirit (ibid., 27f.). But Barth was adamant in insisting that the only way to "read" the traces of God's rule was by reference to Jesus Christ, and like Calvin he had a "predilection for metaphors of sovereignty, royalty

and patriarchal authority," so that God's action in the world was always construed as "controlling" rather than influencing, shaping, persuading, luring, or inspiring (breathing into).

31. See Hans von Campenhausen, *Ecclesiastical Authority and Spiritual Power in the Church of the First Three Centuries* (Stanford, Calif.: Stanford University Press, 1969). "Paul develops the idea of the Spirit as the organizing principle of the Christian congregation. There is no need for any fixed system with its rules and regulations and prohibitions. Paul's writings do as little to provide such things for the individual congregation as for the Church at large. . . . If you are led by the Spirit you are not under the Law." In the church "freedom is a basic controlling principle, for the Spirit of Christ, which is the giver of freedom, urges men and women on not to independence and self-assertion but to loving service" (58).

32. "I should not want 'free will' to be given me nor anything . . . to enable me to endeavor after salvation . . ." (Martin Luther, *Bondage of the Will*, trans. J. I. Packer and O. R. Johnston [Old Tappan, N.J.: Fleming H. Revell, 1957, 313]. For Luther, salvation, or spiritual righteousness, cannot be contingent on the freely chosen endeavors of human beings. On the other hand, civil righteousness—tending to neighbors' needs—is clearly mandated by God as the Christian's responsibility.

33. The subhead modifies a passage from Hodgson, *God in History*, in which he reviews the history of the idea of salvation: "The great challenge of the postmodern world—having inherited from modernity a theoretical grasp of what freedom might mean, but also having glimpsed through the terrors of our time the possibility of utter annihilation, of abject bondage to nothingness—is to take up the history of the praxis of freedom with renewed determination and courage, recognizing how high the stakes are. The future is what we make of it" (50).

34. Again I refer the reader to Kovel, *History and Spirit*. Kovel does not write as a Christian but as a postmodern psychoanalyst who has been liberated from the presumptions of post-Enlightenment modernism.

35. In chapter 6 I will take up satire as a way of plotting the human story. The postmodern claim that there is no plot to what people want to call "history" will be considered again. Satire is not the denial of plot, but its plot runs counter to prevailing assumptions. In such denials there is a positive. These denials have power and can be thought of as the positive work of the Spirit.

36. Perhaps the most articulate, scholarly, and forceful example of a theology of the Spirit in the antirevisionist mode is the recent work of Donald G. Bloesch, *A Theology of the Word and Spirit* (Downers Grove, Ill.: InterVarsity Press, 1992). Bloesch considers all the major twentieth-century revisionist options, especially Tillich, Pannenberg, and the process theologians, and in the end follows Barth. Another major study on the Spirit is Thomas C. Oden, *Life in the Spirit: Systematic Theology*, vol. 3 (San Francisco: HarperSanFrancisco, 1992). Oden's "consensus theology" is an argument that no constructive theology is necessary for the postmodern age. If one knows the tradition as well as Oden seems to, then one would have all that is needed to speak of the Spirit as the presence and power of God. Both Bloesch and Oden impress but do not persuade.

CHAPTER 5

1. Northrop Frye, *The Educated Imagination* (Bloomington: Indiana University Press, 1964), 140.

2. Peter C. Hodgson, *Winds of the Spirit* (Louisville: Westminster/John Knox Press, 1994), 282.

3. Michael Welker, *God the Spirit* (Minneapolis: Fortress Press, 1994), 1.

4. Hodgson, *Winds of the Spirit*, 171f.

5. See my review of Hodgson, *Winds of the Spirit*, and Welker, *God the Spirit*, in *Word and World* 15, no. 5 (1995): 382–86.

6. See David Lan, *Guns and Rain: Guerrillas and Spirit Mediums in Zimbabwe* (Harare: Zimbabwe Publishing House, 1985), and David Martin and Phyllis Martin, *The Struggle for Zimbabwe: The Chimurenga War* (London: Monthly Review Press, 1981).

7. For an especially compelling rendering of the consciousness of early settlers and missionaries in the southern cone of Africa, see Jean Comaroff and John Comaroff, *Of Revelation and Revolution: Christianity, Colonialism, and Consciousness in South Africa* (Chicago: University of Chicago Press, 1991).

8. The reader again is referred to David Tracy, *Plurality and Ambiguity: Hermeneutics, Religion, Hope* (San Francisco: Harper and Row, 1987).

9. David Tracy, "Theology and the Many Faces of Postmodernity," *Theology Today* 51 (April 1994), 106.

10. For example, in *Imagination and Authority: Theological Authorship in the Modern Tradition* (Minneapolis: Fortress Press, 1991), John E. Thiel discusses the classical and romantic paradigms in theology. A major distinguishing feature is how theologians in the respective paradigms speak of authority. Roughly, the *classical* paradigm assumes that authority resides in the objective revelation found in scripture and creeds; the theologian seeks to represent that authority faithfully, but is not in any primary sense the "author." Of the *romantic* paradigm, Thiel writes that "the theologian's task was no longer seen as the mimetic *representation* of an objective revelation but as an imaginative *construction* of the historical experience of salvation." In other words, for the "romantic," authority is not found solely in the received tradition of scripture and creed, regardless of how firmly one argues that God is the author of these texts, but also includes the authorship of the theologian (21). The romantic paradigm was the response of theologians to Enlightenment criticism singling out the Christian tradition's notion of authority as presenting "the greatest obstacle to the success of the Enlightenment's intellectual and political agenda" (25). Schleiermacher is the greatest and earliest exemplar of the romantic paradigm.

One of Thiel's most valuable contributions is his description of the romantic paradigm among theologians of the twentieth century. Barth fits the romantic paradigm, along with the Yale school of Hans Frei, George Lindbeck, Ronald Thiemann, and Stanley Hauerwas. The constructive (thus, "romantic") programs of these theologians are primarily *descriptive*. By recalling the biblical narrative, they believe they can offer an "authoritative measure of the many secular stories which vie for the believers' commitment" (27). "Authorship" resides in these theologians' ability to give compelling renditions or descriptions of the story without relying on extrascriptural categories. Theology is not so much translation as it is fresh transmission, or retelling, of the old story.

Thiel lists a group of *speculative* romantics, including Rudolph Bultmann, Paul

Tillich, and John Cobb among Protestants and Karl Rahner, Bernard Lonergan, Hans Urs von Balthasar, and David Tracy among Roman Catholics. These theologians use extrabiblical resources in order to render the tradition intelligible. A third group consists of *critical* theologians, who use the "hermeneutics of suspicion" as a common method. They do not look for a universal theory on which to build an intellectual bridge to cultured unbelievers, but look instead for "local" implications of the gospel for the socioeconomic, racial, or gender circumstances in which and for which they write. Feminist, Hispanic, Asian, and African theologians give shape to this critical but nevertheless romantic or constructive task of theology (24–30).

For all his stress on theology as an imaginative (and therefore romantic) enterprise, it is curious that Thiel does not attend closely to the structures of imagination that guide such effort. But he is not "doing theology" as much as looking at how contemporary theology differs from theology before the Enlightenment.

11. Northrop Frye, *The Anatomy of Criticism: Four Essays* (Princeton, N.J.: Princeton University Press, 1957).

12. Hayden White, *Metahistory: The Historical Imagination in Nineteenth-Century Europe* (Baltimore: Johns Hopkins University Press, 1973), 8f.

13. See especially Harvey Cox, *Fire from Heaven: The Rise of Pentecostal Spirituality and the Reshaping of Religion in the Twenty-first Century* (New York: Addison-Wesley, 1995). Cox has reviewed the history of Spirit-powered churches in the twentieth century and calls attention to how, in their earliest period, the leadership was egalitarian, nonhierarchical, nonracist, and nonsexist.

14. Different rhetorical styles imagine power and spirit in distinctive ways. By using *metaphor* a speaker represents one thing by referring to another. A metaphor— "my love, a rose"—imagines that a rose adequately represents the beloved, but not as a complete identification—that is, not literally. No reversal is required. *Metonymy* is close to metaphor but does not represent something similar, but different, by association. A metonymy *reduces* but does not represent. That is, "fifty sail" indicates fifty ships by naming a part to indicate the whole. The rhetorical effect is to remind us that behind a ship are necessary parts without which the ship would not be what it is. Political theology uses metonymy to show that the grandest theologies have political motivations which are not so grand. Theology is political.

This section describes the figure of speech known as *synecdoche*, which can be mistaken for metaphor or metonymy. Hayden White shows that the trope works by the way it *integrates*, but I prefer to note how it also *reverses*. (See White, *Metahistory*, 34f.) The stock example is the phrase, "He is all heart." It is literally impossible, but with the phrase one says something about the quality or deepest character of the person. The phrase reverses perceptions of one whom might have thought foolish, wasteful, lacking ambition, and so forth. All of that is reversed as soon as we are persuaded to think differently: "But, really, he is all heart."

15. This is the thesis of Hans von Campenhausen, *Ecclesiastical Authority and Spiritual Power in the Church of the First Three Centuries* (Stanford, Calif.: Stanford University Press, 1969), chap. 3, n. 30. See also James D. G. Dunn, *Jesus and the Spirit* (Grand Rapids, Mich.: Eerdmans, 1997), esp. sec. 57, "The Vision Fades."

16. Following the lead of his teacher Jürgen Moltmann, Geiko Mueller-Fahrenholz summons churches to rethink the doctrine of the Spirit as the life-giving and world-transforming power of God. See *God's Spirit: Transforming a World in Crisis* (New York: Continuum, 1995).

17. "The Spirit is the living God present throughout the world and in the struggle of human history. That being so, whatever is said about the Spirit is in fact the language about the mystery of God" (Elizabeth A. Johnson, *She Who Is: The Mystery of God in Feminist Theological Discourse* [New York: Crossroad, 1992, 146].

18. That "nothing is as natural as it seems" is the well-known aphorism of Romantic poet Robert Burns. Increasingly for scientists and for theologians who have maintained conversations with the scientific community, the statement poses an acceptable way of regarding natural order. Langdon Gilkey's essay, "Nature as the Image of God: Signs of the Sacred," is representative of the new rapprochement (*Theology Today* 51 [April 1994: 127–41]. Of the power of nature coursing through human beings, Gilkey writes: "For, suddenly and irrevocably, modern scientific culture realized to its surprise the ultimacy of this power to be of reality, its transcendent awesomeness, its terrible finality. And with that disclosure of the sacred power of things has appeared a corresponding demand, the unavoidable voice of conscience, of the 'ought,' that has shaken the scientific community and motivated many . . . to control radically our use of this power. . . . As we are discovering, all power, ancient and modern, is hedged about by . . . constraints on our free use of the power our knowledge has given us" (131).

19. Karl Barth, *Church Dogmatics* II.1.31, quoted in Patrick Sherry, *Spirit and Beauty: An Introduction to Theological Aesthetics* (Oxford: Clarendon Press, 1992), 67.

20. See Moltmann's opening remarks concerning Barth in *The Spirit of Life* (Minneapolis: Fortress Press, 1992), esp. p. 6, where Moltmann writes, "In 1929, in his lecture, 'The Holy Spirit and Christian Life,' Karl Barth settled accounts with Idealist notions about the continuity between the Spirit of God and the spirit of human beings."

21. See David Tracy's discussion of "the two basic religious forms in the Bible," the prophetic, in which the prophet speaks the word of the Lord because God demands it, and the meditative (wisdom), which "turns away from the more historical . . . core of the Bible in order to reflect upon our relationships to the cosmos and to face the kind of limit-situations (death, guilt, anxiety, joy, peace, and hope) human beings as human beings will always experience" ("Theology and the Many Faces of Postmodernity," *Theology Today* 51 [April 1994: 112f.]. This distinction informs Tracy's *Dialogue with the Other* (Grand Rapids, Mich.: Eerdmans, 1990). In this chapter I have used this distinction to speak about meditative imagination, rather than prophetic imagination.

22. Daniel Day Williams, *The Spirit and the Forms of Love* (New York: Harper and Row, 1968; Lanham, Md.: University Press of America, 1981), vii. Citations are from the more recent edition. Williams's much-neglected study can be divided into three parts. In the first part he reviews love in Hebrew faith, in the New Testament witness, and in three classical figures: Augustine, whose modern counterpart is M. C. D'Arcy; Francis, whose modern counterpart is Albert Schweitzer; and Martin Luther and the reformers, whose modern interpreters are Anders Nygren and Reinhold Niebuhr. In this section Williams critiques Augustine's doctrine of love which, for all its penetrating insight, is hampered by Augustine's doctrine of God as absolute, nontemporal, impassible, unchanging power. Augustine, along with Thomas, Calvin, and Luther, cannot imagine the love of God as suffering love. "The history of the conception of love is the history of the conception of God" (104). The second section contains Williams's alternative way of imagining power and love in the doctrines of the incar-

nation and the atonement. In the last part of the book he shows how this alternative plays out in Christian life.

23. Ibid., 10.

24. Ibid., 15.

25. Ibid., 137. Emphasis added.

26. This paragraph is my own summation of what is implied by Williams's five categories of love (ibid., 114–22). Reading this section again more than twenty-five years since it was first published caused me to wonder if Williams had not anticipated that his interpretation of love could serve as the main Christian contribution to post-modern theology. Note how love regards the other without any pretension that the other is, to use Tracy's term, "more of the same." Love does not see the other "merely as the illustration of a type. . . . If I am loved merely as one who illustrates a general type, then I know I am really not loved at all" (114).

27. Daniel Day Williams, *The Demonic and the Divine*, ed. Stacy A. Evans (Min-neapolis: Fortress Press, 1990), 71.

28. "The history of love and the history of sin are the same history" (Williams, *Spirit and the Forms of Love*, 192).

29. The subhead is taken from Dostoyevsky, who said, "Beauty will save the world." This somewhat startling quotation proves useful in this study, because it asserts a power by which the world can be saved. It is often quoted by theologians who study beauty. See Patrick Sherry, *Spirit and Beauty: An Introduction to Theologi-cal Aesthetics* (Oxford: Clarendon Press, 1992), 78. Other studies discuss the power of the Spirit as beauty: Hans Urs von Balthasar, *The Glory of the Lord: A Theological Aesthetics*, trans. John Riches et al., 7 vols. (New York: Crossroad Publications, 1982–1991); Paul Tillich, *On Art and Architecture*, ed. John Dillenberger with Jane Dillenberger (New York: Crossroad, 1989); John Dillenberger, *A Theology of Artistic Sensibilities: The Visual Arts and the Church* (New York: Crossroad, 1986); Frank Burch Brown, *Religious Aesthetics: A Theological Study of Making and Meaning* (Princeton, N.J.: Princeton University Press, 1989). See also *Theological Education* 30 (Autumn 1994) on "Sacred Imagination: The Arts and Theological Education," espe-cially the essays by Frank Burch Brown, Gordon D. Kaufman, Wilson Yates, Margaret R. Miles, and Edward Farley.

30. Brown, *Religious Aesthetics*, 26.

31. Ibid., 24.

32. For a careful discussion of the historical development of aesthetics as a secular discipline, see especially Brown, "Can Aesthetics Be Christian?" in ibid., 16–46.

33. There are major exceptions to this statement, as indicated in n. 29 above. Patrick Sherry gives ample evidence for the importance of Jonathan Edwards as a the-ologian of aesthetics (*Spirit and Beauty*, 13ff.). Specialists in theological aesthetics generally agree that the most important twentieth-century practitioner is Hans Urs von Balthasar (see ibid., 7).

34. See the Autumn 1994 issue of *Theological Education*.

35. See Sherry, *Spirit and Beauty*, 67.

36. See Dillenberger's discussion in *Theology of Artistic Sensibilities* (see above, n. 29). "In the Eastern Orthodox Church it was assumed that an icon makes present that which it images. An icon allows for the possibility of the presence of Christ or the saint to the believer. This is not to say that the image is identical with the sacred reality, but that the sacred reality of Christ or the saint is present through the icon. In

this sense, an image is like a sacrament. The icons are viewed spiritually, not aesthetically. A frontal style with a search for transparency characterizes these images of the saints. Thus the style is appropriate to their function, namely to make present without idolatry" (32).

37. See Sherry's careful exposition of von Balthasar's work in *Spirit and Beauty*, especially chapter 4, "The Holy Spirit in the Trinity," and particularly the section, "The Holy Spirit and Beauty."

38. This should not be taken as a plea that all art forms must have a specifically religious subject or function.

39. See Exodus 35:30ff. Bezalel of Judah was full of divine Spirit, "with skill, intelligence, and knowledge in every kind of craft, to devise artistic designs ..." (vv. 31-32). The tabernacle was designed and constructed under his guidance.

40. From John McIntyre, *Faith, Theology, and Imagination*, quoted in Sherry, *Spirit and Beauty*, 122.

41. Sherry offers an insightful discussion of the biblical sources of God's beauty, and argues that God's beauty is closely related to, indeed constituent of, God's glory (*kabod*), which is more central to the biblical witness than beauty. Sherry cites Barth's admission that *kabod* "includes and expresses what we call beauty. But he says that beauty is not a leading concept in treating of the divine perfections, but an auxiliary one, enabling us to see that God's glory is effective" (*Spirit and Beauty*, 67). If Barth's statement is true, it will do for the case I am making here, namely that beauty is one of the effects of God's Spirit in the world. Robert Jenson, a Barthian scholar, writes that "the Spirit is the freedom of universal history . . . the spontaneity of natural process. . . . [T]he Spirit [is] universal creativity . . ." (*Christian Dogmatics* [Minneapolis: Fortress Press, 1984, 2:166]).

42. One is reminded of the early work of Moltmann and his justly influential *The Crucified God* (New York: Harper and Row, 1974). It is noteworthy how he has moved from this early critique of theologies of glory to his most recent explorations of creation and pneumatology.

43. Quoted in Sherry, *Spirit and Beauty*, 83.

44. *Poetics of Music*, trans. Arthur Knodel and Ingolf Dahl (New York: Random House, 1947), 146, quoted in Brown, *Religious Aesthetics*, 30.

45. *First and Last Notebooks*, quoted in Sherry, *Spirit and Beauty*, 57.

CHAPTER 6

1. Victor Paul Furnish, introduction to First Corinthians, *HarperCollins Study Bible* (New York: HarperCollins, 1993).

2. See Gordon D. Fee, *God's Empowering Presence: The Holy Spirit in the Letters of Paul* (Peabody, Mass.: Hendrickson, 1994). Fee writes that even though the terms *power* and *spirit* are not coterminous, the presence of spirit always implies the presence of the power (907). Fee does not say that all power comes from the Spirit of God.

3. I will draw on the work of historian Gordon S. Wood, *The Radicalism of the American Revolution* (New York: Vintage Books, 1993). Parenthetical citations in the text are to this volume.

4. Ibid., 96. "Many like Adam Smith believed that all governments in the world could be reduced to just two—monarchies and republics—and that these were rooted

in two basic types of personalities: monarchists who loved peace and order, and republicans who loved liberty and independence" (97). One could also say that monarchists' imaginations were held in thrall to power as domination, and republicans' imaginations to power as freedom.

5. The preceding paragraph in Wood's book reads: "In the decades following the Revolution, American society was transformed. By every measure there was a sudden bursting forth, an explosion—not only of geographical movement but of entrepreneurial energy, of religious passion, and of pecuniary desires. Perhaps no country in the Western world has ever undergone such massive changes in such a short period of time. The Revolution resembled the breaking of a dam, releasing thousands upon thousands of pent-up pressures. There had been seepage and flows before the Revolution, but suddenly it was as if the whole traditional structure, enfeebled and brittle to begin with, broke apart, and people and their energies were set loose in an unprecedented outburst" (232).

6. Ibid., 276.

7. For a history of ecclesiastical reaction to evidence of the Spirit, see Hans von Campenhausen, *Ecclesiastical Authority and Spiritual Power in the Church of the First Three Centuries* (Stanford, Calif.: Stanford University Press, 1969).

8. Wood, *Radicalism of the American Revolution*, 367.

9. *Metahistory: The Historical Imagination in Nineteenth-Century Europe* (Baltimore: Johns Hopkins University Press, 1973), 10.

10. David Jasper, *Rhetoric, Power, and Community: An Exercise in Reserve* (Louisville: Westminster/John Knox Press, 1993), 144.

11. Douglas John Hall wonders whether the Spirit of God is not at work in the disestablishment of the Christian religion in the West. See Douglas John Hall and Rosemary Radford Reuther, *God and the Nations* (Minneapolis: Fortress Press, 1995).

12. See Rebecca S. Chopp, *The Power to Speak: Feminism, Language, God* (New York: Crossroad, 1989). For Chopp, the power simply to speak is not the point. Her goal is to show how the power to speak must be aimed at changing the social order, namely its power structures. "My discourse attempts, in its own strategies, to criticize and move toward transforming the social-symbolic order" (6).

13. See Herman Waetjen's study of the Gospel of Mark, *A Reordering of Power* (Minneapolis: Fortress Press, 1989).

14. This terse description of "theologies from the underside" appears in Susan Brooke Thistlethwaite and Mary Potter Engel, eds., *Lift Every Voice: Constructing Christian Theologies from the Underside* (San Francisco: Harper and Row, 1990), 77. The work is a collection of writings, with introductions by the editors. Also see *Feminist Theology from the Third World: A Reader*, ed. Ursula King (Maryknoll, N.Y.: Orbis Books, 1994); Justo L. González, *Manana: Christian Theology from a Hispanic Perspective* (Nashville: Abingdon Press, 1990); Chopp, *Power to Speak*; and Rita Nakashima Brock, *Journeys by Heart: A Christology of Erotic Power* (New York: Crossroad, 1991).

15. See especially *In Memory of Her: A Feminist Theological Reconstruction of Christian Origins* (New York: Crossroad, 1983); and *Discipleship of Equals: A Critical Feminist Ekklesia-logy of Liberation* (New York: Crossroad, 1993).

16. Schüssler Fiorenza, *In Memory of Her*, 152.

17. Ibid.

18. Ibid.

19. Ibid., 121.

20. Ibid., 129–30. Fiorenza quotes *Feminist Revolution* (New York: Random House, 1975, p. 205): "We define the best interests of women as the best interests of the poorest, most insulted, most despised, most abused woman on earth. . . . Until Everywoman is free, no woman is free." (132) Subsequent parenthetical references in the text are to Schüssler Fiorenza, *In Memory of Her.*

21. Rosemary Radford Ruether has documented this long story of failure in her most recent study, *Women and Redemption: A Theological History* (Minneapolis: Fortress Press, 1998). She begins with the question of gender equity in the New Testament and then rehearses the history of women in the church to the present. The literature on alterity—otherness—has not only multiplied exponentially, but much of it has become nearly unintelligible except for specialists in postmodern philosophy. Even so, it is not a topic a Christian can avoid if wishing to press the claim of the gospel that God wills all to become one in Christ. All are not one but many, and the many are dazzlingly different and diverse. I have been greatly helped by the work of my colleague, Paul R. Sponheim, *Faith and the Other: A Relational Theology* (Minneapolis: Fortress Press, 1993), and also by David Tracy, *Dialogue with the Other* (Grand Rapids, Mich.: Eerdmans, 1990).

22. See von Campenhausen, *Ecclesiastical Authority and Spiritual Power*, for the best-known demonstration of this phenomenon, already occurring in the earliest period of church history.

23. This is not the place to evaluate the theories and practices of European and American missionaries overseas, nor to deny the great commitment and sacrifice that thousands of people made. But there is no denying that an attitude prevailed among those who took the message of Jesus Christ to places like Africa. Jean and John Comaroff have investigated correspondence of missionaries in South Africa, and demonstrated that they commonly assumed cultural superiority. This did not prevent their converts, however, from becoming Christian in their own way, nor from appropriating the revolutionary power in the Christian revelation. Into the twentieth century, African Christians have benefited from the decentering implications of the Jesus story which the European messengers brought them. See Jean Comaroff and John Comaroff, *Of Revelation and Revolution: Christianity, Colonialism, and Consciousness in South Africa* (Chicago: University of Chicago Press, 1991). See also Lamin Sanneh, *Translating the Message: Missionary Impact on Culture* (Maryknoll, N.Y.: Orbis Books, 1990).

24. This is the title of Moltmann's pneumatology, *The Spirit of Life: A Universal Affirmation* (Minneapolis: Fortress Press, 1992). See especially chap. 3, "Trinitarian Experience of the Spirit."

25. For a wide-ranging description of churches in Africa and their relation to postcolonial governments, see Paul Gifford, *African Christianity: Its Public Role* (Bloomington: University of Indiana Press, 1998).

26. White, *Metahistory*, 38.

27. This point is overlooked in José Comblin, *The Holy Spirit and Liberation* (Maryknoll, N.Y.: Orbis Books, 1989), but one should not expect theologians who focus on the liberating power of the Spirit to construct a new order simultaneously. But do Latin American theologians of liberation really believe that when current oppressors have been turned aside the new order will be able, or willing, to guarantee equality?

28. Moltmann in *The Spirit of Life* refutes what he calls the false alternative between divine revelation and experience of the Holy Spirit. The alternative received

credence from Barth, for whom the Holy Spirit remains on God's side and can there-fore "never be experienced by human beings." Both Barth's neoorthodoxy and secular views of the world would deny the possibility of experiencing the power of the Spirit.

29. See Tex Sample, *U.S. Lifestyles and Mainline Churches* (Louisville: Westminster/John Knox Press, 1990).

30. I owe this phrase to Paul Sponheim, who used it in a paper introducing discussion of his book *Faith and the Other*.

31. Such campaigns have been financed across Africa and in the American media by right-wing conservative groups. See Paul Gifford, *The Religious Right in Southern Africa* (Harare, Zimbabwe: Baobab Books, 1988). For an update on this phenomenon, see idem, "Some Recent Developments in African Christianity," *African Affairs* (1994): 513–34.

32. I dissent from the argument of Charles Davis, whose book closely resembles this one in its use of the structures of the imagination and rhetorical strategies. Unlike him, I do not regard any one of these strategies as normative for, or superior to, all the others. See Charles Davis, *What Is Living, What Is Dead in Christianity Today?* (San Francisco: Harper and Row, 1986).

33. See Francis Fukuyama, *Trust: Social Virtues and the Creation of Prosperity* (New York: Free Press, 1995). Fukuyama is a social scientist at the Rand Corporation, a conservative think tank. His earlier book, *The End of History*, was at the center of controversy for its alleged Eurocentrism. Even if one does not share his conservative views, Fukuyama's basic thesis, that economic systems rise and fall according to the level of social trust, is compelling. Japan is a "high trust" culture; the United States, however, is losing its social capital as churches and schools languish. See also my analysis and theological assessment of Fukuyama, *Trust*, in *Word and World* (Fall 1997).

34. At a book fair in Harare, Zimbabwe, in August 1995, gays and lesbians displayed books concerning equal rights for homosexuals. President Mugabe made public remarks—saying that such material was not acceptable in Zimbabwe—which served his political interests leading up to the presidential election in March 1996. International news services, however, picked up his remarks, which were publicized in San Francisco, Washington, and New York. The power of equality contributed to Mugabe's political ascendancy when the black majority superseded the white minority. Now that black gays and lesbians are a minority, Mugabe's intemperate dismissal testifies to the fact that the power of equality cannot be denied.

35. See David Jasper's discussion of irony in Mark's Gospel in *Rhetoric, Power, and Community*. "In the rhetoric of irony the dead letter of literalism is enlivened by the literary which affirms an authentic faith" (64).

36. See the report on the 1993 Minneapolis "Re-imagining Conference," *Re-membering and Re-imagining*, ed. Nancy J. Berneking and Pamela Carter Joern (Cleveland: Pilgrim Press, 1995).

37. Red Hot Chili Peppers, "The Power of Equality," on *BloodSugarSexMagik*.

CHAPTER 7

1. *The Complete Poetry and Prose of William Blake*, ed. David V. Erdman, rev. ed. (Berkeley: University of California Press, 1982), 231. For this reference I am indebted to Jerry D. Meyer, "Profane and Sacred: Religious Imagery and Prophetic Expression in Postmodern Art," *Journal of the American Academy of Religion* 65 (Spring 1997): 19.

2. See Meyer, "Profane and Sacred," 19. Emphasis added.

3. There are some who would add to the list of totalistic "isms" the rise of global capitalism. See George Soros, "The Capitalist Threat," *Atlantic Monthly*, February 1997: "Because communism and even socialism have been thoroughly discredited, I consider the threat from the laissez-faire side more potent today than the threat from totalitarian ideologies" (48).

4. Anyone with a fleeting acquaintance with contemporary films in theaters and on television will know the appalling sexual violence and physical gore offered. There is no doubt that film technology has expanded the capacity to depict power as coercive force. What is appalling is the seeming failure to imagine other forms of power.

5. I am grateful for a paper by David Frederickson, who argues that the famous Philippians passage discussing Christ's *kenosis* ("emptying") would have been recognized by Paul's readers as politically subversive. In the culture of master-slave relations, political freedom was afforded only those who had slaves. For Paul to tell the Philippians that Jesus was their slave, even until death on a cross, was to ascribe the status of a free person to even the lowliest member of the Christian community.

6. The subhead duplicates the title of an earlier study of the Spirit by Jürgen Moltmann, *The Church in the Power of the Spirit* (San Francisco: HarperSanFrancisco, 1991). It was first published in German in 1975. This section is indebted to the provocative book by Geiko Mueller-Fahrenholz, *God's Spirit: Transforming a World in Crisis* (New York: Continuum, 1995).

7. Jürgen Moltmann, *The Spirit of Life: A Universal Affirmation* (Minneapolis: Fortress Press, 1992).

8. Readers of volume 3 of Paul Tillich's *Systematic Theology* (Chicago: University of Chicago Press, 1963) will detect the influence of his doctrine of the Spirit in much of what I have written, and surely in this sentence. What Tillich designates the universal Spiritual Presence is close to what I mean by the Spirit's presence in all powers. The Spiritual Presence is not lacking anywhere for Tillich, but is manifest everywhere. That manifestation called Jesus as the Christ is therefore not the only manifestation, but is "the criterion" of every manifestation. See especially "The Spiritual Presence in Jesus as the Christ: Spirit Christology," 144–49.

9. One might ask why I have not drawn on Walter Wink's volumes, especially *Naming the Powers: The Language of Power in the New Testament* (Philadelphia: Fortress Press, 1984), and *Engaging the Powers: Discernment and Resistance in a World of Domination* (Minneapolis: Fortress Press, 1992). I have no quarrel with Wink's scholarship nor do I dissent from his moral perspective. But, in the end, these studies give the sense that "the powers" are self-created and independent of the power of God. There is a tilt toward metaphysical dualism, which is probably not intended but which is not sufficiently controlled.

SELECTED BIBLIOGRAPHY

Altizer, Thomas J. J. "Hegel and the Christian God." *Journal of the American Academy of Religion* 59, no. 1 (1991): 71–91.

Anderson, Allan. *Moya: The Holy Spirit in an African Context*. Pretoria: University of South Africa Press, 1991.

Barbour, Ian G. *Religion in an Age of Science*. San Francisco: HarperSanFrancisco, 1990.

Berkhof, Hendrikus. *The Doctrine of the Holy Spirit*. Richmond: John Knox Press, 1964.

Bloesch, Donald G. *Theology of the Word and Spirit*. Downers Grove, Ill.: InterVarsity Press, 1992.

Bosch, David. *Transforming Mission*. Maryknoll, N.Y.: Orbis Books, 1991.

Bourdillon, M. F. C. "The Power of Symbols." In *Religion and Society: A Text for Africa*. Gweru, Zimbabwe: Mambo Press, 1990.

Bracken, Joseph A. *Society and Spirit: A Trinitarian Cosmology*. Selinsgrove, Pa.: Susquehanna University Press, 1991.

Brown, Frank Burch. *Religious Aesthetics: A Theological Study of Making and Meaning*. Princeton, N.J.: Princeton University Press, 1989.

Browning, Don S. *A Fundamental Practical Theology*. Minneapolis: Fortress Press, 1991.

———, ed. *Habermas, Modernity, and Public Theology*. New York: Crossroad, 1992.

Bruner, Frederick Dale. *A Theology of the Holy Spirit*. Grand Rapids, Mich.: Eerdmans, 1970.

Burgess, Stanley M. *The Spirit and the Church: Antiquity*. Peabody, Mass.: Hendrickson, 1984.

Carrol, Jackson W., et al. *Being There: Culture and Formation in Two Theological Schools*. New York: Oxford University Press, 1997.

Case-Winters, Anna. *God's Power: Traditional Understandings and Contemporary Challenges*. Louisville: Westminster/John Knox Press, 1990.

Chopp, Rebecca S. *The Power to Speak: Feminism, Language, God*. New York: Crossroad, 1989.

Chung Hyun Kyung. "Come, Holy Spirit—Renew the Whole Creation." In *Signs of the Spirit*, edited by Michael Kinnamon. The official report of the Seventh Assembly. Geneva: World Council of Churches, 1991.

Cobb, John B. "Two Types of Postmodernism: Deconstruction and Process." *Theology Today* 47, no. 2 (1990): 149–58.

Cobb, John B., and Herman Daly. *For the Common Good: Redirecting the Economy toward Community, the Environment, and a Sustainable Future*. Boston: Beacon Press, 1989.

Comaroff, Jean. *Body of Power, Spirit of Resistance: The Culture and History of a South African People*. Chicago: University of Chicago Press, 1985.

Comaroff, Jean, and John Comaroff. *Of Revelation and Revolution: Christianity, Colonialism, and Consciousness in South Africa*. Chicago: University of Chicago Press, 1991.

Comblin, José. *The Holy Spirit and Liberation*. Maryknoll, N.Y.: Orbis Books, 1989.

Cone, James. *Martin and Malcolm and America: A Dream or a Nightmare?* Maryknoll, N.Y.: Orbis Books, 1991.

Congar, Yves M. J. *I Believe in the Holy Spirit*. Vols. 1–3. New York: Seabury Press, 1983.

———. *The Word and the Spirit*. San Francisco: Harper and Row, 1986.

Cooke, Bernard J. *The Distancing of God: The Ambiguity of Symbol in History and Theology*. Minneapolis: Fortress Press, 1990.

Cox, Harvey. *Fire from Heaven: The Rise of Pentecostal Spirituality and the Reshaping of Religion in the Twenty-first Century*. Reading, Mass.: Addison-Wesley, 1995.

Daneel, M. L. *Quest for Belonging: Introduction to a Study of African Independent Churches*. Harare, Zimbabwe: Mambo Press, 1987.

Davis, Charles. *What Is Living, What Is Dead in Christianity Today?* San Francisco: Harper and Row, 1986.

Dickson, Kwesi A. *Theology in Africa*. Maryknoll, N.Y.: Orbis Books, 1984.

Dillistone, F. W. *The Holy Spirit in the Life of Today*. Philadelphia: Westminster Press, 1947.

———. *The Power of Symbols in Religion and Culture*. New York: Crossroad, 1986.

Ditmanson, Harold H. "The Significance of the Doctrine of the Holy Spirit for Contemporary Theology." In *The Holy Spirit in the Life of the Church*, edited by Paul D. Opsahl. Minneapolis: Augsburg Press, 1978.

Dunn, James D. G. *Baptism in the Holy Spirit*. Philadelphia: Westminster Press, 1970.

———. *Jesus and the Spirit*. Grand Rapids, Mich.: Eerdmans, 1997.

Farley, Edward. *Good and Evil: Interpreting a Human Condition*. Minneapolis: Fortress Press, 1990.

Fee, Gordon D. *God's Empowering Presence: The Holy Spirit in the Letters of Paul*. Peabody, Mass.: Hendrickson, 1994.

Fiddes, Paul. *The Creative Suffering of God*. New York: Oxford University Press, 1988.

Freedberg, David. *The Power of Images*. Chicago: University of Chicago Press, 1989.

Frye, Northrop. *The Anatomy of Criticism: Four Essays*. Princeton, N.J.: Princeton University Press, 1957.

———. *The Educated Imagination*. Bloomington: Indiana University Press, 1964.

Fukuyama, Francis. *Trust: Social Virtues and the Creation of Prosperity.* New York: Free Press, 1995.

Gelpi, Donald L., S.J. *The Divine Mother: A Trinitarian Theology of the Holy Spirit.* Lanham, Md.: University Press of America, 1984.

Gifford, Paul. *African Christianity: Its Public Role.* Bloomington: Indiana University Press, 1998.

———. *The Religious Right in Southern Africa.* Harare: University of Zimbabwe Publications and Baobab Books, 1990.

Gilkey, Langdon. "The Nature and Work of the Spirit." In *Gilkey on Tillich.* New York: Crossroad, 1990.

———. *Through the Tempest: Theological Voyages in a Pluralistic Culture.* Minneapolis: Fortress Press, 1991.

Haroutunian, Joseph. "The Church, the Spirit, and the Hands of God." *Journal of Religion* 54, no. 2 (1974): 154–65.

Hendry, George, S. *The Holy Spirit in Christian Theology.* Philadelphia: Westminster Press, 1956.

Hengel, Martin. *Christ and Power.* Philadelphia: Fortress Press, 1977.

Heron, Alasdair. *The Holy Spirit.* Philadelphia: Westminster Press, 1983.

Hodgson, Peter C. *God in History, Shapes of Freedom.* Nashville: Abingdon Press, 1989.

———. *Revisioning the Church.* Minneapolis: Fortress Press, 1988.

———. *Winds of the Spirit: A Constructive Christian Theology.* Louisville: Westminster/John Knox Press, 1994.

Hoffmeyer, John F. "Absolute Knowing and the Historicity of Spirit." *Journal of Religion* 72, no. 2 (1992): 198–209.

Holmberg, Bengt. *Paul and Power.* Minneapolis: Fortress Press, 1980.

Hood, Robert E. *Must God Remain Greek?* Minneapolis: Fortress Press, 1990.

Jasper, David. *Rhetoric, Power, and Community: An Exercise in Reserve.* Louisville: Westminster/John Knox Press, 1993.

Johnson, Elizabeth A. *She Who Is: The Mystery of God in Feminist Theological Discourse.* New York: Crossroad, 1992.

Kovel, Joel. *History and Spirit: An Inquiry into the Philosophy of Liberation.* Boston: Beacon Press, 1991.

Krieger, David J. *The New Universalism.* Maryknoll, N.Y.: Orbis Books, 1991.

LaCugna, Catherine Mowry. *God for Us: The Trinity and the Christian Life.* San Francisco: HarperSanFrancisco, 1991.

Lampe, G. W. H. *God as Spirit.* Oxford: Clarendon Press, 1977.

Lindbeck, George A. *The Nature of Doctrine: Religion and Theology in a Postliberal Age.* Philadelphia: Westminster Press, 1984.

Lodahl, Michael E. *Shekhinah/Spirit: Divine Presence in Jewish and Christian Religion.* New York: Paulist Press, 1992.

Lukes, Steven. *Power—A Radical View.* London: Macmillan, 1974.

Lull, David John. *The Spirit in Galatia: Paul's Interpretation of "Pneuma" as Divine Power.* Chico, Calif.: Scholars Press, 1980.

Martey, Emmanuel. *African Theology: Inculturation and Liberation.* Mary-knoll, N.Y.: Orbis Books, 1993.

McFague, Sallie. *The Body of God: An Ecological Theology.* Minneapolis: Fortress Press, 1993.

———. *Models of God: A Theology for an Ecological, Nuclear Age.* Philadelphia: Fortress Press, 1987.

McGinn, Bernard. *Presence of God.* New York: Crossroad, 1991.

McIntyre, John. *The Shape of Pneumatology: Studies in the Doctrine of the Holy Spirit.* Edinburgh: T. & T. Clark, 1997.

Midgely, Mary. *Science as Salvation: A Modern Myth and Its Meaning.* London: Routledge, 1992.

Moltmann, Jürgen. *God in Creation.* San Francisco: HarperSanFrancisco, 1991.

———. *The Source of Life: The Holy Spirit and the Theology of Life.* Minneapolis: Fortress Press, 1997.

———. *The Spirit of Life: A Universal Affirmation.* Minneapolis: Fortress Press, 1992.

———. "Theological Proposals towards the Resolution of the *Filioque* Controversy." In *Spirit of God, Spirit of Christ: Ecumenical Reflections on the Filioque Controversy.* Geneva: World Council of Churches, 1981.

———. *The Trinity and the Kingdom.* San Francisco: Harper and Row, 1981.

Mueller-Fahrenholz, Geiko. *God's Spirit: Transforming a World in Crisis.* New York: Continuum, 1995.

Nakashima Brock, Rita. *Journeys by Heart: A Christology of Erotic Power.* New York: Crossroad, 1991.

Nolan, Albert. *God in South Africa.* Grand Rapids, Mich.: Eerdmans, 1988.

Oden, Thomas C. *Life in the Spirit: Systematic Theology.* Vol. 3. San Francisco: HarperSanFrancisco, 1992.

Oliver, Roland, "Pomp and Power." Chap. 12 in *The African Experience.* New York: HarperCollins, 1991.

Olson, Alan M. *Hegel and the Spirit: Philosophy as Pneumatology.* Princeton, N.J.: Princeton University Press, 1992.

Parratt, John. *Reinventing Christianity: African Theology Today.* Grand Rapids, Mich.: Eerdmans, 1995.

Pasewark, Kyle A. *A Theology of Power: Being beyond Domination.* Minneapolis: Fortress Press, 1993.

Pelikan, Jaroslav. *Spirit versus Structure: Luther and the Institutions of the Church.* New York: Harper and Row, 1968.

Placher, William C. *Unapologetic Theology: A Christian Voice in a Pluralistic Conversation.* Louisville: Westminster/John Knox Press, 1989.

Pobee, J. S. *Skenosis: Christian Faith in an African Context.* Harare, Zimbabwe: Mambo Press, 1992.

Poling, James Newton. *The Abuse of Power: A Theological Problem.* Nashville: Abingdon Press, 1991.

Prenter, Regin. *Spiritus Creator*. Translated by John M. Jensen. Philadelphia: Fortress Press, 1953.

Preus, J. Samuel. "Secularizing Divination: Spiritual Biography and the Invention of the Novel." *Journal of the American Academy of Religion* 59, no. 3 (1991): 441–66.

Radford Ruether, Rosemary. *Gaia and God: An Ecofeminist Theology of Earth Healing*. San Francisco: HarperSanFrancisco, 1992.

———. *Women and Redemption: A Theological History*. Minneapolis: Fortress Press, 1998.

Reynolds, Blair. *Toward a Process Pneumatology*. Cranbury, N.J.: Associated University Presses, 1990.

Ritschl, Dietrich. "Historical Development and Implications of the Filioque Controversy." In *Spirit of God, Spirit of Christ: Ecumenical Reflections on the Filioque Controversy*. Geneva: World Council of Churches, 1981.

———. "The History of the *Filioque* Controversy." In *Conflicts about the Holy Spirit*, edited by Hans Küng and Jürgen Moltmann. New York: Seabury Press, 1979.

Rusch, William G. "The Doctrine of the Holy Spirit in the Patristic and Medieval Church." In *The Holy Spirit in the Life of the Church*, edited by Paul Opsahl. Minneapolis: Augsburg Press 1978.

Sanneh, Lamin. *Translating the Message: Missionary Impact on Culture*. Maryknoll, N.Y.: Orbis Books, 1990.

Schillebeeckx, Edward. *Church: The Human Story of God*. New York: Crossroad, 1990.

Schüssler Fiorenza, Elisabeth. *Discipleship of Equals: A Critical Feminist Ekklesia-logy of Liberation*. New York: Crossroad, 1993.

———. *In Memory of Her: A Feminist Theological Reconstruction of Christian Origins*. New York: Crossroad, 1983.

Schweizer, Eduard. *The Holy Spirit*. London: SCM Press, 1978.

———. "What is the Holy Spirit? A Study in Biblical Theology." In *Conflicts about the Holy Spirit*, edited by Hans Küng and Jürgen Moltmann. New York: Seabury Press, 1979.

Sherry, Patrick. *Spirit and Beauty: An Introduction to Theological Aesthetics*. Oxford: Clarendon Press, 1992.

Shorter, Aylward. *The Church in the African City*. Maryknoll, N.Y.: Orbis Books, 1991.

Simpson, Gary M. "Spirit and the Communicative Imagination." Manuscript, n.d.

Sittler, Joseph. *Essays on Nature and Grace*. Philadelphia: Fortress Press, 1972.

Sponheim, Paul R. *Faith and the Other: A Relational Theology*. Minneapolis: Fortress Press, 1993.

Stendahl, Krister. *Energy for Life*. Geneva: World Council of Churches, 1990.

Taylor, John V. *The Go-Between God: The Holy Spirit and Christian Mission*. New York: Oxford University Press, 1972.

Taylor, Mark Kline. "Reflective Ontology in the Land of Postmodern Suspicion." *Journal of Religion* 72, no. 4 (1992): 573–79.

Thiel, John E. *Imagination and Authority: Theological Authorship in the Modern Tradition.* Minneapolis: Fortress Press, 1991.

Thistlethwaite, Susan Brooks, and Mary Potter Engel, eds. *Lift Every Voice: Constructing Christian Theologies from the Underside.* San Francisco: Harper and Row, 1990.

Thompson, John. *The Holy Spirit in the Theology of Karl Barth.* Allison Park, Pa.: Pickwick Publications, 1991.

Tillich, Paul. *On Art and Architecture.* Edited by John Dillenberger with Jane Dillenberger. New York: Crossroad, 1989.

———. "The Problem of Theological Method." *Journal of Religion* 27 (1947): 16–26.

———. *Systematic Theology.* Vol. 3. Chicago: University of Chicago Press, 1963.

Tracy, David. *The Analogical Imagination: Christian Theology and the Culture of Pluralism.* New York: Crossroad, 1981.

———. *Blessed Rage for Order: The New Pluralism in Theology.* New York: Seabury Press, 1975.

———. *Dialogue with the Other.* Grand Rapids, Mich.: Eerdmans, 1990.

———. "Hermeneutical Reflections in the New Paradigm." In *Paradigm Change in Theology,* edited by Hans Küng and David Tracy. New York: Crossroad, 1991.

Victorin-Vangeruud, Nancy. "From Economies of Domination to Economies of Recognition: A Feminist Pneumatology." Ph.D. diss., Vanderbilt University, 1995.

Volf, Miroslav. *Work in the Spirit.* New York: Oxford University Press, 1991.

von Campenhausen, Hans. *Ecclesiastical Authority and Spiritual Power in the Church of the First Three Centuries.* Stanford, Calif.: Stanford University Press, 1969.

Waetjen, Herman. *A Reordering of Power.* Minneapolis: Fortress Press, 1989.

Welker, Michael. *God the Spirit.* Minneapolis: Fortress Press, 1994.

———. "The Reign of God." *Theology Today* 49, no. 4 (1993): 500–515.

Westermann, Claus. *Creation.* Philadelphia: Fortress Press, 1974.

Wilder, Amos Niven. *Theopoetic: Theology and the Religious Imagination.* Philadelphia: Fortress Press, 1976.

Williams, Daniel Day. *The Demonic and the Divine.* Edited by Stacy A. Evans. Minneapolis: Fortress Press, 1990.

———. *The Spirit and the Forms of Love.* New York: Harper and Row, 1968; Lanham, Md.: University Press of America, 1981.

Wink, Walter. *Engaging the Powers: Discernment and Resistance in a World of Domination.* Minneapolis: Fortress Press, 1992.

———. *Naming the Powers: The Language of Power in the New Testament.* Philadelphia: Fortress Press, 1984.

Wisnefske, Ned. "The Mystery of Our Natural Life." *Dialog* 30, no. 1 (1971): 27–35.

Wood, Gordon S. *The Radicalism of the American Revolution.* New York: Vintage Books, 1993.

Wuthnow, Robert. *The Crisis in the Churches: Spiritual Malaise, Fiscal Woe.* New York: Oxford University Press, 1997.

———. *The Struggle for America's Soul: Evangelicals, Liberals, and Secularism.* Grand Rapids, Mich.: Eerdmans, 1989.

INDEX

aesthetics, 89
Africa, views of, 4, 14–16
African-Initiated Churches (AICs), 4
American Revolution, 97–99, 124
animism, 15, 16
Anonymous Christ, 18
atheism, 21
Augustine, Saint, 91–92
authority, 96–97. *See also* power

Barbour, Ian, 30–32
Barth, Karl, 83–84
basileia, 106
beauty
    power of, 80–83, 88–90, 123–24
    and resurrection, 91–93
    spirit as, 83–84
Bible
    Corinthians, 24, 68, 95
    Ephesians, 52–53
    Philippians, 115
    Thessalonians, 13
    See also New Testament; Old Testament
Blake, William, 119
Bonhoeffer, Dietrich, 85
Brueggemann, Walter, 67
Burns, Robert, 154 n.18

calamities. *See* disasters
canonicity, 144–45 n.8
Catholicism. *See* Roman Catholicism
change, 70–73
Christian history, 24, 33, 107, 109–10
church and Spirit, 125–26
civil rights movement, 16–17
classical paradigm, 152 n.10
Cobb, John, 6, 17
comedy, 10, 37, 40–44
Cone, James, 104
Constitution (U.S.), 99
cosmology, African, 1, 4–5, 15, 16, 59

covenant, 47, 51
Cox, Harvey, 4
crucifixion and resurrection, 41, 80, 91–93, 123

death, 82, 91
Declaration of Independence, 98–99, 124
democracy, 45–46, 97
disasters, 13
dissent, 10, 37, 100, 102–3, 124
disunity, 95
divine determinism, 21
dualism, 22

ecology, 127–28
economies of domination, 135 n.1
ecumenism, 128–29
Equal Rights Amendment, 102–3
equality
    among disciples, 103–8
    power of, 102–3, 108–17, 124
evangelism, 127
evil, 10, 33, 75, 82, 86–87
experience, 8, 53, 136 n.15

feminism, 102–3
filioque, 5, 25–27, 84
Flaubert, Gustav, 101
force, 43–44, 49, 52, 55, 96
Foucault, Michel, 13, 71–72, 137 n.5, 139 n.17
freedom and justice, 63–64, 122–23
Fromm, Erich, 71
Frye, Northrop, 75, 80
Fukuyama, Francis, 159 n.33
future, 73–74

Gilkey, Langdon, 60, 154 n.18
God question, 13–14
González, Justo L., 104
Gregory of Nazianus, 25

Hall, Douglas John, 1
health and spirit, 4
Hengel, Martin, 48
Heyward, Carter, 104
Hodgson, Peter C., 77, 79
holiness, 129–30
Holy Spirit. *See* Spirit
homosexuality, 159–60 n.34

icons, 90, 156 n.36
imagination, 10, 16, 18–20, 29–31,
    34–36, 75–79, 81–82, 90, 96,
    119–20
individualism, 135 n.4
inference, 150 n.25
irony, 100, 108, 110, 111, 115–17,
    144 n.6

Jasper, David, 101
Jefferson, Thomas, 97–99, 100
Jesus, 25, 50, 104–5
Jewish community, 105–6
Johnson, Elizabeth, 12, 23
jokes. *See* comedy; irony; satire
Joseph story, 47–48
justice. *See* freedom and justice

knowledge and power, 43–44
Kovel, Joel, 135 n.4, 147 n.2
Kuhn, Thomas, 31

language, religious, 10, 35–36, 41–42
laughter. *See* comedy; irony; satire
literalism, 116
love
    power of, 80–87, 123–24
    spirit as, 83–84
Luther, Martin, 8, 130

Macmillan, Harold, 70
McFague, Sallie, 144 n. 7, 147 n.3
McIntyre, John, 90
Mandela, Nelson, 78
Manichaeanism, 87
metaphor, 144 n.6, 148 n.5, 153 n.14
metonymy, 144 n.6, 148 n.5, 153 n.14
Metzger, Bruce, 68
missionary movement, 107–8

Mobutu Sese Seko, 43
modernity, 2, 9–10, 15
Moltmann, Jürgen, 65–66
    Spirit of Life, 126
monarchy, 96–97, 100, 124
music, 92

new age religion, 15
New Testament, 24, 68
Nicene Creed, 5, 25
Nolan, Albert, 145 n.14

Oduyoye, Mercy Amba, 104
Old Testament, 65–67
other, 108–15

panentheism, 21
pantheism, 21
Pasewark, Kyle, 139 n.17, 145 n.12,
    148 n.8
Paton, Alan, 149 n.24
Paul, the apostle, 24, 39, 69
Pentecostalism, 4, 14, 26, 76
postmodernism, 71–72, 137 n.5
power
    in American experience, 96–99, 124
    force as, 43–44, 49, 52, 55, 96
    knowledge as, 45
    and spirit, 5–6, 9, 10, 19–22, 24, 27,
        40, 49, 53–54, 59–60, 75, 95–96,
        124–25, 135 n.1
    and truth, 50–52, 121
priesthood, 124
prophesy, 67–68
Protestantism, 14, 26, 83

reconciliation, 41
radicalism, 103–7
Reformation, 109, 124, 125
republicanism, 97
resurrection. *See* crucifixion and resur-
    rection
Reuther, Rosemary Radford, 104,
    158 n.21
Roman Catholicism, 14, 26, 83
romance, 10, 37, 79–81. *See also* beauty;
    love
romantic paradigm, 152–53 n.10
Russell, Letty, 104

Satanic Verses, 100
satire, 10, 37, 100–101, 111, 151–52 n.35
Schüssler Fiorenza, Elisabeth, 104–8, 110
Schweitzer (Albert) hospital compound, 1
science, 30–32, 136 n.13, 154 n.18
secularism, 15, 76, 120–25, 137 n.7
Segundo, Juan Luis, 104
shekinah, 66
Sherry, Patrick, 156 n.41
Shona stone sculpture, 137–38 n.9
Sittler, Joseph, 13, 138–39 n.16
Sontag, Susan, 119
Spirit
    as breath of God, 3, 8, 9, 14, 83
    Christ's, 115–17
    and church, 125–26
    defined, 23
    discerning, 11
    evidence of, 1
    as force field, 77, 136 n.12
    intimacy of, 17
    language of, 7
    liberation by, 4
    and power, 6, 9, 10, 19–22, 24, 27, 40, 49, 53–54, 59–60, 75, 95–96, 124–25, 135 n.1
    as practical, 132–33
    re-visioning, 2–3, 4–5, 22, 54, 74
    versus structure, 129
    traditions of, 1–2
    and truth, 50–52
    unity of, 52–57
    witness to, 125–32
spirituality, 15–16
Stravinsky, Igor, 92
synecdoche, 92, 144 n.6, 154 n.14

theism, 21
theocracy, 45–48
theological knowledge, 2, 3–4
Thiel, John E., 152–53 n.10
thinking the faith, 1–2
Thistlethwaite, Susan, 104
Tinker, George E., 104
tragedy, 10, 36, 79
transfiguration, 92, 93
Trinity, doctrine of, 10, 24, 26–29, 104.
    See also Spirit
truth and power, 50–51, 121

Unitarianism, 100, 101
unity, 52–57, 128–29. *See also* disunity

venture, power to, 61–63, 65–70
Victorin-Vangeruud, Nancy, 135 n.1

Welker, Michael, 76–77, 79, 136 n.12
White, Andrew Dixon, 17
White, Hayden, 80, 81
    Metahistory, 36
Whitehead, Alfred North, 9
Williams, Daniel Day, 6, 17, 84–87
    Spirit and the Forms of Love, The, 84
Williams, Delores, 104
witness, 126–32
women, 102–3, 124
Wood, Gordon S., 96–97, 99, 100
    Radicalism of the American Revolution, The, 124
Word of God, 7–8, 30, 83, 141 n.12